P9-CZV-879

Fitness in American Culture

The University of Massachusetts Press, Amherst, and

The Margaret Woodbury Strong Museum, Rochester, New York

Fitness in American Culture

Images of Health, Sport, and the Body, 1830–1940

Edited by Kathryn Grover

Copyright © 1989 by

The Margaret Woodbury Strong Museum

All rights reserved

Printed in the United States of America

LC 89-4772

ISBN 0-87023-681-4 (cloth); 682-2 (paper)

Designed by Edith Kearney

Set in Linotron Plantin at Keystone Typesetting, Inc.

Printed and bound by Thomson-Shore, Inc.

Library of Congress Cataloging-in-Publication Data

Fitness in American culture : images of health, sport, and the body,
    1830–1940 / edited by Kathryn Grover.

        p. cm.

    Papers presented at a symposium held at the Margaret Woodbury
Strong Museum in spring, 1986.

    Includes index.

    Contents: Sport in American life / Donald J. Mrozek — American
advertising and the reconstruction of the body, 1880–1930 / T. J.
Jackson Lears — Iron therapy and tonics / Michael R. Harris —
Eating to win / James C. Whorton — Healthy, moral, and strong /
Roberta J. Park.

        ISBN 0–87023—681–4 (alk. paper) — ISBN 0–87023–682–2
(pbk. : alk. paper)

    1. Physical fitness—United States—History—19th century.
2. Sports—United States—History—19th century. 3. Physical
fitness—United States—History—20th century. 4. Sports—United
States—History—20th century. I. Grover, Kathryn, 1953–   .
II. Margaret Woodbury Strong Museum.

    GV510.U5F58   1989

    613.7′1—dc19   89–4772

                                                          CIP

British Library Cataloguing in Publication data are available.

Contents

Acknowledgments

In a museum as young as the Strong Museum, the project from which these papers emerged seems ancient. Harvey Green, the first and then the only staff historian, proposed the concept of the exhibition later known as *Fit for America: Health, Fitness, Sport, and American Society, 1830–1940* in 1977, five years before the museum opened to the public. Green included both his lifetime batting and earned-run averages with his signature on the proposal, an act that neatly encapsulated the position he has always taken toward these subjects. Having played softball with him, having listened to him analyze innumerable athletic competitions in hallway conversations, having borne his persistent jibes about any Boston club, I feel safe in saying that Green loves sport as much as he understands it. The breadth and richness of his intellectual grasp of the history of health, fitness, and sport made editing the exhibition script, his book *Fit for America* (published by Pantheon Books in 1986 and recently issued in paper by Johns Hopkins University Press), and these papers rewarding enough, but his feeling for these subjects made the project doubly meaningful. Green conceived, helped to plan, and chose the speakers for the 1986 symposium at which these essays were first presented as papers. He has written the introduction that follows. And his guidance on every level of endeavor has been invaluable to this volume.

Inside the museum, many have helped make both the symposium and this book possible. In particular, educator Dorothy Ebersole, now of the Geneva, New York, Historical Society, engineered the April 1986 symposium. Turning the papers into a book involved much illustration research, photography, and diligent work with authors and others. Librarians Elaine Challacombe, Carol Sandler, and Anna Wang were, as ever, cheerful and helpful in the process of locating images; volunteers Christine Daly and Sam LaBue helped with illustration research; Melissa Morgan Radtke, then collections coordinator, and ever-faithful volunteer Frank Warner expedited the process of photography; and James M. Via, the museum's chief photographer, and former museum photographer Thomas Weber shot and printed the photographs that enrich this book. The support and interest of the museum's president, G. Rollie Adams, and its board of trustees sustained us throughout the production process as well. And the book simply could not have been done without Catherine Romano Samson, the museum's editorial assistant. She entered endless corrected manuscripts, handled much of the regular correspondence with authors, bore the responsibility for obtaining permissions to reproduce images, shared in substantive and mechanical editing, helped read proof, and compiled the index. At this museum, she is regarded as the conscience and arbiter of note and bibliographic forms. She encountered trials in researching, locating, and retrieving images for this book that would have thwarted a less persistent person, experiences that she may someday, particularly if she ever owns a car that works properly, find funny.

Seven companies—Beecham Products USA, Campbell's Soup Company, General Foods, Kimberly-Clark, McKesson Corporation, Sterling Drug, Inc., and Timex Corporation—have allowed us to reproduce images of products they have manufactured or continue to manufacture. King Features allowed us to reproduce one of the images that was hardest to find—a *Popeye* comic strip that illustrates spinach's fabled strength-giving ability—and the New Yorker Magazine, Inc., allowed us to use another spinach-related cartoon. Iron Man Publishing permitted the museum to reproduce one of its covers. Several repositories—the Yale University Archives at the Yale University Library, the Archives Center at the National Museum of American History, Smithsonian Institution, the Library of Congress, the Dartmouth College Library, and the Rochester Public Library—provided images from their collections. The rest of the imagery in this book comes from the rich and varied collections of the Strong Museum.

The museum greatly appreciates the assistance and patience of Donald Mrozek, James Whorton, Roberta Park, T. J. Jackson Lears, and Michael Harris, whose essays appear herein. *Fitness in American Culture* is the second in what the museum hopes will be a series of illustrated publications arising from its yearly symposia. I owe much to Bruce Wilcox, Richard Martin, and Pam Wilkinson at the University of Massachusetts Press for their continued interest in the Strong Museum's efforts to sponsor scholarship in the areas of American domestic life and material culture and for the press's co-sponsorship of these volumes.

Kathryn Grover
Editor

Fitness in American Culture

Introduction

Harvey Green

Fifteen years ago, the idea—let alone the reality—of sport history or the history of health and fitness would have provoked varied and not especially complimentary responses in the academy or the museum. For the most part, sport history was thought to indulge the whim of a (usually) tenured professor who happened to be a sports fanatic or, even worse for some, to be another one of those courses intended to fatten the grade-point averages of the lions of the football field or baseball diamond. Health and fitness history did not suffer exactly the same fate at the hands of critics. While it is true that courses in these fields occasionally found their way into curricula on "hygiene," which were often similar in academic rigor to "snap" courses on sport, these offerings were usually buried in the vaults of the history of science or perhaps the occasional history of physical education. The historian's craft was often applied to these subjects, which were yet regarded as vagabond additions to the core of the discipline.

As the end of the twentieth century approaches, inquiries into the histories of these subjects grow in number and in sophistication. Suspicion lingers in the heart of the intensive academic critic, for who does not suspect that such investigations are in fact the result of some sort of emotional or playful calling? Can such work indeed *be* work? The historian of sport, health, and fitness is usually admitted to the party these days, but the Saville Row suits still sense that a trickster has invaded their midst.

It is significant that many of the best works in this branch of history have been second or later books. Nearly all of them have been written after the historian had received tenure, and many have been written by historians who have shifted gears from political or diplomatic or social history. However, more and more senior historians of sport have begun to train succeeding generations of scholars in this field. The subject matter is significant enough so that it, like any specialized branch of knowledge, has its own journal, the *Journal of Sport History*, the publication of the North American Society for Sport History.

There has been a spate of published work in the history of sport, health, and fitness in the past five years, the result of the efforts of this first generation of scholars. They are heir, ultimately, to one of the greatest of twentieth-century European historians, Johan Huizinga, whose original book of 1950, *Homo Ludens*, has escaped the criticism leveled at writing on sport, the great bulk of which was indeed superficial. Huizinga's slender masterpiece analyzed the play element of culture, and the great Dutch historian argued persuasively that play and culture were not only intermingled, but that the former anticipated the latter. His analytical framework was that of the classic cultural historian. He compared the language of play in a variety of ancient and non-Western cultures and proceeded to demonstrate that play was an integral part of such seemingly diverse human areas as law, poetry, war, and religion.

For Huizinga, play was an ordering of experience, even as it was a liberating form of activity. Sport, in the form of organized athletics, had elements of play within it, but it was not necessarily composed only of activities that one might call "play." Competition, which is inherent in most sporting activities, was for Huizinga

a component of play. He was also convinced that sport originated in England because of the nation's town structure, lack of military requirements, educational forms, flat and relatively treeless landscape, and the tendencies of its people to form clubs and associations.

Following Huizinga's lead, historians of modern sport—and the term "modern" has specific meanings for these historians—have found the genesis of most sports in the British Isles. Melvin Adelman, in *A Sporting Time: New York City and the Rise of Modern Sport* (1986), traced the American enthusiasm for horse racing, baseball, football, and crew to the English games of cricket, rounders, and rugby, as well as to the more direct antecedent of rowing. Although it did not originate with his work, Adelman's definition of modernity was similar to that of nearly all his fellow analysts of the topic: "modern" sport is secular, bureaucratic, specialized in the functioning of its players, concerned and perhaps even obsessed with records, rationalized by means of rules agreed upon, theoretically open to all who are able and willing to play, and quantifiable in some fashion.

Adelman's work was influenced by the equally adept investigation of Allen Guttmann, whose *From Ritual to Record* (1978) analyzed the development of sport from ancient ritualistic and religious roots to its contemporary forms. This analytical strain of inquiry has been joined recently by sophisticated works of intellectual and social history that examine sporting and fitness movements in both England and the United States. Bruce Haley's book *The Healthy Body in Victorian Culture* (1978) traced the history of fitness and sport in England and brilliantly linked the political, social, economic, and religious changes of nineteenth-century England to the evolution of sport and public attitudes toward the games and the athletes. Haley was pioneering in his ability to unearth connections between popular and professional medicine and sport. Donald Mrozek carefully examined the linkages among the military, sport, health crusades, body building, and the broad movements of American ideology in the late nineteenth century in *Sport and American Mentality, 1880–1920* (1983).

The history of the various movements to help Americans achieve a more fit existence—usually with the goal of prolonging life—has engaged several astute historians. Ronald Numbers's *Ellen White: Prophetess of Health* (1976) skillfully explored White's contribution to the American quest for health in the nineteenth century and paid special attention to her religious convictions. An energetic woman who was often guided by visions, White was a follower of the faith that ultimately became Seventh-Day Adventism. Stephen Nissenbaum's *Sex, Diet, and Debility in Jacksonian America* (1980) examined the life of dietary faddist and healer Sylvester Graham and placed this quixotic figure in the broader context of the epidemiological history of the United States in the early and mid-nineteenth century. James Whorton's *Crusaders for Fitness* (1982) analyzed the various dietary solutions Americans sought for their ailments, as well as certain aspects of the sport and physical fitness crusades of the nineteenth century. Whorton was particularly attentive to the transatlantic connections that are present in this broad-based series of

movements and demonstrated the connections between such socioreligious concepts as "Muscular Christianity" and dietary reform and faddism.

Numbers's biography of White is one of several important analyses of significant figures in the history of health and fitness. Peter Levine's superb study of the career of Albert G. Spalding, *A. G. Spalding and the Rise of Baseball* (1985), carefully chronicled and analyzed the emergence of one of the first corporate giants of the sporting world. Charles Alexander examined the life of the man many critics think to be the greatest baseball player that ever lived in *Ty Cobb* (1984) and avoided the filiopietism that had characterized the voluminous biographies of the great and otherwise skilled athletes that had become a fixture in bookstores (if not academic libraries) all over the United States. Alexander unearthed information about Cobb's childhood and the traumatic loss of his father (by his mother's hand) and dealt fairly with Cobb's vicious racism, violent tendencies, and generosity, as well as with his greatness on the field. Similarly, Jules Tygiel's *Baseball's Great Experiment: Jackie Robinson and His Legacy* (1983) skillfully chronicled the dramatic moment in the history of the "national game" when Branch Rickey and Jackie Robinson broke baseball's color line in 1947. In each of these works, the connections between the game and the business that the sport had become have been detailed, and the experience has been shown to be part of the larger process of corporate capitalism that has characterized American history.

That sport and the quest for fitness are important parts of the ethos of life in the United States and that they have been so for at least one and one-half centuries is no longer debatable. The enormous popular success of televised sports (there is now at least one television network that airs nothing but sports), the ever-increasing participation of both men and women of all ages in organized and unorganized sports, and the profusion of ordinarily awful books that are either diaries of some winning season or "as told to" autobiographies attest this importance. (There are exceptions to the generally poor quality of the sports diary. Jim Brosnan's *Long Season* [1960], a masterful account of one season of a pitcher who is also an accomplished writer and wit, and Jerry Kramer's *Instant Replay* [1968], the offensive guard's narrative of a championship season of football's Green Bay Packers, are important contributions to American writing.)

The fact that understanding sport and the quest for fitness and health are critical to an understanding of the American past and that this history was but partly revealed was an essential element in the development of an extensive project at the Strong Museum. The project was influenced not only by written primary sources and the scholarly work that preceded its initial formulation in 1977 but also by the undeniable evidence of the material remains of American domestic life that are in the Strong Museum and other collections. From those records, and with the help of two grants from the National Endowment for the Humanities, an exhibition and conference were organized and a book written. These elements were intended as vehicles for presenting a synthesis of new data and earlier work and

aimed at an analysis of the interrelationships of health, fitness, sport, reform, and ideology in the United States between 1830 and 1940. Collectively, these elements were entitled *Fit for America: Health, Fitness, Sport, and American Society, 1830–1940.*

The essays that compose this volume were first delivered as papers at the Strong Museum in the spring of 1986. They have much in common, although each historian brings to his or her analysis a particularly keen set of insights and methodology. Each of the authors perceives a fundamental reorientation of life and culture in the United States occurring at the turn of the century. Donald Mrozek, T. J. Jackson Lears, and James Whorton continue their analysis into the 1930s, and the first two analysts have identified that era as an age in which Americans began to accept the idea of adjustment to social and economic conditions as the cornerstone of popular culture. Each of the essays also establishes that the basis for understanding the ways in which Americans responded to changes in their culture is the enduring concern for and acceptance of individual responsibility for both successes and failures. That this would be a typical American response is in itself no great surprise, but the varying ways in which this concern took shape is a central point of investigation for this volume's contributors.

Individual responsibility was a central tenet of the Puritan faith—God may have made decisions about the fates of the people, but the New England colonies' version of Protestantism nonetheless assumed a close relationship between visible deeds and signs of what the Divine had decided. So too the idea of personal culpability and reward was blended into the more humanistic and optimistic worldview that characterized the gradual (and in many cases grudging) acceptance of Enlightenment ideology that ultimately overtook the free-will–predestination arguments of the older faith. The more optimistic vision of American thinkers such as Jefferson and Madison also carried with it the responsibility to care for and maintain republican government. This relationship—between liberty and responsibility—was both exhilarating and awesome, and it resonated in low rumbling tones with Puritan John Winthrop's warning of 1630: "The eyes of all people are upon us; so that if we shall deal falsely with our god in this work we have undertaken and so cause him to withdraw his present help from us, we shall be made a story and a byword through the world."

The double-edged sword of liberty and responsibility took an altered form in the early decades of the nineteenth century, when more and more Americans began to think of themselves as able to alter the course of human history in a religious environment less accepting of predestination than had existed in the seventeenth or eighteenth centuries. The optimism implied by the Enlightenment faith in political structure combined with the accompanying alteration in religious theory and practice to produce an ideology of millenarian conversion and hope for the advent of Christ on Earth. This altered orthodoxy by and large rejected predestination and held that the human spirit was perfectible by means of individual and social action. Moreover, this perfection was thought to be a necessary step in the pro-

cess that would culminate in the Second Coming of Christ. But, like Winthrop's "bargain" with God and republican theorists' contract between the people and democratic government, this new relationship carried with it the duty to succeed or to face the reality that life's reverses— economic, social, political, even medical—were one's own fault. Amid the joyful music of religious conversion and the dizzying possibility of realizing a heaven on earth was the somber and ever-present minor key of individual responsibility for the failure of that enterprise.

Thinkers of the second quarter of the nineteenth century made the connection between the health of the spirit and that of the body. It is not coincidental that the *Journal of Health*, a publication of two Philadelphia physicians seeking to reach a general public that had little faith in the ministrations of professional men of medicine, began publication in the last months of 1829. Their calls for a greater concern for bodily vigor and strength were joined by those of a variety of crusaders, including William Alcott, Sylvester Graham, Catharine Beecher, Edward Hitchcock, Charles Caldwell, Russell Trall, and Joel Shew. Alcott and Graham had ecclesiastical connections in that both had trained for the ministry: Alcott became a prolific writer on matters of health, and Graham became a famed eccentric in the areas of American dietary habits and social activity. Trall and Shew were commentators on the social and religious implications of Americans' ill health. Both issued tracts and established centers for hydropathy, or the water cure, a popular form of treatment for nearly every form of debility from which Jacksonian Americans suffered. Hitchcock and Caldwell were trained physicians who never abandoned their practices or professional affiliations and who published important popular books in the early 1830s.

Beecher may have been the most important of the group. Her works on domestic economy are probably best known to historians, and with good reason. Her *Treatise on Domestic Economy* (1842) went through numerous editions throughout the century, but so did her *Physiology and Calisthenics*, which was first published in 1856. Like others who wrote about health in her time, Beecher linked the health of the body with that of the body politic and with that of the spirit. A persistent jeremiad about the ill health of Americans was intermingled with her descriptions of exercises and hints for a better diet. Beecher believed that the malaise of Americans was brought about by a diet steeped in grease and spicy condiments, as well as by the evil habits of smoking or chewing tobacco and of drinking spirituous liquors. In addition, Beecher found that Americans were comparatively less healthy than peoples of less developed societies, a shocking fact (she thought) that could be explained by a paradox of economic and political success. The inventiveness and energy evident in the accumulation of wealth that Alexis de Tocqueville noted in *Democracy in America* (1838) had led to the advent of a society in which increasing numbers of people no longer worked with their hands. Success and prosperity were thus a conundrum: the more Americans achieved what they sought in the economic (and related technological) spheres, the more they endangered the future of that society and of their souls.

Other critics agreed, although most were less strident than Beecher, whose father and brother were in succession the most important ministers of mainstream American Protestantism between 1820 and 1880. Caldwell commented on the political "commotion" of the slavery and nullification crises of 1833 and 1834, and Hitchcock was particularly attentive to the problems he saw in zealous students of "literary pursuits." Both were convinced that overinvolvement in politics and study contributed to the development and growth of what they termed a "nervous" population. Shew and Trall thought they had located a panacea—water—for the ills all had identified. Their isolation of that cure distinguished them from their fellow critics, but, like their contemporaries, they found a serpent in the garden of economic, political, and technological delights.

Each of the essays in this volume springs from this basic problem in American history. Roberta Park, Lears, Mrozek, and, to a somewhat lesser extent, Whorton and Michael Harris, find continuing connections between religion and attempts to better the health of Americans. In most cases, the linkage is first one of language: the language of physiological transformation and its promise often parallels that of religious conversion experiences. Second, like earlier reformers, they find that later critics cite the individual's role and responsibility for change in order both to produce a better society and, perhaps more important for twentieth-century Americans, to avoid economic and social failure. The critical difference between the pre–Civil War era and the 1920s and 1930s is that, as both Mrozek and Lears make clear, American popular culture was more directly concerned with convincing Americans to adapt themselves to predetermined standards of social behavior, rather than with providing a force to transform and better that culture.

Roberta Park identifies controlled and organized physical activity as one of the most important components in Americans' quest to achieve a better society and to avert decline in a world that seemed to be changing too quickly and in too threatening a manner. Using both popular and professional sources for evidence, she is able to identify the growth of football as a key element in the change in American attitudes toward physical activity as a solution to health problems and the victory of competitive sport over calisthenics and gymnastics. Football's meteoric rise to prominence as an indicator of "manly" virtue and strength was accompanied by a burgeoning racial nationalism that both assumed the inherent superiority of white Anglo-Saxon Protestants and perceived that this ethnic group was, by its carelessness about matters of health, on the road to committing "race suicide."

Football's curious transition in the eyes of its beholders from the disorganized rabble games of Thomas Wentworth Higginson's Harvard days in the 1850s to the highly organized big-time athletic contests of the heyday of Walter Camp and Loren F. DeLand at the turn of the century is instructive of the changes in American culture in the latter decades of the nineteenth century. Observers and reminiscing alumni regarded the games of the earlier era as joyful, if rough, emblems of disorganization and unpreparedness for what was to become the great crisis of the Civil War. But by the 1890s, as Camp and others revolutionized the game and its publicity, its allegedly controlled violence seemed to signify that men were steeling themselves for battle in the best possible way, whether that fight was to be against foreign (or domestic) adversaries armed with the traditional weapons of war or against others in the corporate boardrooms of the nation and the world. Football was a key to success, because, like the religious devotions of earlier eras and other cultures, it instilled discipline and team spirit. Both were thought critical to success and survival.

The dilemma for the sport's advocates was that, like horse racing, boxing, baseball, and other athletic pursuits, the growth of the sport brought with it the evils of gambling and the specter of the "fix." This notion sprang in part from the reality that sporting contestants were on some occasions caught flagrantly "taking a fall" to enrich sporting profiteers. Only baseball seemed immune, but the revelation of the "fixed" World Series of 1919 eliminated that exception as well. In addition, there was little or no tradition or cultural understanding of what Americans now identify as an "upset," in which a seemingly weaker team manages to beat its opponent. For collegians playing at football, as well as their fans, the compelling pressures of winning led to corruptions and accusations similar to those of contemporary American college sports— athletes recruited not for their academic promise but for their athletic skills, payments to the players, academic dishonesty, and even the use of illicit drugs to heighten performance.

Park points out that one of the ways coaches and other enthusiasts for athletics countered these criticisms was to organize themselves into associations, as their contemporaries in nearly every other professional field had done. In their meetings and in debates published in professional journals and occasionally in newspapers and popular magazines, coaches and physical educators often found themselves at odds. The American Association of Physical Educators (established in 1885) was critical of the emphasis placed on winning in organized sport. Such important national figures as Harvard's Dudley Sargent argued that the college's first responsibility was to its undergraduate students as a whole, and that the college team was secondary in the best of situations. While the physical educators' arguments were powerful and carried with them the ring of student democracy, they were usually overmatched by the coaches, alumni, and politicians' emphasis on training the athletic elite for what was thought to be its parallel positions in business and society.

Popular literature seemed to support a broader acceptance of these ideas, if not consciously then implicitly; certain literary forms about sport have shown enduring strength in the marketplace. The best example of this trend is in the enormous success—more than one hundred titles were published between 1869 and 1924—of Gilbert Patten's almost legendary hero, Frank Merriwell. He was, as Sheldon Messenger points out in *Sport and the Spirit of Play in American Fiction* (1981), an archetypal "school sports hero." His upright, serious, disciplined, and moral leadership made it clear that play and sport had a higher end, born of the continuing celebration and awe of the Civil War's fallen heroes. It was, in addition, a product of the popularization and ultimately the trivialization of Darwinian bio-

logical theory: life is a struggle, and only the fittest can endure. For those fortunate enough to partake of its virtues and mayhem in an organized way, within the confines of the college or university grounds, football became the preparation for that struggle.

That football had become vaguely organized brutality made it something of a problem as well as an activity to celebrate. So dangerous had it become by 1900 that even the staunchest of the advocates of the "strenuous life," including Theodore Roosevelt, were near to condemning it and banishing it from colleges. Led by the venerable Walter Camp, football coaches from major schools altered the game, establishing rules that eased the injury problem while maintaining the disciplinary and testing qualities of the sport. Frank Merriwell was the model athlete for the "new" football, one who played by the rules and played for the glory of the higher good—the team and the school. A descendant of the enormously popular English sporting heroes portrayed in the mid-nineteenth century by Thomas Hughes in *Tom Brown's Schooldays* (1857) and *Tom Brown at Oxford* (1861), Merriwell represented the "balanced" young man who was neither too skilled intellectually nor too committed to success on the athletic fields. He was, therefore, the answer to the criticism of the zealous student that had been a commonplace in advice and reform literature since the 1830s. In Owen Johnson's *Stover at Yale* (1912), however, hero Dink Stover was exemplary of the criticism leveled at American collegiate sport. Johnson's hero implicitly attacked the rapacious competition he encountered at Yale, as well as the elitism of Ivy League play. Stover was a hero of the

Progressive political and social reform agenda: he used information and the skills of representatives from all classes, rather than merely from the elites.

As Park points out, the emphasis on football represented a manifestation of the conviction that "the body had become a symbol and metaphor for expressing . . . a host of cultural concerns and aspirations." The work of Harris and Whorton supports this assertion, which is one of the building blocks of the arguments of both Lears and Mrozek as well. Mrozek perceives a fundamental reorientation in Americans' thinking about the importance of health and the body. By the 1920s, he argues, the capitalist bourgeois culture of the United States was such that pleasure became an acceptable end for Americans to pursue. Personal health became less of a concern than personal amusement. The justification of sport as a means to achieve loftier national ends became less evident in popular cultural forms as traditional leaders in both science and business jettisoned that linkage. This shift in emphasis in the stated goals of sport and physical well-being corresponded to what Lears has described in *No Place of Grace* (1981) as a "quest for disciplined vitality" and "intense experience." This quest explains the late nineteenth-century fascination (among northern elites, at least) with the Roman Catholic and Episcopal faiths. Both seemed to provide a mixture of discipline and intensely mysterious personal experience. For those white Anglo-Saxon Protestants who were in some manner concerned about the rigors and belief systems of Catholicism, Episcopalianism offered something of a compromise—intensity and emotionalism without complete acceptance of the religion that was so

closely linked to the very immigrant groups that seemed to threaten the American establishment from without.

Like the other essayists in this volume, Mrozek perceives a direct connection to the religious history of the nation in his analysis of the emerging "cult of the body" in the culture of the 1920s and 1930s. The critical difference is that this new perfectionist belief and effort was not directed toward social and political ends, but toward the pleasure individuals found in the process and attainment of various stages of perfection. By examining the work of such popular cultural heroes as Bernarr MacFadden and Charles Atlas, Mrozek elucidates the continuing presence of the rhetoric of revivalism, if not the millenarian ends of it. His study offers evidence of the transformation of cultural concerns from the national health and racial nationalism ideology of the late nineteenth century to the emphasis on adjustment found in the popular social culture of the 1920s and after.

The social and economic successes of Frank Merriwell, Dink Stover, and even that nonathletic scion of virtue and money-getting, Horatio Alger's Ragged Dick, were replaced in the ever-growing advertising culture of the United States by the man and woman who best "got along" and "fit in." The emphasis in myriad advertisements that filled the pages of popular magazines from *Physical Culture* to *Good Housekeeping* was on being inoffensive and lively. Cereal manufacturers pitched bran cereals and other forms of roughage to a public worried about "auto-intoxication," a vaguely defined illness in which the poisons produced by the digestion of (usually) "unhealthy" foods led to listlessness, and even to body odor and halitosis. These new "social diseases" became bugbears of a bourgeois elite that had internalized success and failure as their own responsibility, in much the same manner as Winthrop and others had postulated the relationship between piety and position. The problem was also analogous to those of the previous centuries in that the victim of these newly offensive conditions was unaware of them, just as New Englanders were never really certain how God had dealt with them. Thus social self-help books such as Dale Carnegie's *How to Win Friends and Influence People*, first published in 1935, enjoyed enormous popularity.

Carnegie's work and the preachings of popular minister Norman Vincent Peale were summations of tendencies that had been developing in the advertising, popular literature, and cinema of the 1920s and early 1930s. Charles Atlas and other similarly named strong men (Lionel Strongfort, for example) regularly promoted themselves and their systems of body building to reach the fears and dreams of their readers. They and their advertising divisions (or the firms they hired) were not only effective at finding the soft underbelly of American men and women; they also helped shape and exacerbate their fears and longings. Movie stars such as Johnny Weissmuller and Mae West demonstrated not only an ease with their bodies but also the promise of love and sex for the attractive. As Mrozek demonstrates, the fact that Tarzan, Jane, and Boy had connections to the elite cultures of money and position made their condition all the more acceptable to Americans. West's sexual exuberance, and perhaps her dominant role in her come-

dies, was more troubling than the relatively benign nudity and sensuality of Weismuller.

In his essay, T. J. Jackson Lears concentrates on "a fundamental reorientation of attitudes toward the body during the late nineteenth and early twentieth centuries, a collective change of mind that was reflected but also reinforced by the rise of national advertising." He challenges an assumption about the period commonly held by both cultural critics of the turn of the century and their descendants. Lears postulates that Americans of the 1920s and 1930s were no more at ease with their bodies than their Victorian forebears, and he attacks the belief that a pleasure-oriented consumer culture replaced a Puritan "vale of tears." He finds instead a continuity of concern and awareness of the body from the late nineteenth century through the first decades of the twentieth. He also, like Mrozek, finds great changes in the ways and the ends for which Americans responded to their bodies.

Lears cites the important *J. Walter Thompson Book* (1909) as indicative of the advertising world and its prevailing attitudes about American health, fitness, and the human body. Contributors to the book noted that "stupid people . . . move in a rut of tradition," a curious idea to promote for a company that traded on Americans' love of the "traditional" and "colonial" worlds, warmly revered in home furnishings, literature, and iconography. "Modern" Americans were simultaneously looking backward and forward as their culture struggled with its contemporary enthusiasms for both the colonial past, as symbolized by Henry Ford's

Greenfield Village (begun in the 1920s), and the future, as represented by "streamlining" in architecture, industrial design, interior decoration, and popular imagery of all sorts. The discomfiture noted in the quotation is directed at the sort of sloth and sluggishness that, at least in popular mythology, characterized neither the sturdy colonial nor the energetic bourgeois "man-on-the-make." Thus when the W. K. Kellogg Company chose to market its bran-rich cereals in the 1920s, its advertising division shrewdly portrayed an Errol Flynn–like boss (complete with pince-nez) confronting an obviously beaten underling underneath the large headline, "RUTS." The ad went on to explain that without proper roughage no one could expect to get ahead; he would simply lack the energy to do the job to the satisfaction of his superiors.

Studying the staff demographics of important national advertising firms, Lears has found that they were composed primarily of white Anglo-Saxon males. Their ideology not surprisingly appears throughout their work. Like contemporaries in the worlds of politics, education, and business, advertising executives responded to the idea that conservation of energy was important. In a November 1899 *Yale Review* article entitled "The Philosophy of Modern Advertising," Lears finds a pitch for the desirability of "soap and cleanliness over perfumery and enervating pleasures." Here, then, is a version of both the suspicion of pleasure—which Mrozek sees as increasingly important by the 1920s—and the concern for draining the body of vital forces.

This idea had been prominent in American popular culture since at least the middle of the nineteenth century. At first noted in connection with the ill effects of the use of "stimulants" such as spices and alcohol, the idea that the amount of "vital force" was fixed and was even in danger of dissipation gained a solid foothold in the United States. All sorts of devices and panaceas were offered to counter the problem. Electricity, a strange and indecipherable force in the middle decades of the century, was marketed as a way to add new force to the depleted body. All sorts of machines for home use, as well as patent medicines with no electrical properties other than the words on their labels, were produced; consumers gobbled them up. Magnetic machines and gimmicks also traded upon this concern and upon the vaguely mystical associations of "animal magnetism" and clairvoyance popular from the 1840s through the end of the century.

The idea received some attention from the professional medical community but got perhaps its greatest boost from the social sciences. Most important was Brooks Adams's popular book, *The Law of Civilization and Decay* (1895), which postulated that the central characteristic determining the rise and fall of civilizations, as well as their different characters, was the amount of energy with which they were endowed by nature and the degree to which that energy had dissipated. Adams sought to apply the then-current scientific theory of entropy, or energy transference and decline, to the social sciences. While he was never able to develop a comprehensive set of laws for the evolution of cultures that gained widespread acceptance among his colleagues, the idea found a receptive audience in the popular press and in the works of, among others, his brother Henry. In *The Education of Henry Adams* (1907), *Mont-Saint-Michel and Chartres* (1904), and other works, Adams built upon the idea of entropy and the importance of Force in various forms.

The idea of declining energy was also present in the advice literature of the latter decades of the nineteenth century. Young women were advised to limit their studies while in puberty for fear that energy would be diverted from the development of their reproductive organs, thereby endangering the future of their "race." Men were encouraged in similar literature and by educators and stewards of their well-being, such as the YMCA, to conserve their sperm, because many believed that the production and emission of sperm drained energy. The "spermatic economy" became an axiom of medical and quasi-medical theory and athletic training regimen. A more bizarre manifestation of this concern centered around the electromagnetic cosmology of the middle decades of the century. To prevent the loss of "vital force" (a term used to describe the mysterious combination of electricity, magnetism, and other ill-defined forces grouped under the rubric of energy), adherents to the magnetic faith recommended sleeping with the body situated in a north-south alignment with glass casters under bedstead legs to insulate the individual from the silent, imperceptible drain of force to the earth's magnetic pole.

By the end of the nineteenth century, as Lears demonstrates, the impact of a sporting culture had transformed the calculus of health. The celebration of youthfulness and exuberance directed the analytical schema of advertisers to a position

that equated the expenditure of energy—through physical activity and especially sport—with the ability to exert even more of it. Athleticism, rather than exoticism or even nostalgia, became the most important quality to possess. At the same time, as both Mrozek and Lears indicate, Americans became less at ease with certain aspects of their bodies. The need to "fit in" and adjust to social discourse and intercourse led to heightened awareness of and efforts to avoid such conditions as body odor, stained teeth, and halitosis. Thus the paradox: the celebration of the body and its perfectibility resulted in certain freedoms and loosened bonds, but only in a cultural climate that stressed a series of laws for perfection and proper behavior that in turn stifled certain elements of the body's natural state.

Lears points out that the concern for bodily purification and sanitation contained elements of religious zeal that link it to a cycle of revivalism and regeneration deeply embedded in American culture. Anglo-Saxon revitalization, in the form of exercise, sport, cleanliness, or war, was part of the social turmoil at the turn of the century and resulted from the real or perceived threat of immigrants and the implications of Darwinian biological theory. In sum, these activities reflected the need of established mainline bourgeois culture to define parameters and isolate itself from alien "others." Attacks on immigrants were overtly discriminatory; such phenomena as the "Red Scare" of 1919, in which Attorney General A. Mitchell Palmer engineered a series of raids throughout the nation to net suspected anarchists and socialists, exemplify this process. Attempts at legislating immigration quotas finally were successful in

1921: the number of immigrants allowed into the country was limited to 2 percent of their resident populations as established by the federal census of 1890, before which time few newcomers had arrived from southern and eastern Europe.

These activities were closely allied, at least in a cultural sense, with certain aspects of the health and fitness crusades of the early twentieth century. Hostility to immigrants and activists of a socialist or anarchist bent often included the identification of these peoples as "alien filth," a dehumanizing and powerful image. More personally, many Americans concerned about their health and, especially, their nutrition, worried that they were poisoning themselves with "alien filth" that was a result of their own poor eating habits. "Auto-intoxication," as it was called, was a doubly threatening and powerful fear. First, much like the idea of "race suicide," it resonated with the idea of personal responsibility for one's condition. Second, it was an internal condition that worked quietly and invisibly, perhaps until it was too late to reverse it. It was an internal subversion of one's own making.

James Whorton concentrates on the dietary debate that raged in both scientific and popular circles at the turn of the century. The internal subversion of autointoxication and the related malady, "uric acid diasthesis," were countered in some sense by the promise of better health through dietetic righteousness. The perfectionism of the early nineteenth century could be achieved, according to advocates of nutritional balance and care, through diet. Combined with the advances in biochemical understanding of metabolism and nutrition that had been building in the late nineteenth and early twentieth

centuries, this secular regeneration became the "new nutrition."

Whorton cites the dietary transition from food as "aliment," or nonspecific raw materials for supplying the body, to more specialized and distinguishable nutrition forms. This increase of specialization paralleled the increasing specialization in business, the organization of labor in manufacturing, athletics, and everyday commercial products for the home. Office work became more specialized just as the assembly line was developed. At the same time that athletes were increasingly being trained to play specific positions, consumers looking to purchase silver plate could choose from an expanding list of specialized pieces that included such devices as ice cream knives, cucumber lifters, tomato lifters, and berry spoons.

What they ate with those specialized tools garnered the attention of scientists and advertisers, as well as food processors and packagers. Cereal barons such as the Kellogg brothers and Charles W. Post had their fingers on the pulse of a nervous constituency that included not only the established middle and wealthy classes, but also many members of the very classes and ethnic groups that worried the elites and near-elites. But while they noted the desire to avoid the injury to the system that a rich, greasy diet entailed, the cereal kings were astute enough to realize that a vegetarian diet was only for the few (including John Harvey Kellogg). Most Americans wished for an easy answer, one that would not deprive them of all their treasured foods. Part of the quick solution was to be found in the advent of a new compound, the vitamin, so named for the "vital amines" that biochemists considered them to be. These compounds, first isolated in 1912, were a boon to the sluggish American looking for more energy in the struggle to survive and prosper in the socioeconomic reality of twentieth-century America.

Another element in the amelioration of Americans' destructive eating habits, according to the lords of Battle Creek, Michigan (where both Kellogg and Post were located), was fiber, in the form of bran. Roughage could alleviate the problems of constipation, which seems to have bedeviled Americans to the extent that magazines, journals, and newspapers were full of advertisements for laxatives of one form or another. Rather than resorting to patent medicines of dubious composition, or products of the petroleum industry, such as Standard Oil Company's Nujol, consumers could content themselves by solving their autointoxication problems with a "natural" method and product, the bran of grains. Grape Nuts advertisements promised relief for "brain workers," and Kellogg's marketed a variety of bran cereals and flakes. Henry D. Perky's invention, shredded wheat, promised similar relief and health. The key to this campaign, as Whorton points out, was that eating healthy cereals might be enough of an adjustment to allow sound digestion. It was a compromise of sorts: a bowlful of what critics called "grass," "heap-a-hay," or other similar epithets permitted meat-and-potatoes enthusiasts to indulge as usual, sure in the conviction that they would not be hurting themselves, much less the nation.

The popularity of processed cereals was itself a paradox. They were trumpeted as "natural" and as a way to regain equipoise. The advertising pitch suggested that the undoing of Americans was a result of a deviation from or inattention to Nature. Foods themselves, the argument ran, were undone in factories, those symbols of much that seemed wrong with American life. These critics (and Kellogg and Post were vociferous ones) managed to ignore the fact that their own goods were also manufactured in factories. Patent medicine hucksters, as Lears notes, used the allegedly purer and more "natural" Indian as a visual cue to consumers, hoping to suggest that their products were safe and somehow essential to counteract the evils of civilization, cities, and industrialization.

Part of the promotional effort for healthy foods such as bran cereals, yeast, and spinach centered around an ancient set of beliefs about strength and how to achieve and maintain it. Michael Harris demonstrates that iron's position in people's quest for long life and good health has ancient roots. The mineral has folkloristic associations with magical strength, in part because of its properties when smelted and in part because it has identifiable therapeutic uses. Ingesting certain iron compounds alleviated some forms of anemia, and the mineral was successfully used to control bleeding. Like electricity, the water cure, bran, and yeast, iron and its compounds were promoted as panaceas until the 1890s, when the weight of cumulative scientific discovery began to undermine the claims of cure-alls.

The power of iron as a "tonic" for worn-out Americans was difficult to defeat entirely, and for good reason. The practice of taking iron as a spring "tonic" has traditional folk roots, and it endured because iron offered an aid to people whose constitutions may well have been weakened by a winter of iron-poor foods. Thus iron tonics and patent medicines continue to this day to be popular in the marketplace, surviving the attacks of the Food and Drug Administration as most of their competitors have not.

Comprehending the history of fitness and health in the American past eventually brings an analysis to the turn of the century, as each of these essays demonstrates. The web of meanings that characterizes this set of issues involves the intersection of the ideas of public virtue, personal fulfillment, and secular regeneration, as well as the resolution or at least the recognition of paradoxes and conundrums. The debates that raged over health and fitness involved strong social self-criticism and an overbearing and occasionally vicious sense of national and racial superiority; fear and detestation of aliens and a celebration of certain "healthy" primitives; criticism of seventeenth-century "Puritans" for their narrow vision; and a concomitant celebration of all things colonial, especially the discipline of religion and the military. Throughout each of these essays, and characteristic of American culture in the late nineteenth century, is a potent strain of nostalgia for worlds that never were and people who never existed. In the end, each of these responses to the problem of health in the United States was rooted in the persistent need to regenerate the body and spirit, which seemed somehow to have lost or misplaced the strength of the founders of the nation. Perhaps this quest for the idealized past continues because the realities of history are too powerful for the nation to contend with, or perhaps, as Mrozek notes, Americans make the mistake of seeing history as a "warehouse of tools for fashioning a happier present." To view history this way is at best incomplete, and in the end it seems to have resulted in the opposite of the yearning for a happy present. Perhaps that is one of the ultimate ironies of Americans and their history.

Sport in American Life

From National Health to Personal
Fulfillment, 1890–1940

Donald J. Mrozek

Sport emerged as a major institutional force in American life during the latter decades of the nineteenth century, and twentieth-century sporting practices have clearly built on the foundation set in that earlier time. The rise of corporate thinking in the nineteenth century and the growth of scientific management affected sport as much as they did industrial life, and since then the emphasis on order and discipline within a hierarchical society became one of the dominant themes in the history of play, sport, and physical culture.[1] Subordinating the drives of the individual to the needs of the group became intense, as many historians have observed.[2] Almost as a logical corollary, turn-of-the-century Americans showed a deep purposefulness in their sport, justifying their own participation in games and athletic events by the social benefits they supposedly gained from their efforts.[3] Yet, great and consequential though these developments were, they form only one of several "sea changes" in the American practice of sport and play. Between the two world wars, Americans showed a new attitude toward both play and sport, seeing these realms as sources of personal pleasure and fulfillment that needed little, if any, external social justification. The thinking that made sport a major institution in society differed, however, from that needed to justify the culture of pleasure and gratification. Several key aspects of how sport worked upon society at the end of the nineteenth century need to be explored in order to understand the great change in thinking, especially about sport, that was underway before World War II.

The emergence of sport to prominence in America after the Civil War depended largely on a tide of justifications offered by the protectors of old-fashioned respectability, disciplined individualism, self-sacrifice and dedication to common cause, and a code of "real manliness" and "true womanhood." The professed interest in using sport to mold personal character reflected the bias of the genteel middle class that personal character was the basis of public morality and social stability. So, too, it meant that the individual needed to justify his actions by their social value and consequence. The genteel preacher, doctor, or teacher came to tolerate the public display and physical assertiveness of organized sport and athletics by seeing within them new means for ingraining the principles of ethical conduct.[4] Health reformers often justified sports not for the amusement they might bring to participants but for the protection they might afford against illness, and not surprisingly, some reformers railed against the growth of "spectator sport" precisely because it became entertainment more than physical and moral training.[5] Even physical educators sought to keep the exuberance of sport under tight restraint, channeling it to purposes sanctioned by social custom and the new "sciences of the body," such as nutrition and modern physiology. It was as if the Calvinist work ethic permeated the practice of sport, as if the social utility of play and athletics was to be judged according to the criteria of work.[6] Yet the most striking aspect in the whole process by which sport assumed an air of social legitimacy was the notion that it needed a special social legitimation at all. Personal fascination with sport was not enough to allow commitment to it. Clear social benefit was also needed.

If work was not pursued for its own sake, neither was sport. Under the guidance of play theorists, even play was to imitate purposeful work. As long as the traditional, genteel middle class remained an important force in setting the standards of public morality, the rhetoric of self-sacrifice helped to reconcile those Americans who so prized personal character and self-restraint to the obvious vitality and flair of sport. But the rationale for sport that emphasized its rational organization and its encouragement of discipline reflected the values of an older middle class whose power was already in decline by the end of the nineteenth century. The new middle class, as Robert Wiebe has suggested, accepted order as a kind of value in itself. And, to the extent that victory was viewed as proof of effective organization, this attitude contributed to a "win at all costs" attitude which split the practice of sport from its former social purposes. Even more, the new "ultra-rich" industrialists and financiers virtually ignored the older tests of sport's worth, turning instead either to the conspicuous display described by Thorstein Veblen or to the unselfconscious gratification of whims that prefigured the emerging mainstream of twentieth-century American culture. To a large degree, the rich displaced the genteel as the exemplars of moral influence and made material success the test of a new version of character—tested by the accumulation of possessions and the prompt service of one's own desires.

Public professions of the need to use sport to foster social order concealed a more complex underlying reality, where the seeds of a cult of self-gratification and personal pleasure had already been sown. The intermediate state between these two frames of mind lay in what T. J. Jackson Lears has called "intense experience," in which Americans united self-discipline and self-discovery.[7] For an articulate elitist, the discipline entailed in seeking such "intense experience" gave sanction to the pleasures one found in the world in the process of exploring oneself. For the masses of the American people who would soon form the basis of the broad popular culture of the interwar years, "intense experience" gave an ambiguous promise of a future rich in personal happiness and fulfillment. During the early decades of the twentieth century, the rhetorical veil of social benefit began to fall. Self-restraint and self-sacrifice yielded to self-expression, personal taste, and the implicit sense that the pursuit of happiness was the essence of liberty and the purpose of life. This was no mere matter of words, since the change of language reflected a change in the accepted standards for individual behavior in society.

In the first few decades of the twentieth century, the pursuit of enjoyment and the conscious quest for personal satisfaction were becoming legitimate goals in their own right (fig. 1). It was as if fun and personal gratification themselves were somehow socially "useful," perhaps as individual efforts to construct the "good society" and to fulfill the pursuit of public happiness by attaining it one person at a time. And by the 1930s, it was to become a virtual duty to "have fun" and "enjoy yourself." Having fun meant using your body as a vehicle of gratification and pleasure. It meant caring less about personal health than about personal amusement. And it displaced the old focus on national health and well-being as the purpose for an individual's pursuit of fitness and ath-

letic accomplishment with a new turn toward health, fitness, and sportive engagement as their own reward. In decades past, virtue was the reward of one's disciplining athletic pursuits, but by the 1920s and 1930s, the athletic quest and the cultivation of the body were themselves increasingly taken as intrinsically virtuous. Personal fulfillment took on the air of public virtue.

Although the components of a sporting culture were developing in America even during the colonial era, it was in the late nineteenth century that this culture attained institutional status. Its organization was marked by a complex of governing bodies and permanent business enterprises, by extensive ties with other institutions such as religion and education, and by a diversity of specific games and events in which the sporting spirit expressed itself.[8] Critical to sport's achievement of this status was its ability to win respectability in the eyes of both America's traditional cultural leaders and the new scientific, managerial, and plutocratic vanguard. Although these groups did not create the basic interest in games and recreation, they did mark off certain sports for special emphasis, identifying some of them as appealing to old values of discipline and self-sacrificial dedication while promoting the new values of modernism and scientific progress at the same time. But once such groups accepted sport for their own reasons, rooted in the idea of national well-being in physical and moral terms, they lost the power to impose those special goals on others. They lost the power to mold the sporting culture or to contain the sensation-seeking disposition that was sport's inseparable twin. In essence, their acquiescence to sport in gen-

Fig. 1 Bernarr MacFadden's magazine *Physical Culture* celebrated the human body as a magnificent artwork, sculpted and finished until it deserved admiration. In this spread from a January 1933 issue of the magazine, Jack Russell, Louis J. Mazzarella, John P. Nicholas, and Alfred Schuman appear clockwise from the upper right. Characteristic of the spirit in the period between the world wars, the caption described Russell as being "as full of joy as of strength." It is also significant that *Physical Culture* credited wrestling for Nicholas's physique, making the sport more important as a source of physical beauty and self-satisfaction than as contest.

eral undermined their ability to insist upon a particular way of practicing it and cleared the field for a significant rise in the governing power of mass taste.

The measures that various reputable Americans took to reconcile the inner tensions and conflicts they experienced held implications for the future development of American culture other than those they intended. In general, the accommodations undertaken to accept the body—its sensuality and sexuality, its beauties, and its physical accomplishments—gave con-

scious support to the principles of hierarchy and authority. To rely on coaches, trainers, nutritionists, and others was to submit oneself to the control of experts, deferring to their judgment. To seek perfect symmetrical development of one's body as a kind of aesthetic act was to accept the physical culturist's concept of human bodily perfection. Even learning to play meant following the precepts and instructions of professional playground personnel. On the conscious level, then, deference to authority and submission to society predominated. But the unconscious current pulled in a contrary direction. For example, psychologist G. Stanley Hall exhibited a devotion to principle and to strenuous living that reflected the older value structure, but he assumed that human instincts were essentially positive, requiring release and development—a clear anticipation of the twentieth century's enormous emphasis on personality and "getting along."[9] Lears has noted that Hall's "popularization of a *benign unconscious* paved the way for a therapeutic cult of 'letting go'. . . . In general, Hall's valuation of leisure, physical vigor, and psychic health was hardly the stuff of rebellion; it was well suited to the emerging outlook of twentieth-century consumer capitalism" [emphasis added].[10] Quite so—and if natural forces really were benign, as Hall maintained, then one might yield to the natural drives that emanated from one's own body. Society's norms and even the precepts of religion seemed perversely artificial and arbitrary by comparison, and their disciplinary clout waned. If physical vigor and leisure were naturally good, letting individuals enjoy these things in their own bodies became readily acceptable. In the absence of transcendent restraints such as those given by religion, the path to personal excess was open. Linking psychic health to personal well-being made the individual the judge and the criterion of suitable behavior, display, and consumption. In practice, the individual looked to peers for a sense of shared standards. Business experts would seek to mold and manipulate those standards, but they nonetheless originated in the accumulation of personal choices and whims that came to form the newly prominent "mass taste."

Other talented Americans shared many of Hall's concerns and adopted views whose effects were similarly in tension. Members of a self-conscious, educated, cultured elite, such people did not trust the unguided choice of the common American. Without the promptings of the experts and the elitists, the ordinary mass of Americans might degenerate into a mere mob, feeding its whims and drives without discrimination. Such cultivated Americans would have understood Herbert Hoover's caution that man in the mass does not think but only feels. Yet, at the same time, even these elitists refused to suppress the drive to achieve material well-being and physical gratification, seeking to use their own intelligence and personal restraint to turn instinct into a source of benefit. The elitists wanted to have it both ways. They sought the energy and enjoyment of the physical realm while seeking to avoid the mindless, gluttonous excess of a mass taste that was insatiable precisely because it was so thoughtless. As Lears has suggested, the eminent architect Ralph Adams Cram is especially interesting in this regard because of his explicit denunciation of "mass man" who thrived in a culture that deified "purely material and enervating bodily comfort."[11] Cram's cautionary comment that "the suffocating qualities of gross luxuriance are sometimes more fatal than the desperate sensations of danger, adversity, and shame" parallels Freud's perception of the power of unconscious drives and the usefulness of repression in protecting civilization from excesses. But Cram's views—and Freud's, for that matter—had too much subtlety about them. Cram was romantically attached to the mystery and sentiment that flourished in Catholic culture and in the idealized medievalism that he mined in his professional work—and probably the underlying order and structure behind both. Not surprisingly, Cram insisted on discipline, productivity, and linear progress, but it was not clear how many other Americans would take the discipline along with the sentiment. For Cram, as for Freud, discipline worked closely upon the intense energy of experience and emotion, but for a more popular and less intellectually careful audience, the prospect that the restraints would give way grew stronger as years passed.

Various signs of the change underway appeared, significantly in those very institutions that had been citadels of self-restraint and "repression." For example, the United States military made extensive use of sport as a means of maintaining order among the troops in Europe after the end of World War I and before all forces were withdrawn to the United States for demobilization. Using sport for the goals of military institutions was not new, but in past decades the most prized role had been the cultivation of a sense of manliness and knightly character among the officers. Similarly, when sport had been promoted among enlisted men, it had been for the announced purpose of improving their fitness to fight—a fitness understood principally as a matter of physical health. Yet, by the end of World War I, army authorities approved sporting activities and even a "Military Olympics" with the purpose of keeping the troops occupied with activities they quite simply liked. To this extent, an element of "mass culture" had made itself felt, as the values of the mass of the conscripted male citizenry were actually shaping the nature of the recreational programs allotted to them. The criterion for judging these sporting activities was not to be the specific gain the nation would reap in the health and hardihood of its military manpower. Rather, it was simply that rebellion could be averted by loosening restraints and by letting the men do substantially what they wanted, short of returning home.

In the schools, sport became less a means of inculcating the values of self-sacrifice and dedication to some external goals than a way of developing the self (fig. 2). The turn-of-the-century educator sought to ensure discipline and order inside the classroom and was more apt to use organized play and games to regulate the students, to sublimate their instinctive bursts of energy, and to harness them to the yoke of social obligation. After World War I, however, teachers were at least as apt to see the natural side of play as the more precious and fragile one. From elementary schools through universities, sport was a form of self-expression and a vehicle for "getting along" with others (fig. 3). There remained the practical dimension of seeking physical health through sport and seeing it as a means to enhance the ability to work. But the persuasive force of this view faltered before that of personal joy and proper "adjustment."[12] Such shifts in the institutional focus on sport and on the role of things physical in developing a well-adjusted personality signified the extent to which the purported good of the common man guided the nation's cultural character rather than the other way around.

In the 1930s, Americans came to speak specifically of an "American way of life." And if there was a supposedly true

Fig. 2   Even at the high-school level, the casual manner of these Eufaula, Oklahoma, basketball players might have seemed inappropriate to coaches and fans of later decades. But in 1940, their easygoing ways evidently raised no eyebrows. To an indefinite but apparently great degree, sport appears to have been taken often as an enjoyable personal enterprise and a harmless social occasion rather than as an elaborate morality play. Photograph by Russell Lee for the Farm Security Administration. Courtesy Library of Congress, LC–USF34–35418–D.

American way of life, it is hardly surprising that a quest for a specific American way in health, fitness, and sport also developed. Talk of a "Golden Age" of great sports performances has obscured the more important phenomenon of widespread popular commitment to cultivating and enjoying the body. What emerged was a golden dream of individual well-being, a cult of happiness, and a quest for self-fulfillment. This positive attitude toward the body as a vehicle of enjoyment and fulfillment expressed itself in diverse ways, but the commitment itself became a significant component of American culture nationwide.

It is more than a coincidence that self-consciousness about an American way of life emerged at the same time as a golden age is supposed to have occurred in sport. Stabilizing an American way of life required determining the specific components of that life, and the swelling attention to sport marked it as a key building block of the mass culture. The golden age was populated with golden

Fig. 3 The name of the game was clearly "fun" for these youngsters playing in the nursery at the Farm Security Administration's camp for migrant workers in Visalia, California, in 1940. The abundant smiles testify to the playful purpose of the whole exercise, which carries no hint of such societal aims as "character formation" or "discipline." Far from channeling unruliness in children, boxing here seems aimed at letting them enjoy themselves and at giving them an outlet for personal expression. The photograph was taken by Arthur Rothstein for the Farm Security Administration. Courtesy Library of Congress, LC–USF34–24173–D.

young men and women; their bodies and the public attention they sparked celebrated a new cultural disposition.

The rhetoric of a golden age in sport, in a literal sense, gave attention to excellence and the pursuit of the ideal in sports performance. But the enthusiasm that spawned and bolstered the rhetoric was rooted in something much broader and older—an underlying faith that human perfectibility was not only a possibility but even an obligation. More than reaffirming the myth of progress or the rhetoric of individualism in a time when corporatist values were becoming pervasive, the physical achievements of American athletes reflected something near to adoration of the body itself. If Americans had needed only a means to compensate for the loss of individualism in industrial society, there would have been an abundance of alternatives. The specific characteristics of those options that proved sufficient to the actual task, however, are themselves suggestive. For example, the inheritors of leadership in fields previously dominated by nineteenth-century gentility—such as education and the arts—may have had the most genuine potential to exemplify individualism for their time. Yet the attention they attracted was negligible if compared to that of

Analyzing Douglas Fairbanks

By Carl Easton Williams

THE mystery of Douglas Fairbanks. For some years now the entire world has contemplated that mystery—how "Doug" does it.

We have seen him make all kinds of more or less impossible jumps; sometimes up, sometimes down, sometimes from roof to roof. We have seen him climb walls and porches and bridges and other seemingly inaccessible places. We have seen him dive over fences and through windows in the apparently most reckless and devil-may-care fashion. We have seen him fight whole bunches of villains, sometimes empty-handed, sometimes with swords—never with custard pies. And we have wondered how he did it. So let's look him over. What is Douglas Fairbanks, anyway? He is, first of all, a personality — one of the two or three most unique personalities on the screen. He is

an exponent of whimsical comedy. He is, indeed, the embodied spirit of refined comedy, with the distinction that his is a special brand of the same—light comedy with a dash that represents the spirit of American youth, and then some.

Then, also, he is our most versatile stunt performer, and while we revel in his comedy, just as we delight in that of Mary Pickford, Dorothy Gish or Taylor Holmes, we also marvel at his stunts. At first glimpse these stunts seem purely athletic in character. But the truth is that this same spirit of dashing, whimsical comedy is a big factor even in the performance of those stunts. For the thing that we call Fairbanks, the thing that makes "Doug" what he is, is both muscular and mental. The things he does, athletically and acrobatically, are not merely a matter of strength and speed, but of spirit. They are an expres-

Showing both what he can do and why he is able to do it. This is the Fairbanks physique in action—very much in action. "Doug" jumped five feet into the air for this picture, which was taken expressly for PHYSICAL CULTURE.

Fig. 4   Film actor Douglas Fairbanks contributed much to linking the athletic image to the popular American notion of personal satisfaction, self-expression, and joy. Fairbanks was actually quite accomplished as a gymnast and acrobat, and he routinely did his own stunts in his films. Analyzing Fairbanks for the November 1921 issue of *Physical Culture*, Carl Easton Williams wrote that the actor had "a dash that represents the spirit of American youth." Exuberance, energy, and enjoyment became the fashion in sport, far different from the concept of character formation so dear to Victorian America—and far different from the "cult of toughness" that developed in the 1940s and after.

sports figures and movie stars—for whom the cultivation of the body was central (fig. 4). This preeminence of the body becomes even more obvious when one recalls that movies were silent for decades and that acting was consequently nonverbal and physical. The use of "sight gags" and slapstick in comedy also focused on the body as a communication device. Similarly, sports stars were more talked about than listened to—images frozen on glass plates. Indeed, individualism was less the point than celebrity, which supplied a means of being noticed and made no chal-

lenge to the existing social order; celebrity was actually facilitated by submission to that order.[13] Not only a compensation for something lost, the rush to sport also showed a positive embrace of something quite new as a pivotal element in society—the unabashed love of the human body and the quest to bring it to its highest fulfillment as an act of personal and social joy.

Much like the early Puritans—and much like later revivalists—the physical culturists espoused a perfect way of life. But the perfect life, precisely because it was an ideal (even if people thought they could achieve it), had to stand as a model for everyone to fulfill. The Puritans had separated from the imperfection of the old world and had espoused community for the true believers—that is, what made them very different from the outsiders made them very much the same among themselves. And so, too, the physical culturists appeared very different from those not committed to the new cult of the body. But physical culturists advocated faithful pursuit of the same "devotional" exercises for all the believers. In this way, the quest for perfection permitted an intense apparent denial of self-will, even as it simultaneously demanded extraordinary attention to the body as an ersatz, material self.

Between the two world wars, the forces creating this optimistic view and the rhetoric expressing it—and to some degree an actual social context of optimism—remained diverse and sometimes conflicting. A key tension was the one between popular instinct about the body and the body of formal knowledge about health. But the apparent conflict between science and imagination diminished in light of the scientific basis behind some psychosomatic illness. "Mood," for example, is partly a matter of chemistry. "Endorphins come to mind" is an awful pun, but, in fact, they do—in both senses of the phrase. Much else that has been dismissed as spurious in one era is discovered to have some physical basis at a later date. For example, new research has established the effect of various vitamins on apparent cases of mental derangement. But despite all the efforts to develop a scientific literature in defense of physical culture in the decades after World War I,

the ultimate test of validity became simply the feelings spawned by one's fellows in the culture and ingrained into one's own self.

The Culture of Pleasure

The interest in pleasure was much more revolutionary than the quest for health, largely because it required a much more significant change in basic values.[14] This transformation in popular morals gathered force through the 1920s and 1930s, sanctioned by the critiques of puritanical restraint offered by intellectuals. In *The Wine of the Puritans* (1908), Van Wyck Brooks blamed the Puritan tradition for diverting all American energy into utilitarian pursuits, both expressing and reinforcing a fear of pleasure.[15] Public morality and the legal structure supporting it changed drastically, as bans against smoking among women collapsed, speakeasies became commonplace, and open discussion of sexual matters became frequent. Precisely what form the new code of sexual behavior might take was not obvious—a measure of abstention was advocated by some feminists but nearpromiscuity was allowed by less fastidious thinkers. In all events, the role of the body and the roster of acceptable physical behavior became centerpieces of concern in American life. And if Freudian psychologist A. A. Brill's public lectures on masturbation were not an explicit pitch for a culture of pleasure, they demonstrated the matter-of-fact acceptance of the body that was central to the creation of such a culture.[16]

The timelessness that philosophically inclined observers have found in sport made it an ideal match for a culture that itself rejected time and history, a culture that, in fact, reconceived history as a warehouse of tools for fashioning a happier present that conformed to the sway of current taste. A group of intellectuals including Hart Crane and Kay Boyle asserted flatly that "time is a tyranny to be abolished," and Gertrude Stein's writing gave a clear indication of what an art based on time's abolition might look like. "The future is not important any more," Stein said. Even the apparent interest in history suggested by Henry Ford's so-called historic site at Greenfield Village withered when subjected to a closer look. Ford wrenched cottages once occupied by Noah Webster and Patrick Henry from the original locations that had actually given them their genuine context and meaning. "We want to live in the present," Ford said, "and the only history that is worth a tinker's dam is the history we make today."[17] Joseph Freeman has cited the new American effort to "find a frank and free life for the emotions and senses," and historian William E. Leuchtenburg has summarized the dominant tone of the age as commitment to the "ideal of hedonism"—living for the moment.[18] The President's Research Committee on Social Trends said the focus on the present reflected the desire for pleasure and promoted its attainment; committee members looked with curiosity and concern at "the new attitude towards hardship as a thing to be avoided by living in the here and now."[19] Sport was seen to be above and beyond time. It was at once unswervingly physical and sensual, pulling powerfully at the emotions.

In some measure difficult to quantify, the intense enthusiasm for sport in the decades between the world wars—an enthu-

siasm that gave vitality to the notion of a golden age—depended upon the vogue of psychology and likely gave it reciprocal support. Mental health was not only a part of comprehensive health. It was seen as an important form of health in its own right. Activities that promised to create good feelings, therefore—activities that seemed to produce positive affective consequences—gained value. Sport clearly rated high on the list.

Being healthy had been a part of American culture for some time, but feeling healthy now became at least as important. However, feeling good was separable from strictly physical health. The medical facts of proper health, to the extent that they could be established, provided a social norm for a vast range of behaviors at a time when metaphysical moral norms were largely discarded. But the affective matter of "feeling good," or at least seeming to do so, paradoxically provided still more norms outside oneself. Self-gratification was a socially determined priority, and precisely what was supposed to feel good to the individual depended profoundly on publicly communicated models, such as those that sports and movie stars provided in the popular press and on radio (fig. 5). Feelings, sentiments, and sensibilities are a part of health, too. In the 1920s and 1930s, physical fitness, sport, and exercise were expected to be a source of such good feelings. Dr. Earle C. Lindeman, national director of the WPA's Community Organization for Leisure, called for "light" and "joy" through recreation and leisure, claiming that the "old American dream" was "a good life for everybody."[20] Moreover, recreation and leisure were expected to offer more than a guarantee of the absence of serious

Fig. 5   Charles MacMahon's exercise book *The Royal Road to Health and Strength* gave readers of *Physical Culture* a highly personal definition of health. In essence, "the way you feel" was most important. Although such familiar words as "strength" and "endurance" and concepts as immunity from sickness all appeared, the individual became the judge of whether he possessed these elements of "health" sufficiently. Even more significant, MacMahon's advertisement emphasized personal appearance and the ability to create a positive impression. In short order, the dedicated student of MacMahon's method would "have people exclaim, 'My, what a *finely built chap*' after one glance at the broad shoulders, deep chest, trim waist, and beautiful proportions which are noticeable even when you are fully dressed." What the man did was less important that what he was—his accomplishments less commanding than his appearance. Advertisement in *Physical Culture* (January 1926).

ailments and disease; they were to be a source of positive joys and pleasures as well (fig. 6).

Psychiatry and the concept of mental health were not clear components of "popular" life until some time into the twentieth century, but popular psychiatry was surely an important aspect of the popular culture of the 1920s and after, even though it was something of a fad as well. The popularity of psychiatry also helped to set the ground for later matters, such as the resurgence in the 1930s of the notion of individual responsibility for corporate or social problems. The self-reliance espoused by Norman Vincent Peale, Dale Carnegie, and others was a giant step away from guilt. Yet making such a step meant accepting responsibility, even for public events, in an intensely personal and individual way. Public renewal and transformation depended on personal development in mind and, ever more, in body.

Fig. 6 In 1939, Juanita Coleman, left, helped adults learn to play during a recreation period outside the church at Gee's Bend, Alabama, where she conducted a class in the fundamentals of education. Coleman's role suggests the importance given to experts during the 1930s and in other times as well. But the purpose to which her expertise was put was based on the belief that Americans deserved personal happiness and fulfillment. Photograph by Marion Post Wolcott for the Farm Security Administration. Courtesy Library of Congress, LC–USF33–30355–M5.

Body Love

The early decades of the twentieth century witnessed a sharp rise in public praise of the body—indeed, in love for the body as a component of the self. Although one cannot precisely measure it, the vogue of psychology clearly supported greater attention to the body. Rather than being a source of temptations that violated moral precept, the body became much more a vehicle for relationships and a means of gratification—not a matter of fear, but a matter of fact. The physical side of humanity was not a regrettable accident but an essential instrument of identity.

As Leuchtenburg has observed, Sigmund Freud's concept of "repression" proved especially useful because it allowed Americans to dismiss as psychological defects any inconvenient social and personal restraints.[21] Although sexual taboos and social customs were part of any culture almost by definition, American intellectuals tended to see them as distinctively American problems, extending the notion of "American exceptionalism" to the realm of morals. To the degree that Americans focused on the body as an object of repression, it became the ready means to demonstrate liberation from old psychological shackles. They turned away from Victorian "respectability," and they rejected the "high diction" tinged by moralism and sentimentality that had prevailed before World War I.[22] Ripping away one veil of values after another, Americans were finally left with nothing by which to ennoble actions, and so their actions, no longer standing for anything else, had to stand on their own.

Physical contact—incidental, sexual, athletic—became a vehicle through which relationships were established, not as symbols of something else but as the actual building blocks of personality. As Warren Susman has suggested, the psychosocial agenda of the 1920s and 1930s included the elimination of guilt and the transcendence of shame; the devices for dealing with them were, respectively, the debunking by popularizers (or distorters) of Freud and Adlerian adjustment.[23] Popular Freudianism took away the air of mystery from human relationships, imposing a nearly mechanistic logic on what had previously been considered the soul and the emotions. In essence, Freud developed a science of emotions, but the risk was that individual responsibility would seem lessened if humans shared an underlying psychological inheritance that motivated them and guided their primary affections. To the extent that Freud's work was made to explain all feelings and drives, it deprived personal guilt of its logical underpinnings and enabled the liberated American to regard shame as a peculiar vestige of puritanical ignorance.

Although this popularized Freudianism was the dominant psychological theory in the 1920s, in the 1930s the ideas of Alfred Adler came into greater prominence. Adler disagreed with Freud's seeming reduction of human relationships to a few underlying mechanistic processes, and he emphasized the importance of each individual's network of personal relationships and associations. By reaffirming the worth of individual relationships in constructing one's own personality, Adler made social contacts a matter of individual choice—and hence kept them from being subject to a divine or even social mandate. It was not quite that there were no rules, but it did mean that the rules could never be regarded as absolute. Freud freed people *from* God, but Adler freed people *for* other people.

The vehicle for shedding traditional ways and the old morality in the 1920s was a cult of objectivity, supported by the ideas of Freud. If human behavior was driven by the rules that Freud believed to be resident in the mind—rules that meshed with the impulses of the body— then creeds rooted in religion and other transcendent sources lost their power. Indeed, to a network of thinkers, reformers, and social agencies, the very idea of transcendent values seemed to be bunk. Freud offered a sense of power over human drives, which he neutralized by describing in scientific terms. But if physical drives were innate, then shame became merely a social creation. What Freud considered an objective science made the individual option to feel guilt for transgressing a social code almost an act of eccentricity.

In other fields, too, there was a strong effort to impose some sort of objectivity and to avoid the vagaries of purely personal choice. The manner in which one dealt with others thus became a more apt object of study than the substance of what one meant to say. In other words, the importance of what one said yielded to the importance of how one communicated, as interest in the works of S. I. Hayakawa, Stuart Chase, and Thurman Arnold suggested. In child rearing, behaviorists warned about the dangers of hugging and kissing one's offspring— behavior that would supposedly kill the freedom of choice and association that the child could otherwise develop. But this kind of "freedom" really restricted the parents, diminishing their role as models of character and moral action. Paradoxically, this sort of freedom also exaggerated the importance of social context.[24] This challenge to traditional networks of familial feeling and mutual affection may have served to banish some form of guilt, such as that born of past ingratitude toward one's parents. But this challenge compelled obedience to new norms that were widely thought to be neutral even though they were actually dictated by society. Actions did thus serve to create identity for the individual, but to make that identity distinctive became painfully difficult.

Similarly, the 1930s saw the concoction of cures for newly invented social "diseases"—centered on the body—such as bad breath, body odor, stained teeth, and dishpan hands.[25] The awareness of oneself as a creature of culture was coupled with the passion for commitment— indeed, this awareness made commitment to some group, ideology, or cause the key to firming up personal identity. Shorn of precepts and codes that had traditionally been viewed as permanent, the individual now suffered the anxiety of complete relativity, which was resolved, ironically, by submission to the culture itself, despite the fact that it was the source of the relativity in the first place.

If Freud's psychology insisted that the body's needs must be known and its functions accepted, then Adler's psychology urged that the body be seen as a focus of relationships and as a means for cultivating them. In such a realm, the sensory fulfillment in sport loomed important— the physical, the sexual, and the sensual all increasingly confused. The interpenetration of these diverse undercurrents accounted for the odd mixture of acclaim and hostility faced by those various proponents of physical culture and sport whose love of the body was so ambivalent.

Bernarr MacFadden advocated "body love" with such fervor that the term became one of his nicknames. Touted as the hero of a rags-to-riches story by his biographer, MacFadden carried the mythic aspects of Horatio Alger tales into the realm of the body and its performance (fig. 7).[26] Yet his greatest success lay not in the accumulation of wealth but in his own personal development. As American culture gave increasing attention to the body and its potential, the aim was not to learn moral precepts in order to win the eye of the contented business leader but to learn "proper regulation" of the body so as to infuse the individual with vitality. Discovering MacFadden's solution to personal weakness

Fig. 7 Editor of *Physical Culture* and many other magazines, "Professor" Bernarr Mac-Fadden emerged as one of the most ardent proponents of health and fitness in early twentieth-century America. He regarded the human body so highly, and so strongly urged caring for it as an inherent good, that he won the nickname "Body Love." For MacFadden, a person's main goal was to fulfill individual potential; what society gained from individual health was derivative and secondary. Photograph by F. W. Guerin of St. Louis, Missouri, 1893. Courtesy Library of Congress, portrait file.

resembled the experience of a religious conversion; regular exercise was a sweaty act of revival. "At fifteen years of age," biographer Clement Wood claimed, "he was frail and emaciated, and threatened with the same trouble [tuberculosis] from which his mother had died." He became a "modern Old Testament prophet" proclaiming "nature's laws of eating and doing and mating," all for the sake of "man's physical salvation, on which depend also his mental salvation, his spiritual salvation, his happiness, his health, his very life." His regimen had transformed him into "an erect, happy, successful Samson at sixty whose life has been devoted to making of his fellow men a race of Samsons." A key tenet in the creed of the new Samson was that the body could purify itself, availing itself of healthy exercise and small quantities of natural food. "Drugless healing" had a measure of common sense about it, but the passion for purification made physical culture smack of religion and gave exercise and diet the aura of sacred rituals. Thus, too, the body was both the means and the goal of adoration. "Promotion of the health and happiness of a people is a paramount object of proper government," MacFadden proclaimed. "Nothing is worth while without buoyant health! . . . Health is the greatest thing in the world." With the conviction and sweep of a faith healer, MacFadden quoted British novelist Bulwer Lytton, author of such works as *The Last Days of Pompeii* (1834): "Never tell people you are ill; never own it to yourself. Illness is one of those things which a man should resist on principle at the outset."[27]

MacFadden looked like an obsessive and mercurial eccentric to those who were not his followers. Yet the key to his significance lies in the blinding consistency of his views. Outsiders tested each of his pronouncements against their own standards, against traditional social values, and against established law. For MacFadden, however, all such criteria were irrelevant—the body and its natural demands were the one and only standard. His passionate love of the body often met with little sympathy from other Americans, but for him it was the standard by which to make sense out of his life. He spoke positively about Soviet society's encouragement of women's physical development. He defended sex education (although he discouraged "excessive" sexual activity), and he advocated that women marry only for love and that men be impetuous lovers of the "cave man sort." The unifying thread of his philosophy was knowing natural processes and giving them highest priority. He promoted nudity—or at least baring all but the most delicate parts of the body—because he distinguished between sexuality and sensuality. He railed against "petting parties," not because there was too much sexual activity but because, in a sense, there was too little: the emotion of love must not be toyed with but pursued with diligence and élan. He did not conceive of himself as a "liberal" in such matters. In all the appetites and all sensual expression—in food, sex, exercise, sport—his answer remained consistent: "Let nature be the guide."[28] Everything depended on the physical side of man, released from inhibition and repression.

MacFadden meant to have it both ways—seeing the care of the body as a means to pleasure and the achievement of pleasure as a good reason for caring for the body. And his rhetoric makes clear that he could, in fact, have it both ways without losing coherence because he regarded the body as a fit object of care in its own right. "Health has become popular," he wrote in 1924 in the introduction to one of his cookbooks; "a strong and beautiful body has become a thing of honor and glory, and the proper feeding of the body a duty recognized and a pleasure to be enjoyed by all."[29] He elevated the cultivation of the body to the level of a virtual religion. "Sickness is a sin," he proclaimed in *Physical Culture*; "don't be a sinner. Weakness is a crime; don't be a criminal."[30]

The transformation that MacFadden's life embodied was imitated by other notable cases including that of Charles Atlas, who must be regarded as something of a protégé of "Body Love" MacFadden. Charles Atlas, whose real name was Angelo Siciliano, was born in Italy on October 30, 1893. His parents separated when he was ten, and his mother took the boy with her to New York. On Halloween night in 1908, he was attacked by a neighborhood bully; when he got home, his uncle chided him for getting into a fight and gave him another beating. Many years later he recalled, "I went to my room and cried myself to sleep, but before I fell asleep, I swore an oath to my God that I would never allow any man on earth to hurt me again." The next year, he actually had sand kicked in his face on the beach at Coney Island—the victim of "a big husky lifeguard—maybe there were two of them."[31] The odd combination of vivid memory and imprecision on so basic a fact as the number of bullies underscores the centrality of the adolescent's own feelings and desperate need for identity—to the point where the number, let alone identity, of his assailants slipped into relative unimportance. Young Angelo supposedly found a solution for his need in a chance viewing of classical statuary at the Brooklyn Museum. Soon he pasted a picture of strong man Eugene Sandow on the mirror of his dresser and became an avid reader of Bernarr MacFadden's *Physical Culture*. He pursued an exercise program drawn from what he read, aiming to emulate the well-muscled Sandow. According to legend, a friend thought the results so successful that Angelo had come to look like a statue of Atlas atop a hotel named after the mythological figure. Angelo had long been nicknamed Charlie, and so the new professional name of Charles Atlas was born. A new identity, based in the body, had been won. A "conversion experience" had been achieved—a conversion not through moral reflection and spiritual conviction of sin but through the banishment of the physical sin of muscular weakness.

The subsequent successes of Charles Atlas were many and varied. He went the route of other strong men and physical culturists, such as MacFadden and Earle E. Liederman, and with the latter he founded a vaudeville act called Orpheum Models. They combined feats of strength with posing, expressing delight not only in the achievements that bodily development might give but also in physical beauty as a proper goal in its own right. When the act folded, Liederman started a mail-order physical culture course, using Atlas as one of his promotional testimonies. Then, in 1921, Atlas won the "World's Most Beautiful Man Contest" sponsored by Bernarr MacFadden— "Body Love" promptly gave Atlas a check for one thousand dollars and pro-

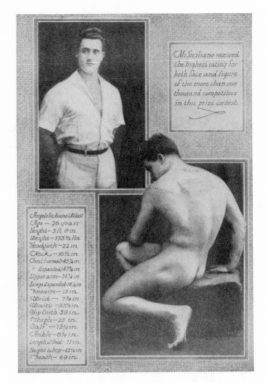

Fig. 8   Smooth, "aesthetic" poses evoking classical sculpture set the standard for the "ideal human body" of the 1920s and 1930s— a standard emphasizing personal grace and suggesting ease, quiet confidence, and contentment. A durable exemplar of the physical style was Angelo Siciliano, known professionally as Charles Atlas. He is seen here in an October 1921 issue of *Physical Culture* as victor in the magazine's "World's Most Handsome Man" contest.

claimed him "the living realization of my lifelong battle for the body beautiful" (fig. 8). In the following year, Atlas swept to quick victory in MacFadden's search for "America's Most Perfectly Developed Man." (MacFadden then called off plans for further contests, fearing that he would simply bankroll Atlas.)[32]

Atlas's work as a promoter of physical culture thrived under the management of Charles Roman, who took on his ac-

Fig. 9 There was a cruel persistence in the way physical culturists sought to badger and embarrass Americans into buying their books and taking their courses. Here, for example, Charles Atlas tells the potential student that he can be "AD-MIRED instead of *pitied*"—playing a variation on the theme of "peer pressure" that grew more intense in the 1920s. Atlas promised strength and vitality. But the leading concern remained personal appearance—to be "beautiful" and "symmetrical," to wear a bathing suit well so that "YOU needn't be one of those they scorn and poke fun at!" The body was to be trained and shaped—but mostly just to be pleasing to oneself and to others. Advertisement for Charles Atlas's *Secrets of Muscular Power and Beauty* in *Muscle-Builder* (March 1924).

count at the Benjamin Landsman Advertising Agency in New York in 1928. According to writers working from the recollections of Charles Roman, the key to selling Charles Atlas was to "reach into where people live, not into their abstract thoughts about good health and leverage over objects, but into their fears and longings, and dreams for themselves." They needed to distinguish Atlas from his competitors, and the key was for Atlas to "embody a collective dream of manhood through strength and health." The insis-

tent reference to dreams and longings properly evokes the spirit of the time—a striving for personal transformation and an anxious quest for the regard of others (fig. 9). Always, despite Atlas's interest in his personal financial success, the enrichment of one's own body remained the goal so surpassingly attractive that positive side effects of physical culture seemed almost trivial. Atlas claimed that during the Depression he was often called by wealthy men who had "gone bust" and threatened suicide. His answer was telling: "I say,

'You ought to stick your head under water for that statement. Get to exercising. Forget it. Burn your bonds. Tear up your stocks. Give away your property. Get on a healthy basis. My God, man, it's your body that counts. The hell with your possessions.'"[33] Spoken like a true zealot of the body.

Atlas's focus on full, balanced development did not lead to exaggerated musculature, and in this respect he embodied the same aesthetic as the streamlined objects appearing in the material culture of his day.[34] So, too, his plan for achieving "perfect manhood" included a broad array of prescriptions, dealing with personal grooming and manners as well as exercise and diet. In this way, he echoed the peculiar variation on self-reliance represented in the work of Dale Carnegie and other advocates of self-improvement. He spoke of posture, how to sleep and how to rise, why the solar plexus and genital organs must be bathed in cold water every morning, on gaining "physical magnetism" through such measures as stretching, and on rubbing olive oil into the scalp.[35] One's salvation was manifestly an intimate as well as an individual matter.

Atlas's career consistently depended on the celebration of his body. In 1939 a committee of artists at the New York World's Fair proclaimed him to be the best male physical specimen alive.[36] Still, an objective assessment of Charles Atlas's physique at the time of some of his greatest successes might be disappointing—especially if he was compared with other physical culturists, even with his own student Tony Sansone. What Charles Atlas sold was less his body itself than the image of confidence in one's physical self—an ebullient "body love" in which the body seemed less important than the freedom to love it.

The Rhetoric of the Body

It is said that "there are words for things," but there are also things for which the meanings of words change. As consciousness of one's world alters, the change may create an awareness of things previously taken for granted as part of an unseen background. The conscious celebration of the body and the intentional pursuit of pleasure spawned certain new uses of words, and certain other usages gained far greater frequency. Talk of "shaping up" came into American speech during the 1880s, at which time it referred to the preparation of cattle hides and, later, to the fattening of stock before slaughter.[37] From the outset, then, the rhetoric of "shaping up" focused on physical rather than emotional and affective dimensions. Even when someone was later told to "shape up" (or else to "ship out"), there was enormous emphasis on behavior, grooming, and other physical attributes as the test of proper "shape." During the 1920s and 1930s, the idea of "being in shape" had assumed special association with physical fitness and conditioning—as well as with sport, in which case the notion of being "in form" also held sway.[38]

The increasing use of terminology derived from sport to give metaphorical vitality to other fields of endeavor suggests the growing importance of sport in American life. But the more specific shifts in vocabulary—and in the meaning of words—hint at the underlying enthusiasm for the body. So, too, the manner in which the language was used, casually and comfortably, shows the matter-of-fact embrace of the body and what it could do—without explanation or justification.

Visions of Joy

The language of the body was accompanied by an iconography that reflected the esteem and fondness people felt toward it. Where late nineteenth-century imagery drew on the objectivity of science, the photographs and films of the interwar years abounded with the rich personality of star performers and other celebrities. Where the older iconography extolled discipline, the newer one was rich with action. If the imagery of decades past drew strongly on the tradition of self-denial, the "new era" fostered visions of joy.

The coach became a visual symbol of paternal affection, guiding his athletes with fondness even more than with firmness. In a 1939 *Look* article about the swimming team of Pennsylvania's Mercersburg Academy, the coach appeared as a smiling father figure, joking with the young men in his care. The Mercersburg swimmers exuded a sense of commitment and confidence. The photographers did not portray them as if in pain—as if they were sweating out the sins of the flesh in thinly disguised masochism. So, too, the coach was presented as kindly and warm. In one photograph, he is shown riding a bicycle in the midst of his team as they took a training run; they smiled as their coach poked them and urged them on. No one seemed uncomfortable at the coach's attentions. In another photograph, the coach leaned over at poolside to counsel a swimmer in a mild-mannered way. In yet another, the coach personally gave doses of honey to his team.[39] In short, human kindness and consideration suffused physical effort; the pervasive tone was *Kraft durch Freude*—strength won through joy rather than through the pain of training and competition.

The portrayal of the Mercersburg coach and athletes is especially telling when compared with the picture given in other eras, whether of the technocratic expert of the turn of the century or of the militaristic disciplinarian of the decades after World War II. In 1964, for example, *Life* illustrated an article on the newly fashionable isometric contraction with photographs of swimmer Lary Schulhof, as captions explained that he was at the highest stage of training when he ascended from mere "hurt" and "pain" and achieved "agony." Pain was not shown as a mere accident of training but as its very core. The centrality of pain for the swimmer made Coach Jim Counsilman, by extension, the master of "All-Out Agony at Indiana U."[40] A 1962 article proclaimed "Football Is Violence," emphasizing that pain must be welcomed as a means of displaying stoicism. Even "an occasional fatality" was embraced as a part of the situation, and a coach expected an injured player who "[grimaced] in pain" to welcome his suffering as a badge of honor.[41] For such coaches, sport was life, and life was war. One coach told a researcher that he expected injured players to "behave as my boys in the service—Brave—and not go into any fanfare for the People."[42] However obvious their appeal to later Americans, such words would not have been persuasive in the 1920s and 1930s.

"Teamwork," after all, was an apotheosis of "getting along." The enormously popular football coach Knute Rockne made this clear in promotional speeches he gave to car dealers and salesmen after he signed on with the Studebaker Corporation in 1928. What worked for Rockne in football, he thought, would apply in business as well. Key was the "ability to cooperate"; he disparaged a number of personality types who he thought hindered all real accomplishment: "the swelled head," "the chronic complainer," "the quitter," those with an "inferiority complex," those who make up alibis, "the mucker, who tries to get by by playing unfair."[43] Hints of late nineteenth-century concern over individual character lingered, but Rockne added a perspective well suited to the era of his greatest triumphs—that the winning power of the team depended on building warm interpersonal relationships among its members.

Important champion athletes who emerged as lasting celebrities exuded enthusiasm and joy rather than self-denial and suffering. Even the bodily form of the retired athletic competitor could become an emblem of unselfconscious ease. The case of Johnny Weissmuller is a notable example. When director W. S. Van Dyke began his search for someone to play Tarzan after MGM acquired rights to an Edgar Rice Burroughs property, he said he wanted "a man who is young, strong, well-built, reasonably attractive, but not necessarily handsome, and a competent actor." But the kind of acting Van Dyke demanded was telling. "The most important thing is that he have a good physique." Looking for "someone like Jack Dempsey," Van Dyke hoped to sign Olympic shot-putter Herman Brix, who lost the role when he suffered a broken shoulder while making another movie. But instead of a Dempsey, Van Dyke chose the leaner, smoother look of a swimmer. What finally sold Van Dyke on Weissmuller was his physical ease and grace, his unaffected acceptance of his body. Before he made the final selection, Van Dyke had complained that "most actors without clothes are undressed rather than naked and are too self-conscious to act naturally." Van Dyke's publicity touted Weissmuller as the "only man in Hollywood who's natural in the flesh and can act without clothes."[44]

Praise for Weissmuller's realization of Tarzan on the screen clearly placed higher priority on his physical gifts than on his acting talent; the final basis of his emerging status as a celebrity was not his dramatic skill but his appeal as a sex object. Thornton Delehanty of the *New York Evening Post* remarked, "However credible or interesting Tarzan may be on the printed page, I doubt very much if he emerges in such splendor as he does in the person of Johnny Weissmuller. . . . There is no doubt that he possesses all the attributes, both physical and mental, for the complete realization of this son-of-the-jungle role. With his flowing hair, his magnificently proportioned body, his catlike walk, and his virtuosity in the water, you could hardly ask anything more in the way of perfection." In *Photoplay*, however, Katherine Albert insisted that "the most vital statistic of all is the fact that a lad who had never been in a picture before, who had been interested in nothing but swimming all his life, and who frankly admits he can't act, is the topnotch heart flutterer of the year."[45]

Ease with his body not only made Weissmuller a credible Tarzan; it also made him the kind of Tarzan who could be credible in the interwar years by presenting a flowing, supple body that reflected the streamlined sensuality of the modernist aesthetic. Like the designs of Walter Lescaze, Norman Bel Geddes, and Raymond Loewy, Weissmuller's body showed strength in smoothness, curve overcoming angularity, and a celebration of appearances instead of the guts that made things work.[46] Weissmuller's body did not display the bold muscular development and fine "rippling" or detailing of a man like Eugene Sandow; his had a far smoother look—a style favored even by acknowledged physical culturists such as Charles Atlas and Tony Sansone. So removed from the thought that "gain" required pain, Weissmuller exemplified the view that "gain" was natural (fig. 10). His body showed not the look of hurt but the look of joy and—if *Photoplay* was right— perhaps even the look of love.

Despite challenges from unprincipled ivory hunters and even an occasional Nazi, Tarzan showed a life-style that recaptured primitive beauty and physical contentment, if not quite Eden. Affectionate talk between Tarzan and Jane was often eclipsed by exuberant swinging in the vines and splashing in the waters. *Tarzan the Ape Man* (1932) and *Tarzan and His Mate* (1934) showed Weissmuller at his sensuous best—still close to the physical form that had carried him to Olympic triumphs in 1924 and 1928. Critic Francis Birrell praised *Tarzan the Ape Man* for making no pretense at accuracy and fell for its enthusiasm. "It is just a terrific piece of gusto in the romantic manner," he wrote.[47] Notably, what really did ring true in the film was the "gusto"—the

Fig. 10   The athletic look of the 1920s and 1930s may best be seen in champion swimmer Johnny Weissmuller's smoothly balanced body. Shown here in 1930 with former heavyweight boxing champion Jack Dempsey, Weissmuller seemed a "natural athlete" who performed well by realizing his inherent gifts. Even boxer Dempsey shows relatively little of the bulk and distinct musculature that became common in later notions of what an athlete ought to look like. In contrast to a later cliché in sport, it was as if "gain" did not require "pain." Courtesy Library of Congress, biographical file.

spirit and enthusiasm of sportive, happy display and of intense, energetic activity.

In these movies the theme of the corruption of civilization comes to the fore, sharpening the audience's taste for the gratifying "natural" life of "The Family Tarzan." In *Tarzan's Secret Treasure* (1941), deceitful visitors pit Jane against Tarzan in a plot to steal "Boy" away from his jungle haven—or heaven—so they can govern his multimillion dollar inheritance. Still later, in *Tarzan's Desert Mystery* (1943), the hero stands as emblem for a mythic America shedding its isolationism to fight the Nazis, who not at all incidentally seem set upon imposing an artificial system of social compulsions on a natural and otherwise unspoiled realm.

In films explicitly dealing with sport in the decades between the world wars, affectionate sentiments predominated; the spirit of play and humane regard held its own against competitiveness and a gross fixation on victory. To be sure, winning is much prized; but in "winning [the game] for the Gipper," the victory is one of memory and comradeship—not a tick on the card en route to a title. In *Knute Rockne—All American* (1940), this feast of mutual respect and regard, this triumph of personal relationships, is laid out under a coach played with compelling warmth by Pat O'Brien. The personal side of fulfillment reigned supreme, even in the much-noted scene in which Ronald Reagan simulates the death of Notre Dame player George Gipp.

Even when sport turned sour and threatening, the film athlete still aimed at personal fulfillment and achievement through his relationships. A notable example is *The Champ* (1931), in which Wallace Beery plays an over-the-hill boxer who risks fatal injury to support his son and keep his admiration. Here, too, sport is the arena of achievement and fulfillment, but the substance of achievement is personal in the relationship of father to son. *Ex-Champ* (1939) also centers on a father-son relationship, overshadowing the downbeat feeling of a boxing career in eclipse. In *Kid Galahad* (1937), the success of a boxing promoter, played by Edward G. Robinson, is offset by the loss of his girlfriend to a naive fighter, portrayed by Wayne Morris. The most trenchant story is in the personal side of human relationships rather than in the public side of sporting competition.

To be sure, there was a darker side to the presentation of sport. In *College Coach* (1933), for example, Pat O'Brien—years before his transformation into the warm and winning Knute Rockne—plays the coach as a domineering and merciless martinet. Dick Powell portrays a star athlete who wants to get an education, angering the coach by not sharing his singleness of purpose. But such films actually prove the commitment to the kindly coach during the interwar years. *College Coach* exposes and challenges the worth of a victory that comes at the expense of a fuller life, family relationships, personal regard, and friendship.

In *They Made Me a Criminal* (1939), John Garfield plays boxer Johnny Burns who is duped into thinking he has killed a man so that his manager can pocket the boxer's fight winnings. Yet, even here, Garfield is redeemed by his encounters with the Dead End Kids and Ann Sheridan, and the focal point remains how well people manage to get along. Although Burns boxes for greed in the early part of the film, he uses his skill at the end as a sign of his love and concern for his newfound friends—risking disclosure of his identity to win one last purse literally to "save the farm." Sport thus serves as an "arena" in which one may reach the deeper personal fulfillment of lasting human relationships. In this sense, even athletic victory pales before shaping a happy, well-adjusted personality—although it is still better to have both, as Garfield's Johnny Burns ultimately does. In his own way, perhaps Burns exemplifies an inner conflict experienced by many Americans in the 1930s—a conflict different from that between personal identity and corporate loyalty that had troubled Americans a few decades earlier. Yet now, the achievement of victory—or the transcendence of the need for it—was more likely to strengthen the identity of the individuals on a team than to subsume that identity in deference to the social group.

Perhaps it was symbolically apt that the era's treatment of sport in film should have included musical comedy, such as *Pigskin Parade* (1936) with Judy Garland, Jack Haley, Stuart Erwin, and Betty Grable. Sport could serve as grist for humor in such films not because sport was ephemeral but rather because it had become an integral part of American life. As portrayed in the popular culture, sport strengthened personal relationships—those relationships ultimately centered not on working together for the good of society but on "feeling good" for oneself.

In the first few decades of the twentieth century, Americans took to sport with new zest and a fresh desire for enjoyment and personal development. In this shift in tone, sport was like many other elements of the new mass culture—both a form of entertainment and a plan for self-improvement. At times, the enthusiasm for sport in old bastions of elitism and high thought, such as the universities, has been styled as an unusual "anti-intellectualism."[48] Even more, though, this enthusi-

asm marked the importance of "getting along," of individual relationships rather than the social polity, and of the place of the body in the process. Less important than a general anti-intellectualism was the specific turn from logical analysis and the tradition of rational criticism. As Paula Fass has observed, establishing personal identity and a claim to worth in such a manner had clearly conservative implications.[49] Sport itself had already become a part of a new "establishment," not at all popular in governance and yet catering to popular taste; developing one's self through such sport mandated a deference to existing outside authority. Nonetheless the perception remained strong that it was the individual whose needs and desires set the standard of what made activities worthwhile.

The final belief that what is good for the individual must benefit society seems the ultimate in presumptuousness, but it is an integral premise of twentieth-century sport. And if there is a presumption even more dazzling in its sweep and aspiration, it may be the equation of the individual's good with his conscious sense of feeling good: content, fulfilled, and happy (fig. 11). "Enjoy Yourself," a popular song of the 1940s urged, giving voice to this new tone cultivated in the 1920s and 1930s. The time to do so was while one might have youth, probably had vitality, and certainly had good health: "Enjoy yourself, while you're still in the pink." The lyrics warned against deferred gratification—"It's later than you think"—and told the value of the present by noting its frailty: "The years go by as quickly as a wink."[50]

Sport was a joy, but it was also a duty—a peculiar but essential paradox not unlike that arising in religious conver-

Fig. 11 College football was one of America's biggest sports in the 1920s and 1930s, but there is no grim dedication to be found in this scene at Duke University in November 1939 during a game between Duke and the University of North Carolina. Popular bandleader Kay Kyser joins a UNC cheerleader, spreading joy and enthusiasm. Photograph by Marion Post Wolcott for the Farm Security Administration. Courtesy Library of Congress, LC–USF33–30683–M3.

sion. Liberation from the sin of physical sloth always came at the cost of sweat, often with a tax in tears, and sometimes even with a surtax in blood. Yet the tears had to be those of joy, whether in reality or only in pretense. The mastery of one's body, then, allowed a curious mastery of one's self and one's place in society. Freedom became not an unending realm of variables requiring new choices at every turn but a voluntary commitment to fixed regimes undertaken day after day that made health just one tool to use in achieving self-fulfillment.[51]

Notes

1 The interpretation of the "rise of sport" as a response to the pressures of industrialization first emerged forcefully early in the twentieth century. See Frederic Paxson, "The Rise of Sport," *Mississippi Valley Historical Review*, September 1917, 143–68. Historian John Betts continued the study of how industrialization and modern technology affected the growth of sport. His works culminated in the textbook *America's Sporting Heritage, 1850–1950* (Reading, Mass.: Addison-Wesley, 1974). The interplay of technological advancement, industrial development, and the growth of cities in fostering sport is discussed in such case studies as Dale A. Somers, *The Rise of Sports in New Orleans: 1850–1900* (Baton Rouge: Louisiana State University Press, 1972); Stephen Hardy, *How Boston Played: Sport, Recreation, and Community, 1865–1915* (Boston: Northeastern University Press, 1982); and Steven A. Riess, *Touching Base: Professional Baseball and American Culture in the Progressive Era* (Westport, Conn.: Greenwood Press, 1980).

2 An early influential study of the impact of industrial notions of efficiency on society is Samuel P. Hays, *Conservation and the Gospel of Efficiency: The Progressive Conservation Movement, 1890–1920* (Cambridge: Harvard University Press, 1959). A later synthetic view of the era emphasizing corporate values and the subordination of the individual is Robert H. Wiebe, *The Search for Order, 1877–1920* (New York: Hill and Wang, 1967).

3 Donald J. Mrozek, *Sport and American Mentality, 1880–1910* (Knoxville: University of

Tennessee Press, 1983), explores the various justifications for sport used by middle-class, genteel, and wealthy Americans. Social rather than personal standards were used to legitimate sport, and these reflected the corporate values of society in general.

4 A discussion of each of these various "constituencies" appears in ibid.

5 Harvey Green, *Fit for America: Health, Fitness, Sport, and American Society* (New York: Pantheon Books, 1986).

6 That such corporate values persisted in the twentieth century is clear in studies of the American playground movement. See, for example, Dominick Cavallo, *Muscles and Morals: Organized Playgrounds and Urban Reform, 1880–1920* (Philadelphia: University of Pennsylvania Press, 1981).

7 See T. J. Jackson Lears, *No Place of Grace: Antimodernism and the Transformation of American Culture, 1880–1920* (New York: Pantheon Books, 1981).

8 On the emergence of sport to respectability, see Mrozek, *Sport and American Mentality, 1880–1910.*

9 On the shift from a nineteenth-century concern with character to the twentieth-century interest in personality, see Warren I. Susman, " 'Personality' and the Making of Twentieth-Century Culture," in his *Culture as History: The Transformation of American Society in the Twentieth Century* (New York: Pantheon Books, 1984).

10 Lears, *No Place of Grace*, 249–50.

11 Quoted in ibid., 208.

12 The routine dismissal of the "play days" held for school girls as a sign of sexism misses the fact that the specific focus of these days— that is, the spirit of play itself, joyous and celebratory—was not restricted to females. Quite clearly, boys' and men's sporting events were staged in much more keenly competitive formats, but even there the sense of sport as a joyous and happy pursuit ran strong—certainly much stronger than in many other eras.

13 The much-mentioned notion, espoused in *Knute Rockne—All-American* (1940), that football players in a big game should "win it for the Gipper" meant that the individual should subordinate himself to the group and to the demands of the team (or to the socially sanctioned order of things). Implicit was the notion that one's ability to perform grew not out of one's own private resources but from the acceptance of one's social context. Examples of "excessively individualistic" movie stars and sports stars are readily available. The case of Frances Farmer warns us that some observers might see an extreme case of personal independence but interpret it as mental collapse, and the erratic popular views of Ty Cobb indicate how far Americans had already departed from the scientific, technical bent that based respect upon one's expertise. The transformation of Babe Ruth into the lovable "Bambino" reflects how much the essence of success came to depend on "getting along" rather than on performance alone. Also, as may become clear in the broader context of society's development, Ruth's sexual escapades and tremendous appetites actually conformed to the new ethos of accepting the body as a dictating fact rather than as the creature of external morals.

14 The quest for health could be justified by considerations external to the body, such as the capacity for work and the demands of social cohesion and order, but the search for pleasure was a goal in itself. Using the body as a vehicle of pleasure similarly made it an object of affection, interest, and care in its own right.

15 Van Wyck Brooks, *The Wine of the Puritans* (London: Sisley, 1908).

16 William Leuchtenburg refers to Brill's lectures in the context of the rise of interest in Freudian psychology in America in *The Perils of Prosperity* (Chicago: University of Chicago Press, 1958), 163–64. The rapid popularization of Freudian ideas and the parallel acceptance of the body and its functions are reflected in book titles such as *Psychoanalysis by Mail*. Sears, Roebuck offered such works as *Ten Thousand Dreams Interpreted* and *Sex Problems Solved*, evidently reflecting an eclectic adherence to both Jung and Freud.

17 Quoted in Leuchtenburg, *Perils of Prosperity*, 174, 176.

18 Ibid., 174, 176.

19 Quoted in ibid., 174. Also see Jesse Fred-

erick Steiner, *Americans at Play: Recent Trends in Recreation and Leisure Time Activities* (New York: McGraw-Hill, 1933).

20   Earle C. Lindeman, "Recreation and the Good Life," *Recreation* 29 (December 1935): 436. Judith A. Davidson deserves credit for bringing the story of WPA recreation programs in New York to greater attention. Her dissertation and publications in progress also provide a solid sense of the national system of which the New York case was a part. See Judith Anne Davidson, "The Federal Government and the Democratization of Public Recreational Sport: New York City, 1933–1943" (Ph.D. diss., University of Massachusetts, 1983). Although some talked of baseball's embodiment of American virtues, in defending the continuation of professional baseball during World War II, Fiorello H. LaGuardia may have been more in tune with popular temperament when he called it simple "fun" for the common man. See Ronald F. Briley, "Where Have You Gone William Bendix?: Baseball as a Symbol of American Values in World War II," *Studies in Popular Culture* 8, no. 2 (1985): 20.

21   Leuchtenburg, *Perils of Prosperity*, 144.

22   Leuchtenburg especially notes Randolph Bourne's spurning of the idea of "respectability" (ibid.). The idea of "high diction" comes from Paul Fussell, *The Great War and Modern Memory* (New York: Oxford University Press, 1975).

23   Susman, "The Culture of the Thirties" and " 'Personality' and Twentieth-Century Culture" in Susman, *Culture as History*, 164, 284–85.

24   Susman, "Culture and Civilization: The Nineteen-Twenties," in ibid., 108–11.

25   Susman, "The Culture of the Thirties," 165.

26   Clement Wood, *Bernarr MacFadden: A Study in Success* (New York: L. Copeland, 1929; reprint, Woodstock, N.Y.: Beekman Publishers, 1974). MacFadden is a difficult man to simplify, one whose career included both mainstream and fringe activities. His publications never lacked enthusiasm, but they sometimes lacked respectability. Thus, in addition to *Physical Culture*, MacFadden's line of

magazine publications included *True Story*, *True Detective Mysteries*, *Airplane News*, *Dream World*, *Ghost Stories*, and others. Although it would be churlish to expect MacFadden to have been one-tracked, it is hardly surprising that some contemporaries found it hard to distinguish "the wheat from the chaff." On MacFadden's career, see also Mary MacFadden and Emile Gauvreau, *Dumbbells and Carrot Strips: The Story of Bernarr MacFadden* (New York: Henry Holt and Co., 1953).

27   Wood, *Bernarr MacFadden*, 17, 19, 22–23, 25, 188, 210.

28   Ibid., 239. It is worth noting that Mac-Fadden was hardly a Spartan of self-denial when it came to diet and the foods he recommended to his followers. The emphasis on whole wheat flour was predictable. But he did not shy away from the use of chocolate, heavy cream, natural cooking fat, salt, and many other ingredients typically dropped from "fad" diets. See Bernarr MacFadden, *Physical Culture Cook Book* (New York: MacFadden Publications, Inc., 1924).

29   MacFadden, *Physical Culture Cook Book*, iv.

30   *Physical Culture*, June 1947, cover.

31   Quoted in George Butler and Charles Gaines, *Yours in Perfect Manhood: Charles Atlas* (New York: Simon and Schuster, 1982), 17, 19.

32   Ibid., 57–59.

33   Ibid., 67–69, 90.

34   Some historians have assumed that the emphasis on "softness" in women during this era constituted a form of discrimination against them. See, for example, Lois Banner, *Women in Modern America* (New York: Harcourt Brace Jovanovich, 1974), 167. This criticism ignores the extent to which "soft," smooth, and sleek looks were male ideals during this period, too.

35   Butler and Gaines, *Yours in Perfect Manhood*, 113.

36   A separate judging at the Westchester Biltmore Country Club identified Dorothy Wilson as the best-developed female.

37   Mitford M. Mathews, *A Dictionary of Americanisms on Historical Principles* (Chicago:

University of Chicago Press, 1951), 1510. It is intriguing that so many words that came to have special meaning for sport and human fitness originally had to do with animal husbandry.

38   The *Oxford English Dictionary* records the use of "shape" for "excellence of form" or "beauty" in many centuries and the notion of "shape" as efficient performance, in sport especially, from the end of the nineteenth century.

39   "Mercersburg: Its Swimmers Are Prep-School Champions," *Look*, 20 March 1939, 33–36.

40   "All-Out Agony at Indiana U.," *Life*, 10 April 1964, 94–96. For more complete remarks on the stoic and militaristic themes in sport after World War II, see "The Cult and Ritual of Toughness in Cold War America," in *Rituals and Ceremonies in Popular Culture*, ed. Ray Browne (Bowling Green, Ohio: Bowling Green University Popular Press, 1980), 178–91.

41   "Football Is Violence," *Look*, 28 August 1962, 72–78.

42   See Frances P. Noe, "Coaches, Players, and Pain," *International Review in Sport Sociology* 2, no. 9 (1973): 47–61.

43   Quoted in Robert Sklar, ed., *The Plastic Age, 1917–1930* (New York: George Braziller, 1970), 261–62.

44   Gabe Essoe, *Tarzan of the Movies* (Secaucus, N.J.: Citadel Press, 1968), 67, 70.

45   Quoted in ibid., 73–74.

46   A convenient survey of streamlined design appears in Martin Greif, *Depression Modern: The Thirties Style in America* (New York: Universe Books, 1975). An obvious example of how the appearance of things—their surface— took priority over the display of what made those things operate is the streamlining of railroad engines. Quite contrary to the aesthetic of the late nineteenth century, the streamlining aesthetic of the interwar era disguised the steam boilers and pipes that had once been a focus of deliberate attention.

47   Quoted in Essoe, *Tarzan of the Movies*, 73.

48   See, for example, Paula S. Fass, *The Damned and the Beautiful: American Youth in the 1920s* (New York: Oxford University Press, 1977), 173. Fass does not oversimplify the phenomenon, nor does she mistake the important emphasis on psychological interests. The psychological dimension of the turn to sport, however, needs more elaboration.

49   Ibid., 189–91.

50   Herb Magidson and Carl Sigman, "Enjoy Yourself, It's Later Than You Think" (1948). For general access to song references, see Patricia Pate Havlice, *Popular Song Index* (Metuchen, N.J.: Scarecrow Press, 1978).

51   The phenomenon recalls the curious but clever notion that "freedom is wanting to do what you have to do."

American Advertising and the Reconstruction of the Body, 1880–1930

T. J. Jackson Lears

I want to begin in the spirit of advertising, with a startling revelation about body odor. As late as 1930, deodorant users had to follow a demanding and cumbersome procedure, particularly if they used Odorono, the earliest and up to then most successful product in the field. They had to apply the ruby red paste to their underarms before going to bed, then hold their arms up for ten minutes or so until the deodorant dried. They had to be careful not to let the deodorant touch their clothing while it was still damp, because it would eat into the fabric. This was powerful stuff, as Dr. John B. Watson told a J. Walter Thompson Company staff meeting in 1928. Watson, the "founder" of behaviorism and the first prominent psychologist to work for an advertising agency, advised the company that Odorono (which J. Walter Thompson advertised) was "pretty hard on sensitive skins"—it frequently caused "a mild dermatitis." So we begin with what to me is a striking image: a young woman, arms aloft, waiting for the Odorono to dry, hoping it won't irritate her skin or eat her slip (fig. 1).[1]

For a cultural historian, the image is worth pondering. What made people willing, even eager, to do this to themselves? Had they always been intolerant of body odor and by the 1920s finally had the technology available to stop it? Or had there been a fundamental reorientation in attitudes toward the body during the late nineteenth and early twentieth centuries, a collective change of mind that was reflected but also reinforced by the rise of national advertising? I want to suggest

A version of this essay first appeared in *The Missouri Review* 10, no. 2 (1987).

Fig. 1 "Underarm odor, so offensive to others, is almost always imperceptible to the person guilty." This May 1934 advertisement for Odorono deodorant in *Good Housekeeping* offers clear, "instant" Odorono as an option to the original paste product.

that this sort of change did in fact occur, though it was halting, uncertain, and impossible to measure. I want further to suggest that by scrutinizing this change in attitudes toward the body, we might be led to rethink some of our most cherished ideas about the "revolution in manners and morals" that occurred as the nineteenth century became the twentieth.

The most common interpretation is that the passage from the nineteenth to the twentieth century was marked by movement from a puritanical vale of tears to a hedonistic consumer culture, from stiff-backed propriety to casual exuberance. Even our most sophisticated cultural historians have accepted this framework. Warren Susman, for example, adducing evidence for the rise of a pleasure-oriented "culture of abundance," notes the changing connotations of the word "comfort": in the mid-nineteenth century, "comfort bags" containing a Bible and a bottle of whiskey were sent to Civil War soldiers at the front; a hundred years later, "comfort stations" promised immediate relief to visitors at amusement parks and sports arenas.[2] This is surely a problematic view: Susman describes a development that could as easily be described as the trivialization of comfort. But even if one defines comfort in purely behaviorist, physiological terms as release from tension, the evidence suggests that Americans in the 1920s and 1930s were probably no more at ease inside their own skins than their parents or grandparents had been.

What I want to do in this essay is to make two modest proposals. First, the Victorians may not have been as unacquainted with erotic pleasure as their twentieth-century critics have assumed.[3] Second, the repression that did exist did not necessarily disappear and may have reappeared in new idioms and cultural forms that were sometimes more subtly coercive than the old moralism had been.[4] Overall, I want to call into question the simple model of a passage from puritanism to hedonism and to imply that the transition from Victorian to post-Victorian mores is more complex than historians have supposed.

My focus will be on advertising and the way it collaborated with other cultural institutions in redefining the body as a universe of discourse—recasting the ways Americans conceived of sensual pleasure, physical attractiveness, and bodily health. One reason to concentrate on the advertising industry is that its leaders claimed to be spearheading a cultural transformation. In a typical statement, the *J. Walter Thompson Book* asserted in 1909 that "advertising is *revolutionary*. Its tendency is to overturn preconceived notions, to set new ideas spinning through the reader's brain, to induce something that they never did

before. It is a form of progress, and it *interests only progressive people*. That's why it thrives in America as in no other land under the sun. Stupid people are not much impressed by advertising. They move in a rut of tradition." Later in the same pamphlet, the authors defined progress more specifically. "The chief work of civilization," they wrote, "*is to eliminate chance*, and that can be done only by foreseeing and planning." The tendency to endow advertising with a high civilizing mission and to equate that mission with the elimination of chance pervaded the literature of advertising apologetics in the early twentieth century. And the preoccupation with systematic control of one's environment linked ad men with social scientists and other would-be "professionals."[5]

In concrete terms, advertisers defined their civilizing accomplishments in terms of health, cleanliness, and hairlessness: the elimination of the American carnivore's traditional greasy breakfast; the plumbing of bathrooms from Maine to California; the disappearance of beards and expansive stomachs among men, of body hair and facial blemishes among women. The overarching emphasis on grooming and cleanliness was no small matter; it amounted to a "Philosophy of Advertising." As a writer for *Yale Review* claimed in 1899, "It is no exaggeration to say that next to teaching a people to read and write, if not equal to it in importance, is teaching them to prefer soap and cleanliness to perfumery and enervating pleasures." The juxtaposition of "soap and cleanliness" with "perfumery and enervating pleasures" was revealing: it implied not merely the familiar Enlightenment paradigm of civilization over barbarism, but also the triumph of a particular kind of civilization over a false and decadent version. It also suggested that advertising was concerned with something more than the simple pursuit of pleasure.[6]

To begin to puzzle out the significance of the civilization defined by national advertising, we need to look first at the changing social background of the ad men themselves. Until the late nineteenth century, most advertising was done by local or regional entrepreneurs. On the whole, they were Anglo-Saxon Protestant businessmen, members of the established middle and upper classes, but their advertising efforts remained relatively modest, constituting a kind of vernacular tradition of commercial iconography embodied in trade cards, calendars, and almanacs. The coalescence of a national market and the growing dominance of large corporations brought a new kind of advertising into prominence—the advertising of brand-name products to a nationwide market. During the 1880s and 1890s, advertising agencies arose as middlemen between the corporation and the new consumer audience, providing services to businessmen who thought they needed expert counsel. These agencies were staffed by a remarkably homogeneous group of WASP males. Small-town northeasterners or midwesterners, many of them ministers' sons, they were highly educated—often at Ivy League colleges. One could argue that they were trying to keep the faith of their fathers by conceiving their work as a civilizing crusade, just as Protestant missionaries had often done. Whatever their intentions, the ad men became part of a national corporate elite, extraordinarily insulated from the rest of the population.[7]

By the 1930s, this insulation from the common life had led to some soul-searching. Wallace Boren of J. Walter Thompson, conducting an in-house survey of New York copywriters for the company in 1936, discovered that not one belonged to a lodge or civic club; only one in five went to church except on rare occasions; half never went to Coney Island or any other popular public resort, and the others only once or twice a year; more than half had never lived within the national average income of $1,580 per family a year, and half did not know anyone who ever had. While 5 percent of American homes had servants, 66 percent of J. Walter Thompson homes did. The profile was affluent, metropolitan, secular, and sophisticated, and this was typical of the most prestigious agencies with the biggest accounts.[8]

My intent here is not to reduce the complex rhetoric and iconography of advertising to a mere reflection of its social origins. But the social background does provide some insight into the changes in attitudes toward the body that advertising helped to shape. Admakers were part of a WASP upper class, asserting national dominance through the reassertion and refinement of progressive ideology. That ideology drew on familiar Enlightenment themes—rationality over ignorance, culture over nature—but it took a while to get into its twentieth-century shape. There was a mix of continuity and change in transit from nineteenth-century advertising and its symbolic universe.

The chief continuity was the persistent promise of physical and psychic revitalization that allegedly would occur with the use of the commodity being advertised. The promise had its earliest roots in the evangelical culture of nineteenth-century rural America, and the patterns of revitalization resembled those of Protestant conversion. The central agent of the process was the patent medicine vendor, who partook of the aura of the confidence man: he was not only a trickster but—like the evangelical minister—a man on the threshold between nature and the supernatural, a purveyor of miraculous cures and magical self-transformations. The testimonials he assembled were themselves rooted in patterns of evangelical culture—the cries of the converted, testifying to the soul's deliverance from suffering. Soul-sickness, everyone knew, could take bodily form, and testimonials reflected the mingling of body and soul. Whether suffering was caused by constipation, catarrh, bilious liver, seminal losses, or the ubiquitous "tired feeling," the conditions from which the sufferer was saved could sound remarkably like the boredom, lassitude, apathy, and overwhelming depression that preceded the sinner's conviction of sin and discovery of the path to salvation. In 1875, a Mr. Karl Barton of Buffalo, New York, recalled his life before he ingested his first bottle of Dr. Chase's nerve pills: "It was a pretty hard matter for me to call attention to anything in particular. It was a general, debilitated, languid, played-out feeling, and while not painful, depressing." And here are the effects of catarrh as told by Childs' catarrh remedy in 1877: "The patient becomes nervous, his voice is harsh and unnatural; he feels disheartened; memory loses her power; judgment her seat, and gloomy forebodings hang overhead, —Hundreds, yea, thousands in such circumstances feel that to die would be a relief—and many do even cut the thread of life to end their sorrows." Patent medicine ads habitually intertwined

physical and psychic corruption. "Be a real man—a live man," a Dr. Phillips advised readers in 1900. "Don't be satisfied to be a lump of half-dead, rapidly decaying flesh"—which is what you are, he implied, when you are constipated. Or to take another example, this one from 1923, a young woman was finally rescued from the Slough of Despond: "At last she found out. Something was amiss. Her animation and buoyancy, once so marked, were giving way steadily, to lassitude, indifference, and depression." Then she tried Yeast Foam tablets. This manic-depressive cycle of despair followed by dramatic self-transformation, long a butt of satire and a source of bemused wonderment to European advertisers, was rooted in the rhetoric of conversion pervading our Protestant culture.[9]

The same could be said for the promise of "more abundant life," which recalls the "second blessing"—the ecstatic attainment of "entire and perfect sanctification" that might follow years after an authentic conversion. In advertising, "more life" could be achieved (for example) through the use of Mosko's silver pills (1900), which were probably cocaine-based and were especially designed for "lawyers who would be eloquent, commercial travellers who would be jovial," and so on. Yet even shredded wheat (1908), Lifebuoy soap (1917), and Gillette razors (1926) promised a feeling of exhilaration, a sense that it was "great to be alive," nothing less than a kind of personal regeneration.[10]

The further one moved from evangelical origins, the greater the possibilities for self-parody. Reverend Henry Ward Beecher's endorsement of Pears' soap in 1885 was a straw in the wind. "If Cleanli-

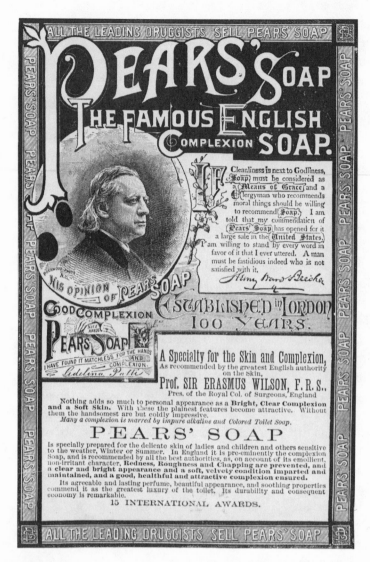

Fig. 2   According to
Henry Ward Beecher,
whose portrait appears in
a *Harper's Weekly* (2 May
1885) advertisement for
Pears' soap, "A Clergy-
man who recommends
moral things should be
willing to recommend
soap."

ness is next to Godliness," said Beecher, "then surely SOAP is a means of GRACE" (fig. 2). A Dr. Tyrrell, explaining in 1924 in a pamphlet of the same name "why we should bathe internally," warned that "the Colonic is a worse menace to society than the Alcoholic": irritable and ineffi-cient, the colonic had forgotten that "the first requisite to sanctity is to keep the in-testines open." Religious vessels were filled with strange elixirs. It was not sur-prising that the vessels gradually began to lose shape as regeneration became less a unique and shattering experience than part of the daily routine, experienced while showering, shaving, or sitting astride the commode.[11]

As religious language was diluted and drained of spiritual significance, the quest for health deepened and intensified. The battle against pain began to be waged with unprecedented ferocity. In part, this re-flected the abandonment of traditional stoicism and fatalism. "What higher aim can man attain than conquest over human pain?" asked Eno's fruit salts in 1891, posing a question that would hardly have been considered rhetorical a century earlier. From the traditional Christian view, there were of course several aims far higher than the conquest of pain. Alongside the abandonment of stoicism, there were increasing attempts to seek out, name, and cure even the vaguest of maladies. As early as 1873, Tarrant's seltzer observed that "thousands of people who are not absolutely sick complain that they are NEVER WELL." A spreading preoccupation with the blues, that tired feeling, and other forms of ennui justified the brisk promotion of opiates and revealed a greater sensitivity to physical or psychic discomfort.[12]

At the same time, the ubiquitous references to fatigue in the promotional literature suggest that vast numbers of Americans wanted to lie down and rest, to be left alone with their aches and exhaustion for a little while, but that they were constantly being prevented from doing so by a small band of activist cheerleaders—many of them in advertising—who were promoting a more rigorous definition of well-being, not merely steady-state equilibrium but dynamic, efficient performance. In 1908, an advertisement for Grape Nuts warned:

An overloaded ship makes slow headway against the heaving, rolling sea. It's the same with the man who overloads his system with a mass of heavy, indigestible food. It means a heavy, foggy brain, and a tired, sleepy feeling when you ought to be making "things hum"—skimming along on the high road to success. Are you going to remain in the slow-going "freighter" class, or would you

prefer to be one of the Ocean Greyhounds?[13]

(If the latter, try Grape Nuts.) The preoccupation with efficient performance points to the largest change in health and beauty advertising from the nineteenth century to the twentieth: the shift away from primitivism and exoticism and toward what might loosely be called scientism, as the worldview animating the iconography.

Throughout the nineteenth century, patent medicine advertising was steeped in herbalist lore—incantatory references to the product's magical effects and closeness to nature. Astrological charts, with parts of the body linked to the signs of the zodiac that governed them, were common in patent medicine almanacs until the early twentieth century. An overwhelming number of patent medicines claimed a primitive tribal origin—kola from the heart of Africa, coca from the mountains of Peru, "sagwa" from the North American Indian herb doctors: elixirs that cured everything from impure blood to sexual debility to indigestion. In 1893, the Kickapoo Medicine Company promised its customers "a stomach like an Indian—he never worried about dieting. Why can't we live like the Indian, in a healthy, hearty, natural way?" Answer: we can, with sagwa.[14]

Much of the promotional literature followed an imperialist pattern: the white man enters the dark interior of a tropical land, extracts mysterious remedies, and puts them to the service of "civilization." The clearest example of this formula was a pamphlet dating from about 1890 that describes the discovery of Peruvian Catarrh Cure. The story of the cure was allegedly told to the narrator by Dr. Edward Turner, "an adventurous and daring Englishman," on the eve of his death by ambush at the hands of "black devils" in Zululand, Africa. Troubled with catarrh since boyhood, Turner had received a hot tip from Father de Rossa at the Sacred Heart Mission, Indian Territory (now Oklahoma), after enduring the failures of "medical men, with whom I got disgusted" throughout the old and new worlds. De Rossa tells him of mosca, a red root from Peru, then gives him some in powdered form. Mosca, it appears, was discovered by the Cotahuasi Indians; in their language, it means "new life." Turner loves it and heads for Peru. The chief of the Cotahuasi likes Turner's pluck and, even more, his apparent desire to help others. In the chief's view, Turner is not like the other palefaces, who care only for money. The irony is that Turner wants to make a business of the cure, but he conceals that fact because he fears the chief might want too many presents in exchange for the secret ingredient. "I therefore left him with the idea that I was one of the few palefaces who don't care for money. That, you know, may work among the Indians, but not with us." The secret is rescued from Turner on his deathbed and imported to North America, where it brings relief to millions. The pattern of the shrewd Caucasian outwitting the natives is repeated often and is perfectly captured in an 1888 advertisement for Warner's Safe Remedies, which shows a respectable white man's head on a muscular brown body, paddling a canoe toward the heart of primitive darkness (fig. 3).[15]

Cosmetics as well as food and even laxative advertising wallowed in exoticism during the last two-thirds of the nineteenth century. Breath and body per-

Fig. 3   A number of patent medicines, including Warner's Safe Remedies, were sold as "natural" and "primitive cures" used in tropical regions by uncivilized tribes whose vitality and healthfulness were legendary. Detail of advertisement for Warner's Safe Remedies in *Warner's Artistic Album* (1888). Photograph by T. J. Jackson Lears; courtesy Warshaw Collection of Business Americana, Archives Center, National Museum of American History, Smithsonian Institution.

fumes, talcum powder and toilet water, all were placed in exotic settings redolent of luxuriant sensuality (fig. 4). There is a strikingly overt eroticism about many of these images, especially in the aura of languorous ease displayed by the full-figured, mature, and voluptuous woman—whom historians of fashion have identified as the belle ideal of the late nineteenth century. She was hardly a sexless Victorian, and her origins lay in a subculture of sensuality inhabited by actresses, prostitutes, pimps, and gamblers.[16]

Even the corset, long since dismissed

Fig. 4 Trade cards of the late 1800s for personal care products such as Ayer's hair vigor, said to restore "gray hair to its natural vitality and color," were often illustrated with voluptuous women in exotic, even mythological, settings. Trade card for Ayer's hair vigor, Dr. J. C. Ayer and Co., Lowell, Massachusetts, about 1885.

as an emblem of male dominance and female repression, could fit into the erotic picture. Corsets were often associated with images of explosive fecundity and sexual energy, as well as peep-show-style prurience (fig. 5). The removal of the corset offered possibilities for protracted foreplay, amatory expertise, erotic build-up of tension. Opponents of the corset recognized this, attacking its capacity to stimulate sex excitement. Tightlacing could be as much an emblem of exotic decadence and rebellion against feminine quiescence as a sign of patriarchal prudery.[17]

At the turn of the century, there were dramatic changes in advertising iconography. Exoticism and primitivism persisted in the entrepreneurial tradition, inscribed on the walls of fashionable restaurants and metropolitan movie theaters; but, in the corporate iconography of national advertising, exotic and primitive impulses were channeled into safer, more productive outlets. The advertisers who promoted the early twentieth-century vogue of tanning, for example, detached dark skin from its overtones of lush tropical sensuality and linked it instead with bracing

Fig. 5 As illustrated by this 1880s trade card for the "Celebrated Thomson's Patent Glove Fitting Corsets," these female accoutrements were sometimes displayed in settings inviting, rather than discouraging, sexual activity.

outdoor vigor; through this psychic screen, forbidden longings for the dusky, nubile maidens of imperialist lore were disguised and rendered respectable. ("Our" maidens could never be openly defiled; a tanned Caucasian lady exuded health rather than seductive sensuality.) Cultural imperialism was gradually redefined: it became less an attempt to extract mysterious potions from primitive interiors than an effort to impose civilized values on "inferior" native populations. And those values were invariably defined in terms of cleanliness and good grooming. In an Ivory soap series from 1900, for example, an assembly of Plains Indians recalled their old ways of dirt and disorder:

> Our blankets smeared with grease and stains,
> From buffalo meat and settler's veins . . .

Then:

> Ivory soap came like a ray
> Of light across our darkened way
> And now we're civil, kind, and good
> And keep the laws as people should
> We wear our linen, lawn, and lace,
> As well as folks with paler face.

This newer version of imperialism was nothing if not universal in its ambitions, as Babbitt's soap proclaimed that "cleanliness is the Scale of Civilizations" and Gillette announced its razors' hegemony "from Boston to Bombay."[18]

In one sense, there was nothing new going on here. A preoccupation with cleanliness, often carrying racial import, had been a central theme in bourgeois culture for at least half a century. It intensified as technological advances made soap and running water more widely available. Cleanliness became a crucial piece in the puzzle of respectability that upwardly mobile strivers were constantly trying to assemble. Clean hands had joined white skin, white bread, and white sugar as emblems of refinement as early as the 1850s.[19]

By 1900, though, soap had begun to acquire a nearly numinous quality, and bathing seemed a sacrament.[20] The issue was not cleanliness per se but a certain kind of cleanliness, purged of any decadent, hedonistic associations, oriented toward productive activism and a broader agenda of control. As *Yale Review* had noted, "the philosophy of advertising" played a key role in that reorientation, elevating soap and water over "perfumery and enervating pleasures." What the *Review* failed to note was that through most of the nineteenth century, advertising itself had celebrated "enervating pleasures"—it was only with the corporatization of advertising at the turn of the century that the iconography of the body became sterilized and controlled.

The most obvious change was the growing emphasis on standardized, sanitized images of youthful physical perfection—"perfect specimens of the human type"—on the Anglo-Saxon model. The voluptuous woman and the bearded man yielded to smoother, cleaner, more activist and athletic models of beauty. Exotic settings faded in favor of the more immediate and familiar—the soda fountain and the suburban neighborhood (fig. 6).[21]

All this was part of a broader, less ambiguous reassertion of culture over nature, best seen (or smelled) in the growing intolerance of odors. With the coming of an urban society and the increase in person-to-person contact, there was growing concern about offensive breath, per-

Fig. 6 After the turn of the century, images in advertisements of tropical forests and tribal men and women were replaced with more familiar settings. Advertisement for Mennen's borated talcum toilet powder, Gerhard Mennen Company, Newark, New Jersey, 1908. Photograph by T. J. Jackson Lears; courtesy Warshaw Collection of Business Americana, Archives Center, National Museum of American History, Smithsonian Institution.

Fig. 7 Magazine advertisements of the 1930s frequently depicted men and women grimacing at the horrors of unpleasant smells from such diverse sources as breath, gelatin, perspiration, and sneakers. Advertisement for Hood Hygeen Insole in *Good Housekeeping* (May 1934).

spiration odors, and the like. One can find scattered advertisements for breath and body perfumes from the 1830s on, but, in general, genteel folk put up with a lot more in the nineteenth century than in the twentieth. Dress and suit shields, marketed in the 1880s, were designed to stop perspiration stain but not odor. Yet by the 1930s, odor was virtually an obsession. Popular magazines were full of faces (male and female) contorted with disgust over everything from "sneaker smell" to "smelly hands" (fig. 7).[22]

Within advertising's symbolic universe, the recoil from odor was part of a general revulsion against biological processes, an itch to extirpate all signs of organic life from a sterile home environment. A Kleenex ad from 1934, for example, described washing dirty handkerchiefs as "Revolting!" It was "the worst job on earth!" according to a nearly nauseated housewife, but it was no longer necessary thanks to throwaway tissues (fig. 8). At bottom, this impulse seemed animated by a desire for a perfectly controlled and sanitized world. As a copywriter for Zonite antiseptic (also peddled as a contraceptive douche) observed in 1931, "The feminine world now demands an absolute cleanliness of person, a real surgical cleanliness." And a long-running Lysol ad from the early 1930s presented a cellophane-wrapped guest at the front door: "If callers also arrived in sanitary packages, we wouldn't need Lysol." But of course they don't, so we do (fig. 9).[23]

What was once a set of pious maxims about cleanliness and godliness had become a nearly obsessive preoccupation with controlling biological processes. How does one account for the change? There were, I think, several related reasons for it.

One involves the social experience of ad men themselves, as local and entrepreneurial production of advertisements gave way to national, corporate control. The big agencies were staffed by an educated upper class with a national outlook. But for all their apparent power and influence, they were still employees of bureaucratic enterprises; their most cherished and creative copy was constantly carved up by supervisors and clients. They lacked personal authority and autonomy. In that lack, they resembled many other organization men in the early twentieth century, team players all. The advertisements' new model of masculinity—smooth-shaven, collegiate boyishness—reflected a broader shift in male authority from the paterfamilias to the paternalistic corporation. As Gillette proudly pointed out in a 1926 pamphlet, it was much harder to be a raging parent in a beardless era: "The best a smooth-shaven dad can do is crease his brow and compress his lips." The boyish man was in part a projection of copywriters' everyday lives, in an era when familial patriarchy was yielding to corporate bureaucracy.[24]

Fig. 8   In the July 1932 issue of *Good Housekeeping*, the manufacturers of Kleenex tissues singled out the virtues of disposability with the warning that "germ-filled handkerchiefs are a menace to society." Courtesy Kimberly-Clark Corporation.

Another development that reshaped the iconography of the body was the dramatic rise in prestige of scientific medicine. Up to the 1890s, medical authority was constantly in dispute; laboratory research had produced no highly visible

If callers *also* arrived in sanitary packages

FORTY-SIX states have abolished the public drinking cup, and forty-six the common roller-towel. Milk is delivered in sealed, individual bottles. Bread, cereals and a host of other products now reach your home in sanitary wrappings.

Why?

To protect you from germs—from the bacteria of the diseases that all of us dread, the minute organisms that are spread by the very dust in the air.

But the *people* who come into your home—they can't be sealed up. And they bring in the same germs on their hands and breath and clothes and shoes.

Only *you* can help protect your home and family against these germs that you can't keep out. That's why health authorities and doctors urge the regular use of "Lysol" Disinfectant in all home cleaning processes.

It's easy enough: just add a tablespoonful of "Lysol" to each quart of cleaning water—and *every day* disinfect the telephone, doorknobs and other places that hands are constantly touching.

Get a large bottle today. Tomorrow may be too late.

Sole distributors: LEHN & FINK, Inc., Bloomfield, N. J.

Lysol Disinfectant

Fig. 9 The makers of Lysol recommended that housekeepers use the product to protect "home and family" against the germs on visitors' "hands and breath and clothes and shoes." Advertisement for Lysol disinfectant in *Good Housekeeping* (April 1930). Courtesy Sterling Drug Inc.

therapeutic breakthrough. But in 1894, the development of diphtheria antitoxin marked a major advance against a dreaded killer of children; in subsequent years, there seemed less need to look for primitive or exotic alternatives to regular medical practice.[25]

Popularization of germ theory also promoted the sanitizing of bodily discourse. To take one of many possible examples, Hood's sarsaparilla (in 1908) evoked a vision of "swarming myriads of tiny, but powerful enemies of life, those

soldiers of death's dark legions" that "always and everywhere . . . surround us, and incessantly make war upon us. . . . The wonder is not that we are ever ill, but that we are ever well." There was a swelling desire to repel the soldiers of death's dark legions, even after they had broached the citadel of the body itself. By 1930, Dr. Watson was excitedly telling the J. Walter Thompson Company staff about S.T. 37 mouthwash: "If one could be taught to rinse the mouth in the morning after breakfast, after lunch, and at night, one would have, ALMOST ALWAYS, a sterile mouth!" Hopes for sterility centered on the scientist, who became a popular authority figure in advertisements—so much so that the white lab coat became a necessary prop even for floor wax ads. The popular ideology of scientism offered techniques for total control of the self and the environment, total imposition of culture over nature—though a carefully constructed ideal of "naturalness" survived. It was as if, in trying to retreat from the chambers of death, we backed into his anteroom.[26]

These developments embodied the much broader process Max Weber identified as "the disenchantment of the world," the reduction of nature—including one's own body—to a commodity, a manipulable thing. One can see the process of disenchantment most clearly in advertisements for farm implements, which around the turn of the century suggest a reorientation of attitudes toward dirt, the ground of biological life. Up to around 1900, farm implement catalogs celebrated the fecundity of the earth with a profusion of buxom female images, reminiscent of Ceres and other mythic emblems of agricultural bounty—not to mention "buxom" fruits and tumescent vegetables surrounded by apple-cheeked cupids and maidens. Then, abruptly, those images disappeared: chromolithography became black-and-white photography, and the slogan "Every farm a factory" appeared over row on row of gleaming, sterile milking machines. The iconography of agriculture, as well as that of the domestic interior, reflected a desire for increasing insulation from the dirt and disorder of biological life.[27]

But along with the process of disenchantment, there were other more specific historical reasons for the reorientation of body imagery. Given the class and ethnic composition of the corporate ad industry, it is not surprising that we should find a link between the new youthful and athletic ideals of beauty and a broader agenda of Anglo-Saxon revitalization among the ruling elites. The turn of the century was a time of nearly continuous social disorder and cultural tension—disorder and tension that often had racial undertones. Swarming immigrants and anarchist assassins populated the bourgeois imagination, as well as the streets of Chicago and New York. But the rise of racism reflected personal as well as social tensions. The popularization of Darwinian biology, along with the opening of "unexplored" territory in what Conrad called "the dark places of the earth," promoted increasing ambiguity about what it meant to be "truly human." If one had apes for ancestors and hottentots for cousins, the old boundaries between civilization and barbarism, body and soul, no longer seemed quite so clear.[28]

Amid restless immigrants and Darwinian theories, Anglo-Saxon elites may well have felt the need to distance themselves from primitives, exotics, the "lower races," the whole lot of brute creation. The anthropologist Mary Douglas has shown how a concern with bodily purification can reflect broader anxieties in a period of social turmoil: pollution taboos are part of an effort to reassert the reality of established social boundaries. It is not stretching the point to suggest that the American preoccupation with sanitized, hairless bodies and sterile households constituted just such an effort, a reassertion of cultural boundaries in a period of critical social stress.[29]

It was no accident that the ideal males in advertisements began to look like heroes from that burgeoning realm of upper-class revitalization, the college football field, or that ideal females looked like their co-ed admirers. Respectable Americans who sought to exorcise subversive demons had long focused on the masterless bestial Other, from Indians in the Jacksonian Era to immigrants and anarchists in the Gilded Age. A standardized model of physical perfection acquired more appealing resonance as an alternative to the simian stereotypes of immigrant ethnic groups, the people who were the targets of Attorney General A. Mitchell Palmer's raids in 1919, whom he characterized as "alien filth" with "sly and crafty eyes . . . lopsided faces, sloping brows, and misshapen features."[30] Correct appearance became a mark of political normality and, ultimately, of civilization itself.

"Woman," meanwhile, retained her central role as civilizer, guiding man between bestiality and effete decadence. "She does not approve the ladylike massage finish of the tonsorial artist," Gillette claimed in 1910. "If it were not for her, man would revert to whiskers and carry a club." The struggle between barbershop and blade manufacturer involved an interesting reversal of masculine and feminine signifiers: the barbershop, a traditional male domain, became—at least in this text—the bailiwick of the effeminate "tonsorial artist." Advertisers, like other leaders of the dominant culture during this period of flux in gender roles, re-

tailored images of masculinity to fit a new and more organized social environment. The alternative, for "Progressives" as for Victorians, was reversion to barbarism. Civilization, it appeared, hung by the wispiest of threads.[31]

The changes in advertising iconography were part of broader shifts in our social, intellectual, and psychic history. The mingling of themes can be seen in laxative advertising. Constipation runs like a black thread through the advertising of both the nineteenth and twentieth centuries. There was much material reason for it: Americans notoriously bolted huge quantities of heavy, greasy food. The older advertising for laxative products, from the mid- and later nineteenth century, echoed ancient medieval obsessions with bodily putrefaction ("Don't be satisfied to be a lump of inert, half-dead, rapidly decaying flesh") as well as puritan and evangelical conversion rhetoric on the need to make the body a fit dwelling place for the Lord's divine grace. By the 1920s and 1930s, the material causes of constipation had abated—eating habits had significantly improved—but the rhetoric had, if anything, grown shriller with the emergence of a new preoccupation—"auto-intoxication." This term referred to the buildup of proteins in the blood stream; dozens of advertisers insisted that the condition was a foe to efficient performance and a threat to life itself. The "auto-intoxication" scare developed at about the same time as the Red scare and the movement for immigration restriction: both were preoccupied with eliminating alien filth from the American body politic.[32] A pollution taboo coincided with the reassertion of cultural boundaries, but it was formulated in a new, entirely secular language. The religious mists had lifted; the body and its "performance" had become the sole focus of concern.

What lay behind the redefinition of bodily discourse was not a hedonistic quest for pleasure but a pervasive anxiety and fear—fear of the masterless, subhuman Other, and, increasingly, fear of the biological processes in one's own body that might give offense to others and bring the precarious self to social ruin. The tale of Frances and Millie, told by Ivory soap in 1932, illustrated this uneasiness:

Together after ten years. It seemed like old times to them both until—

Tom has done very well,

she said

. . . her HANDS told a different story.

It happened just about the middle of luncheon. Frances, charming in Paris clothes. Millie, describing her ten happy years of married life.

"Tom has done awfully well," she was saying. "He's manager of the new factory, and people say . . ."

Just then Frances' eye fell to Millie's hand resting on the snowy linen. A fleeting glance—but Millie noticed. Her voice died away as she looked at her own hands. How red they were. How rough. How *scrubby* looking. *They didn't look like the hands of a successful man's wife.*

She couldn't go on to tell about the dear little house they'd bought and the new car. It would sound as though she were trying to make up for those poor, hardworking hands.[33]

This may seem peculiar to the depression, but one can find similar social anxieties well into the post–World War II

era—the dingy yellow teeth, the five-o'clock shadow become staples of advertising lore and prominent butts of satire. In the end, these ads acquire a claustrophobic quality, based not merely on a correct perception of the world as a fearful place (especially in the thirties and forties) but also on a fear of imprisonment in one's own body, and ultimately betrayal by it—perhaps, as well, on a realization that the effort to elevate culture over nature was finally doomed in death, the ultimate betrayal by the body, the ultimate taboo in advertising and in the culture advertising embodied (fig. 10).

None of this is an attempt to reverse the conventional wisdom and argue a shift from nineteenth-century hedonism to twentieth-century puritanism. Clearly, there are some ways in which we probably are more at home in our bodies than our great-grandparents were. But the symbolic universe of advertising is less concerned with solitary pleasures than social relations in private and public. And the persistence of the motif of control down to the present, in ads for everything from hair spray to computers, suggests the continuation of the patterns described here. As the public world outside the self becomes diffuse, distant, governed by institutions we cannot control or even influence, the body remains important as an arena we actually can control—or think we can. It becomes a domain of self-expression, a field for developing one's own set of cultural meanings, and a source, quite naturally, of anxiety.

So the point is not to reverse the conventional wisdom but to suggest that the progressive paradigm of liberation is grossly inadequate. Remember that Odorono user, holding her arms aloft

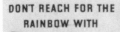

Fig. 10 Soap and hand cream makers linked rough, chapped hands to social alienation, embarrassment, and even inferiority complexes. "Why be miserably self-conscious," asks this advertisement for Hinds honey and almond cream from *Good Housekeeping* (April 1932), "over a condition that is so easily corrected?"

while the ruby red paste hardens. Pleasure and pain are as much mental constructions as they are physical experiences—elusive, ambiguous, impossible to chart precisely. Of happiness and despair, we have no measure.

Notes

1   Advertisement for Odorono in *Good Housekeeping*, March 1930, 173; John B. Watson, quoted in minutes of J. Walter Thompson Company representatives' meeting, 1 June 1928, in J. Walter Thompson Company Archives, New York, New York (hereafter cited as JWT Archives). For the early years of Odorono, see an advertisement for J. Walter Thompson Company excerpted from *Printers' Ink* (May 1917) in JWT house ads collection, JWT Archives.

2   Warren Susman, *Culture as History: The Transformation of American Society in the Twentieth Century* (New York: Pantheon Books, 1984), xiv.

3   Here I follow the lead of some of our most energetic cultural historians, such as Carl Degler, "What Ought to Be and What Was: Women's Sexuality in the Nineteenth Century," *American Historical Review* 79 (December 1974): 1467–90; and Peter Gay, *Victoria to Freud: Education of the Senses*, vol. 1 of *The*

Bourgeois Experience (New York: Oxford University Press, 1981), and *The Tender Passion* (New York: Oxford University Press, 1984).

4   I have begun this argument in "From Salvation to Self-Realization: Advertising and the Therapeutic Roots of the Consumer Culture, 1880–1930," in *The Culture of Consumption: Critical Essays in American History, 1880–1980,* ed. Richard Wightman Fox and T. J. Jackson Lears (New York: Pantheon Books, 1983), 3–38.

5   *The J. Walter Thompson Book* (New York: J. Walter Thompson Co., 1909), 8–9, 22, in JWT Archives. The preoccupation with efficiency and control pervades the literature generated by professionalizing elites around the turn of the century; for a good introduction to the idiom see Samuel F. Haber, *Efficiency and Uplift* (Berkeley: University of California Press, 1958).

6   "The Philosophy of Modern Advertising," *Yale Review* 8 (November 1899): 229–32. For two later examples of this remarkably consistent apologia, see "We Have to Be Told," *Collier's,* 31 August 1929, 58; and "Messenger to the King," ibid., 3 May 1930, 78.

7   On the social background of advertising agency people, see Lears, "Some Versions of Fantasy: Toward a Cultural History of American Advertising," in *Prospects: An Annual of American Cultural Studies,* ed. Jack Salzman (New York: Cambridge University Press, 1984), 349–405; and Roland Marchand, *Advertising the American Dream: Making Way for Modernity, 1920–1940* (Berkeley and London: University of California Press, 1985), 130–38.

8   Wallace Boren, "Bad Taste in Advertising," *J. Walter Thompson Forum,* 7 January 1936, unpaginated, in JWT Archives.

9   Karl Barton, quoted in *100 Special Receipts Selected from Dr. A. W. Chase's Receipt Book* (ca. 1875), in Patent Medicines, Box 5, Warshaw Collection of Business Americana, National Museum of American History, Smithsonian Institution, Washington, D.C. (hereafter cited as Warshaw Collection); T. P. Childs Company, untitled pamphlet on Childs' catarrh remedy (Troy, Ohio: privately printed, 1877), n.p., in Patent Medicines, Box 5, Warshaw Collection; Dr. Pierce, *A Badge of Sym-* *pathy* (Buffalo, N.Y.: privately printed, 1900), unpaginated, in Patent Medicines, Box 25a, Warshaw Collection; advertisement for Yeast Foam tablets in *American Magazine* 95 (January 1923): 15. On the frequency of ministers' testimonials for patent medicines, see James Harvey Young, *The Toadstool Millionaires: A Social History of Patent Medicines in America before Federal Regulation* (Princeton: Princeton University Press, 1961), 69.

10   Advertisement for Mosko's silver pills (ca. 1900) in Patent Medicines, Box 7, Warshaw Collection; Natural Food Co. (makers of shredded wheat), *More Life* (n.p.: privately printed, 1908); advertisement for Lifebuoy soap (1917) in Soap, Box L-M, Warshaw Collection; advertisement for Gillette razors (1926) in Barbering, Box 1, Warshaw Collection.

11   Advertisement for Pears' soap in *Harper's Weekly,* 2 May 1885, 288; *Why We Should Bathe Internally* (New York: Tyrell's Hygienic Institute, 1924), unpaginated, in Baths and Bathing, Box 2, Warshaw Collection.

12   Advertisement for Eno's fruit salts, quoted in James W. Turner, *Reckoning with the Beast: Animals, Pain, and Humanity in the Victorian Mind* (Baltimore and London: Johns Hopkins University Press, 1980), 81; advertisement for Tarrant's seltzer aperient in *Harper's Weekly,* 31 May 1873, 472.

13   Advertisement for Grape Nuts (1908) in Cosmetics, Box 110, Warshaw Collection.

14   Kickapoo Medicine Co., *Almanac* (1893), in Patent Medicines, Box 18, Warshaw Collection. For other examples of primitivism, see the advertisement for Wright's Indian Vegetable pills in Patent Medicines (1844), Box 33, Warshaw Collection; Lyon Mfg. Co., *Morning, Noon, and Night* (n.p.: privately printed, 1872); Centaur Co., *Atlas, Almanac, and Receipt Book* (1884–85), in Patent Medicines, Box 5, Warshaw Collection. For the persistence of astrological charts, see (for example) Ayer's Cherry Pectoral Almanacs in Patent Medicines, Box 2, Warshaw Collection. In nearly every patent medicine advertisement in the Warshaw Collection, there is some reference to the product's "magical effects." This is true even in publications aimed at an educated elite, such

as the *Atlantic Monthly Almanac* for 1868 (in Almanacs, Box 64a), which contains an advertisement claiming that Turner's universal neuralgia remedy "works like magic."

15 Pamphlet for Peruvian Catarrh Cure Co. (ca. 1890) in Patent Medicines, Box 25, Warshaw Collection; advertisement for Warner's Safe Remedies in *Warner's Artistic Album* (Rochester, N.Y.: Warner's Safe Remedies Company, 1888) in Patent Medicines, Box 34, Warshaw Collection. For another example of this pattern, see the advertisement for Oregon Indian Medicine Co. (ca. 1890) in Patent Medicines, Box 24, Warshaw Collection.

16 Advertisement for F. J. Taney Co. angostura bitters (1876) in Patent Medicines, Box 31a, Warshaw Collection; advertisement for Love's Incense in Cosmetics, Box 108, Warshaw Collection; advertisement for London Toilet Bazaar Co. in ibid.; advertisement for Taylor's premium cologne in ibid. On the voluptuous woman as belle ideal, see Lois Banner, *American Beauty* (New York: Knopf, 1982), 111.

17 Advertisements for Warner Bros. Coraline corsets (ca. 1890) in Corsets, Box 4, Warshaw Collection. Here I follow the argument made by David Kunzle, *Fashion and Fetishism: A Social History of the Corset, Tight-lacing, and Other Forms of Body-Sculpture in the West* (Totowa, N.J.: Rowman and Littlefield, 1982).

18 Advertisement for Mennen's borated talcum powder (1909) in Cosmetics, Box 110, Warshaw Collection; pamphlet for Ivory soap, "What a Cake of Soap Will Do" (ca. 1900), in Soap, Box "Procter and Gamble," Warshaw Collection; advertisement for B. T. Babbitt's Best (ca. 1885) in Soap, Box A–B, Warshaw Collection; advertisement for Gillette safety razors (1910) in Barbering, Box 1, Warshaw Collection.

19 Ruth Schwartz Cowan, *More Work for Mother: The Ironies of Household Technology from the Open Hearth to the Microwave* (New York: Basic Books, 1983), 51–53.

20 Advertisement for Ivory soap (1900) in Soap, Box "Procter and Gamble," Warshaw Collection.

21 Advertisement for Mennen's borated talcum powder (1908) in Cosmetics, Box 110,

Warshaw Collection; Weingarten Bros., *Beauty Book* (ca. 1910) in Corsets, Box 4, Warshaw Collection; advertisement for Coca-Cola (1927) in Beverages, Box 1, Warshaw Collection. Banner, in *American Beauty*, 130–31, discusses the upper-class counterattack on the voluptuous woman.

22 Banner, *American Beauty*, especially 39–47; advertisement for Dewey's dress and coat shields (1887) in Corsets, Box 2, Warshaw Collection; advertisement for Hood canvas shoes in *Good Housekeeping*, May 1933, 175; advertisement for Royal gelatin in *Good Housekeeping*, March 1934, 150–51.

23 Advertisement for Kleenex tissues in *Good Housekeeping*, July 1932, 160; advertisement for Zonite antiseptics in *Good Housekeeping*, April 1931, 126; advertisement for Lysol in *Good Housekeeping*, April 1930, 143.

24 "The Gillette Blade" (September 1926) in Barbering, Box 1, Warshaw Collection.

25 On the consolidation of medical authority, see Paul Starr, *The Social Transformation of American Medicine* (New York: Basic Books, 1982), especially chapters 1–3.

26 Michael Williams, "Our Billions of Invisible Friends," reprinted by Hood's sarsaparilla from *Success*, May 1908, in Patent Medicines, Box 14, Warshaw Collection; John B. Watson, quoted in minutes of J. Walter Thompson representatives' meeting, 30 April 1930, 7–8, in JWT Archives.

27 Compare, for example, the Wood farm implements catalog of 1889, in Agriculture, Box 6, Warshaw Collection, with the advertisement for International Harvester Co. (formerly McCormick Reapers), in *Farm Mechanics* 8 (February 1923): cover, in Agriculture, Box 4, Warshaw Collection. The concept of disenchantment is ably (even poetically) explicated in Peter Berger, *The Sacred Canopy: Elements of a Sociological Theory of Religion* (Garden City, N.Y.: Doubleday, 1967).

28 These issues are ably discussed in Turner, *Reckoning with the Beast*, 63–69, though Turner does not explore the imperial resonances of the subject.

29 Mary Douglas, *Purity and Danger* (London: Routledge and Kegan Paul, 1966).

30 A. Mitchell Palmer, quoted in Michael

Rogin, *Ronald Reagan, the Movie and Other Episodes in Political Demonology* (Berkeley: University of California Press, 1987), 238–39. Rogin's essays are masterful explorations of recurrent themes in countersubversive demonology.

31 Advertisement for Gillette blades in Barbering, Box 1, Warshaw Collection.

32 See the insightful essay in this volume by James Whorton, "Eating to Win."

33 Advertisement for Ivory soap in *Good Housekeeping*, March 1932, 133.

Gentlemen of the clerical profession, are peculiarly subject to those diseases which result from the digestion becoming impaired by cerebral excitement and body inactivity. Not only excessive intellectual labor, but also extreme tension of the moral and emotional sentiments, tends to produce this effect. Sympathy with sorrows and joys of a parish, the excitements of the chamber of sickness and death, and the ceaseless demands on the clergyman's mental and physical energy, slowly but surely interfere with the healthful performance of the organic functions.

Iron Therapy and Tonics

Michael R. Harris

In this "Letter to Clergymen on the Preservation of Health," published in Boston in 1858, an anonymous patent medicine promoter extolled the curative powers of Peruvian syrup, which he identified as "a protected solution of protoxide of iron."[1] About thirty years later, the Brown Chemical Company of Baltimore featured the opinions of "a leading Medical Professor" on the back of an advertising trade card as an indirect endorsement for its product, Brown's iron bitters (fig. 1). "The preparations of *Iron* which are termed in medicine as *Ferruginous* or *Chalybeate*, are by far the *most important of all tonics*—in fact, there is no tonic, either mineral or vegetable, which meets so many requirements of man . . . ," the professor was quoted as stating. "The diseases in which Iron is especially serviceable are those which come from want of richness in the blood, strength in the muscles and tone in the nerves, such as Weakness, Inactivity, Depression, Loss of Appetite, Dyspepsia, Indigestion, Neuralgia, Hysteria, and all other diseases so distressing to ladies." "With such medical authority," Brown observed, "the use of Iron cannot be too strongly urged."[2]

Whether the American public knew what ferruginous, chalybeate, or protoxide preparations of iron were, the fact that these solutions included iron in any form seemed to be sufficient recommendation for their use. Throughout the nineteenth and early twentieth centuries, iron tonics and other iron preparations sold vigorously, although it is not possible to give even approximate production figures for medicines containing iron manufactured in the United States. Of the few records of nineteenth-century drug manufacturers that are known to have survived, none contains information on the quantities of drugs produced, although some do contain overall sales figures. Even in the 1980s, it is difficult to determine total production figures for many classes of drugs.

Wholesale catalogs provide sketchy evidence of the amounts of drugs produced, however. In the 1907 catalog of the Milwaukee Drug Company, a wholesale supplier to Wisconsin and northern Illinois, 133 over-the-counter patent medicines either featured the word "iron" in their brand names or were composed of formulas that are known to have included the metal. The company offered druggists iron in the form of such products as Baker's nitrogenized iron, Dietrich's iron peptonate, Iron-ox, Iron-up, Maltine Ferrated, New York Pharmacal Elixir Phosphate Iron, and Wyeth's Beef, Iron and Wine.[3]

These 133 preparations with known iron content are a small number of the six thousand items listed in the company's catalog, yet it is possible that many other preparations contained the substance. For instance, we know that Hooper's female

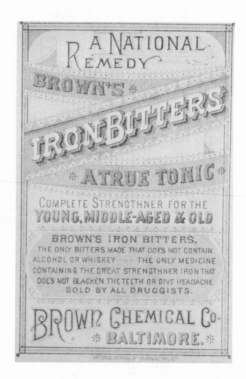

Fig. 1   Trade card for Brown's iron bitters, engraving by National Bureau of Engraving, Philadelphia, 1880.

pills contained a mixture of iron, aloes (a cathartic drug), hellebore (a North American plant yielding a toxic alkaloid with medicinal value), myrrh, soap, and ginger. More than fifty female pills are listed in the wholesaler's catalog, and only about 25 percent of the formulas listed in a sample of recipes from formulary and receipt books contained iron (fig. 2).[4] Some tonics, anemia preparations, bitters, cough syrups, and other types of patent medicines also contained iron. Taking into account that 20 percent of the patent medicines manufactured are listed in these formular books, it is probably safe to conclude that another three hundred of the Milwaukee Drug Company's products would have contained iron. Thus, 7 per-

Fig. 2 Promoted as a cure for female weakness, Hooper's pills were manufactured in Great Britain and imported to the United States. A combination of iron and six botanical ingredients, the pills were used for more than two hundred years in both countries and were effective in the treatment of anemia. They were sold in both bottles and wrapped pill boxes as late as the 1940s. Courtesy Smithsonian Institution.

cent of the six thousand listed preparations might have contained iron.

However, the sheer number of iron preparations provides no insight into the prevalence of their use. In the 1800s as today, each patent medicine receives just one line in a catalog. In the 1980s, drug wholesalers' catalogs list Tylenol only once, yet its sales are in the hundreds of millions of dosages. In 1907 or 1980, 7 percent of the over-the-counter drugs sold would indicate substantial popularity. In addition, the same 1907 Milwaukee wholesaler listed fifty-seven salts or compounds of iron that pharmacists could buy to fill prescriptions or to put up their own house-brand iron tonic or female pill, a practice that was popular at the turn of the century.

By that time, iron was included in more than fifty official drug products and in hundreds of patent medicines.[5] Pro-

moted for use among the sick and infirm, iron tonics have also been claimed to fortify the strong. The strongest metal of the ancient world, iron's connection with images of strength has persisted to the present day (fig. 3). In part because of its real therapeutic value, it has been used continuously in Western medicine and has frequently been recommended in standard domestic medicine manuals and in folk medicine.

However, like other drugs such as penicillin and heroin, iron has a public personality, a value related to its perceived medicinal virtues or vices. Heroin has an image as a toxic addictive drug, but it is also an excellent antitussive or cough suppressant. During the 1920s, it was widely used with terpen hydrate (a cough medicine) until its constant abuse forced its removal from the market.[6] Penicillin, by contrast, has a respected and respectable

Fig. 3 Subtitled "the quality magazine for all bodybuilders," *Iron Man* was first published in 1937 and is still in print. This May 1953 cover showed the ideal developed male figure. Courtesy Iron Man Publishing Company; photograph courtesy Smithsonian Institution.

public image. It was the miracle drug of the 1940s and 1950s, but it can cause death by anaphylactic shock in a small percentage of the people who take it. And Tylenol, through no inherent flaw in the drug itself, is widely perceived as too risky to take, especially in capsule form. Yet it had earlier been perceived to be different, even better, than similar pain-relieving drugs, collectively known as analgesics. The truth is that acetaminophen—the active ingredient in Tylenol—is also the active ingredient in Panadol and Anacin 3. Only advertising has created the perceived difference among the public.

Over time, iron has developed an image in the medical profession and the public in general that, I will argue, has been directly influenced by eighteenth-century concepts. Compared to most other natural substances, iron has only recently been mastered and manipulated by humans. When it was first used, it was viewed to be a magical metal because of its superiority over stone and bronze, especially in battle. Tribes that clung to older ways and materials had good reason to dread its use.

This belief in iron's wonder-working properties persisted long after it passed into general use and still survives in many of our superstitions. Iron was believed to have therapeutic effect, even if it was not taken internally. Witches, fairies, and evil spirits were believed to fear iron and to be powerless against it. In Egypt, a man entering a dark and unknown place would often cry, "Iron, you devil!" in order to drive away any malevolent jinn who might be lurking there. Iron horseshoes have been and continue to be hung up in houses to avert evil and bring good luck. People making rash boasts would touch iron instead of the more common wood in order to protect themselves from evil. Scissors have been concealed under cushions or floor coverings to keep witches away from a house. In a dairy, iron objects were thought to prevent witches from enchanting the churn or stealing milk from the cows. The application of a piece of cold iron, similarly, was thought to cure cattle of disease. Iron nails thrust into the wooden parts of the bed were considered essential to ward off demons

Fig. 4 Trade card for Nichols' Bark and Iron, lithograph by Donaldson Brothers, New York, about 1890. One brand of the popular combination of iron and quinine in alcohol, Nichols' Bark and Iron partly relied upon the metal's association with warfare to promote the tonic. It was used both as a nerve tonic and a body-building preparation. Courtesy Smithsonian Institution.

and fairies during childbirth. The Romans are said to have driven nails into the walls of houses as an antidote to the plague. Pliny, the great Roman encyclopedist, remarked that an epileptic patient could be cured by driving a nail into the ground on which he had fallen during his seizure. An iron door key dropped down the back of a patient was thought to end nose bleeding.[7]

Such legends illuminate why iron was so often resorted to as a drug. The metal has also played a role in the ancient and still-popular system of astrology. The planet Mars was said to have an influence over the power and use of iron. The standard term for iron in pharmaceutical texts up until the nineteenth century was Mars or Martis; in some patent medicine advertisements, the term was used until the 1920s. Mars is also the god of war in Greek and Roman mythology. Because iron became the preferred substance for weapons, its association with war is understandable (fig. 4).

An iron cure was presented in the most often-read literary work of the an-

cient world, Homer's *Iliad*. "The rust of the spear of Telephus" could cure the wounds that the weapon itself had inflicted. It is not clear from Homer's description whether the spear was made of iron or copper; the rust could have been either iron oxide or copper sulfate. Both preparations could be used to stop the bleeding if applied in powdered form to the wound. Iron oxide in powder or solution was commonly used to stop bleeding from wounds or after childbirth until the end of the nineteenth century.

Apollodorus, whose writings predate Homer's, described the use of iron in his account of Melampus of Argos, the most ancient Greek physician of whom we have knowledge. Melampus was said to cure the sterility of Ipyclus, one of the argonauts, by administering the rust of iron in wine for ten days (the Greek word for sterility might also be translated as "impotence," or lack of strength).[8] The wine of iron could have acted like a placebo and a belief in the powers of an iron preparation could have cured the argonaut of psychologic impotence, but it is also possible that the preparation did indeed have a therapeutic effect. The legendary warrior could have been suffering from anemia, and the wine of iron would then have been the drug of choice.

Wine was a very common vehicle for medicines from ancient times up to the twentieth century. Its alcoholic content would dissolve most constituents in plants, thereby making it an almost ideal solvent for plant drugs. It made mild solutions of many metals thought to have therapeutic effects. Even if the active ingredient in a wine preparation did not have an effect, the action of the wine would more than compensate for this shortcoming. It is likely, therefore, that a therapeutically viable preparation could be formed of iron in wine. Over a short period of time, the iron is adsorbed into solution by the action of the tartaric acid in the wine, forming ferrous potassium tartrate, which is highly soluble and more easily assimilated by the body than pure iron. Whether the argonaut was really cured is a moot point: the *Iliad*'s assertion that iron had cured him helped ensure its widespread use for centuries, if not millennia.

Iron also had a place in the humoral theory of Hippocrates and Galen, a system that is thought to have been created by Empedocles of Agrigentum (504–433 B.C.). Medical historian Erwin H. Ackerknecht has offered a concise description of this humoral theory, which dominated Greek and Roman medicine and continued to influence Western medicine through the Renaissance:

[Empedocles] was probably the originator of the theory that replaced the one fundamental element of the former philosophers with

four: air, fire, water and earth. Empedocles imagined that the elements came into being through a combination of the four fundamental qualities: hot, dry, wet and cold. A further step was to identify the four basic elements with the four constituent humors of the body: blood, phlegm, yellow bile, and black bile. These four humors originated in the heart, brain, liver and spleen respectively. This theory, through its incorporation into Hippocratic writings and its development through Aristotle and Galen, became the ruling medical theory of the Middle Ages and the following centuries. It provided the "reasons" for techniques of evacuation used long before, such as venesection, cupping, cathartico, emetics, sneezing, sweating, urination, and so on. Its popularity can probably be attributed to its simplicity. A disease of the black bile, for instance, which was "dry" or "cold," would logically be treated by "hot" and "wet" remedies.[9]

Iron, because it was derived from the earth, was considered a "dry" and "cold" substance. It therefore would have been used to counteract diseases of the blood, which were "hot" and "wet." In Galen's *Galeni Opera Omna*, written in the second century A.D., the application of iron was suggested to heal mucous membrane wounds and malignant ulcers, uses similar to those described six hundred years before in the *Iliad*.[10]

At the height of the Greco-Roman period, then, iron had few but very effective uses. By the latter part of the seventeenth century, the therapeutic uses of iron had grown considerably. William Salmon's *New London Dispensatory*, a popular text originally published in 1676 that physicians and apothecaries consulted to research drugs and their uses, listed more than twenty applications for iron. It was thought effective when used as an astringent (to contract organic tissues or to arrest hemorrhages), when applied in all diseases proceeding from corruption of the "humors" and from obstruction of the stomach, bowels, kidneys (or reins), and when used to combat all "fluxes" such as dysentery, diarrheas, lienterias (evacuation of half-digested food), hemorrhages, and terms (menses). Iron was considered "an excellent thing against all diseases of liver, spleen, and womb," gonorrhea, and bleeding at the nose. It was also assumed to cure "melancholy, jaundice, quartans [intermittent fever with a four-day cycle], and the Green sickness."[11]

In the fifteen hundred years from Galen to Salmon, iron had come to be viewed as a panacea. At first glance, it does not seem possible that the metal could have ameliorated all of these conditions, yet a good number of them are affected positively by iron. It does act as an astringent: that is how, I believe, the rust from Telephus's spear healed wounds. In low dosages, iron acts as a laxative; in higher dosages, it will bind up the patient and therefore stop fluxes, or the discharge of large quantities of fluids from a bodily surface or cavity. Because of its astringent quality, it could be used to stop a bleeding nose or external and vaginal hemorrhages. However, it could not be used to stop internal bleeding; similarly, it would have no effect on diseases of the liver, spleen, and womb.

Two disease states listed in Salmon—melancholy and the green sickness—are relevant to the discussion of the use of iron to cure nineteenth- and twentieth-century disorders. It is possible that some

of the melancholy of the seventeenth century was due to anemia, which was called the green sickness when it afflicted young girls and women. The accepted medical term for this disease at the time was chlorosis, derived from the Greek for yellow-green, the purported color of the affected woman's skin. Burton, in his book *The Anatomy of Melancholy* (1621), described chlorosis as one of the symptoms and signs of love-melancholy. Burton observed that "the green sickness often happeneth to young women," a condition that resulted from the fact that the mind was distracting the spirits and thus preventing the liver from playing its role of turning food into blood (fig. 5).[12]

Although the true cause of the green sickness was not understood, some physicians knew how to treat it properly. The leading doctors of the period used iron in mild dosages to effect a cure. Renowned seventeenth-century physicians Thomas Sydenham (1634–1689) and Georg Ernst Stahl (1660–1734) recognized that iron would be needed in small dosages over a long period of time—that is, for thirty or forty days; the common practice in the seventeenth through the mid-nineteenth centuries, however, was to give a single dosage of a medicine. Sydenham, when recommending iron for a tonic, dropsy, or hysteria, suggested a most pleasant form for prolonged use. His favorite iron compound was an infusion of iron or steel filings in Rhine wine. This infusion was almost the same as the preparation used by Melampus thirty-six hundred years before.[13]

Iron became increasingly important in medicine during the eighteenth century due to the development of a new theory of therapeutics based on stimulation and de-

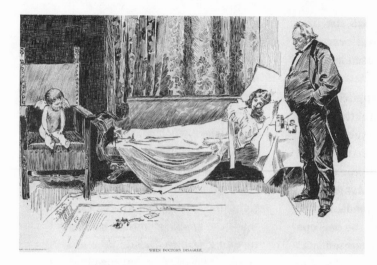

Fig. 5 "When Doctors Disagree," drawing by Charles Dana Gibson in *The Gibson Book I* (1897). Nineteenth-century physicians sometimes labeled lovesickness "green sickness," or chlorosis, a condition that is today diagnosed as anemia.

pression. This system, which largely supplanted traditional humoral theory, had a tremendous effect on medical thinking during its own time. It still influences prevalent thought about disease, which, at least in popular culture, is characterized by metaphors (and therefore beliefs) that equate disorders with greater or lesser amounts of energy. There were many theories about the "vital force" within living organisms and about why people and animals became sick. Such systems as homeopathy and hydropathy were based on the concept of the body reacting "too weakly" or "too strongly" to a disease. This idea was the basis of the theories of European physicians Friedrich Hoffman (1660–1742), Stahl, William Cullen (1710–1790), and Cullen's student John Brown (1735–1788). Each of these physicians had his own classification of disease and his own extreme system.

Brown in particular had a great influence on American medical thinking at the end of the eighteenth century, in part through his student Benjamin Rush (1745?–1813), signer of the Declaration of Independence and leading American phy-

sician. In his *Elementa Medicinae* (1780), Brown divided all diseases into two kinds, the sthenic (produced by too strong stimuli) and the asthenic (produced by too weak stimuli). According to Brown, most diseases were asthenic and had to be treated very actively with stimulants. His main medicaments, used very generously, were alcohol and opium, both drugs known to the ancients.[14] The simplicity of Brown's system and the charms of his two favorite drugs led to the tremendous success of Brownism, or Brunonianism, as it is more popularly called.

The work of Brown, Cullen, Hoffman, and others in their search for stimulants led to a classification of drugs called tonics. Hoffman viewed all disease as a disruption of the functional readiness of bodily tissues, or tonus, from which term the word "tonic" arose for those substances that remedied disease. These preparations were believed to increase the general strength of the body. There were two subgroups of tonics—bitters and astringents. Bitters were claimed to promote appetite and digestion by increasing the tone of the gastric muscular fibers. The most popular bitter preparations contained Virginia snakeroot, wild cinnamon, wormwood, chamomile, quashia, ginger, and angostura.[15]

Metallic bitters were also used, although they were less plentiful than botanical products. Arsenic, strychnine, and iron were most commonly used. At least nine brands of iron bitters appear to have been available, the most popular and heavily promoted of which was Brown's iron bitters. The influence of the concept of a bitters tonic on American popular therapeutics during the nineteenth century is reflected in the successful sale of German bitters, celery bitters, Lydia Pinkham's blood bitters, and more than five thousand other brands.

The tonics of the second group were called astringents, drugs capable of local effects and able to increase fiber density. Of the botanical astringents, cinnamon, logwood, pomegranate, snakeweed, lemon juice, and quinine were the most popular (fig. 6). The metal astringents included copper, lead, arsenic, and iron. It was this tonic use of iron that gave it wider application beyond its earlier associations with anemia and the healing of wounds.

The concept of iron as a general tonic came to this country with immigrants from Europe and from the young American doctors who studied in Edinburgh at the turn of the eighteenth century. A major medical education center from about 1780 to 1830, Edinburgh was also the city where Cullen and Brown practiced and taught. American physicians and the American people in general seized upon iron in both its newfound uses as a tonic and in its earlier applications. During this period, there seems to have been little difference between "regular" medicine ad-

Fig. 6   Reverse of Nichols' Bark and Iron trade card shown in fig. 4. Nichols' tonic was an astringent, not a bitter, but the distinction was probably lost on most users. Like many bitters, this combination of quinine and iron was claimed to promote appetite, though its manufacturer made no claims for its ability to cure indigestion. Courtesy Smithsonian Institution.

ministered by trained professionals and the tonics used by amateurs and people healing themselves. Most domestic medicine handbooks of the nineteenth century were written by physicians, and a strong central medical education system was not in place before 1890. Therefore, no apparatus existed to challenge systematically the concepts put forward by both physicians and lay persons. In addition, many of the patent medicines marketed in America were either sold by, endorsed by, or based on formulas of "regular" physicians. There was no regulation requiring proof of a drug's therapeutic value until 1938.

Fig. 7 Bottles of iron preparations, United States, 1890–1940. With the exception of the tall Brown's iron bitters bottle in the rear, all these combinations were single iron salts, not patent medicines. Photograph by Laurie Minor; courtesy Smithsonian Institution.

Several standard therapeutic textbooks of the nineteenth century provide information about how iron was used at the time, uses that are similar to those proffered in folk medicine and patent medicines. The *Dispensatory of the United States of America* (1860) lists more than eighty forms of iron for therapeutic use; in 1864, Harry N. Draper listed some sixty-six forms in which iron could be prescribed in his *Manual of the Medicinal Preparations of Iron.*[16] Iron was used in its free state and in combination with a large number of other nonmetals such as salts, acids, tinctures, solutions, or mixtures (fig. 7).

Of the eighty forms listed in the 1860 *Dispensatory*, one-third were combinations that were used in this country until the 1950s. Iron was put up with other metal tonics such as arsenic, with a botanical tonic such as quinine, or with quinine and strychnine, a commonly used nineteenth-century cardiac stimulant (fig. 8). These combinations were attempts to decrease the dose of iron and to introduce the effects of other stimulants. Overdoses of iron were known to cause stomach upset, constipation or diarrhea, bitter taste, blackening of the teeth (when ferric chloride was used), and even, occasionally, death. Medicinal chemists attempted to develop a safer form of iron. Binding saccharin to iron was attempted as an antioxidant, for example. Between 1871 and 1900, there were more than 270 articles on iron in medical journals alone, more than double the number that had appeared between 1840 and 1870.[17] But even with all this "modern" interest and research, the most popular salts of iron were still the oxides and sulfates, the forms used by Egyptian, Greek, and Roman physicians in the ancient world. Ferrous sulfate is the most common salt used in iron supplements today.

If there were many forms and combinations of iron, there were equally many uses. The 1880 *Dispensatory* described them:

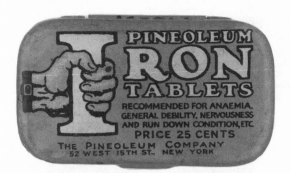

Fig. 8 Tin of Pineoleum iron tablets, Pineoleum Company, New York, about 1930. These iron tablets were actually a combination of iron and strychnine. Despite the imagery of the man's strong hand, the product was primarily recommended for women for general debility, anemia, and menstrual disorders. Photograph by Laurie Minor; courtesy Smithsonian Institution.

The preparations of iron were preeminently tonic, and peculiarly well fitted to improve the quality of the blood, when impoverished from any cause. Hence they are useful in diseases characterized by debility especially when the consequence of inordinate discharges. The diseases in which they are usually employed are chronic anemia or chlorosis, hysteria, flur albus, scrofula, rickets, passive hemorrhages, dyspepsia when dependent on the deficient energy of the digestive function, and neuralgia.[18]

The *Dispensatory* listed only some of iron's uses; standard medical texts of the period had more indications for the metal. In his *Materia Medica and Therapeutics* of 1882, Charles Phillips added cancer, uterine hemorrhage, injections, aneurism, hemorrhoids, relaxed throat, gonorrhea, spermatorrhoea, catarrh, herpes, ringworm, in-growing toenails, gangrene, tumors, rheumatism, diabetes, cholera, and, as a catch-all, hypochondriasis to the list

of ailments iron could ameliorate. Phillips deemed eleven other uses peripheral.[19]

Together, these two sources list almost all the known diseases of the nineteenth century. How iron can have been thought to cure everything seems attributable to two conditions. Because, like other substances, iron was successful in treating a few diseases, it was accordingly administered to assuage all diseases. Other successful drugs, such as quinine and digitalis, were similarly viewed as panaceas at certain points in history. Iron also was perceived as a general tonic, a stimulant to the entire system; thus, it was thought, it could be used to correct any weakening of the body (fig. 9). Today, we know that iron is good for only certain types of anemia and as an astringent.

One of the popular ways of making medicinal use of iron in the nineteenth and early twentieth centuries was to imbibe it as a tonic in the spring of the year, a practice that had apparently been popular from the sixteenth century on. The need created by poor diet for a dietary supplement was common, particularly after a long cold winter during which people ate root crops, cured meats, and dried vegetables and fruits. A popular American home remedy used as a spring tonic was sulphur and molasses, the latter a very potent source of iron. Growing children have a high need for iron; thus, this folk remedy had real value. The interest in molasses increased during the 1920s and 1930s after major breakthroughs in food research discovered it to be a source of iron and recommended its use over iron tonics and pills. Brer Rabbit molasses advertisements in popular magazines, for example, drew on the new research. Not all

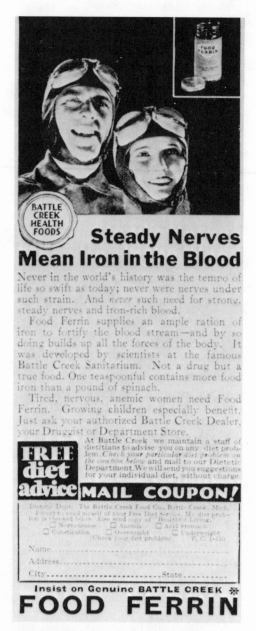

BATTLE
CREEK
HEALTH
FOODS

Steady Nerves
Mean Iron in the Blood

Never in the world's history was the tempo of
life so swift as today; never were nerves under
such strain. And *never* such need for strong,
steady nerves and iron-rich blood.

Food Ferrin supplies an ample ration of
iron to fortify the blood stream—and by so
doing builds up all the forces of the body. It
was developed by scientists at the famous
Battle Creek Sanitarium. Not a drug but a
true food. One teaspoonful contains more food
iron than a pound of spinach.

Tired, nervous, anemic women need Food
Ferrin. Growing children especially benefit.
Just ask your authorized Battle Creek Dealer,
your Druggist or Department Store.

FREE diet advice

At Battle Creek we maintain a staff of
dietitians to advise you on any diet problem. *Check your particular diet problem on
the coupon below* and mail to our Dietetic
Department. We will send you suggestions
for your individual diet, without charge.

MAIL COUPON!

Dietetic Dept. The Battle Creek Food Co., Battle Creek, Mich.
I want to avail myself of your Free Diet Service. My diet prob-
lem is checked below. Also send copy of "Healthful Living."
☐ Nervousness   ☐ Anemia   ☐ Acid Stomach
☐ Constipation   ☐ Overweight ☐ Underweight
(Check your diet problem)   P. C. 1-330

Name..
Address...
City...State..........

Insist on Genuine BATTLE CREEK ✳
FOOD FERRIN

Fig. 9   The January 1932 issue of *Physical
Culture* featured an advertisement for Food
Ferrin, a food additive that was claimed to
"fortify the blood stream." Battle Creek Food
Company, its manufacturer, used aviation imagery to amplify its promotional claim that
such iron supplements were vital if Americans
were to step to the quickening pace of
twentieth-century life.

spring tonics contained iron: sarsaparilla,
for example, was a popular botanical
spring tonic for more than three hundred
years. However, the interest in iron was
so great that it was added to many brands
of sarsaparilla, thereby combining two
powerful folk remedies.

The physical culture movement and
scientific research into the nutritive constituents of food led to greater popular interest in and use of vegetables and certain
animal organs. Liver was promoted as a
natural and a more easily assimilated
source of iron for anemics. Spinach was
also promoted as a natural way to take
needed iron. Many children tended to re-
ject the green vegetable, probably because
of its slightly bitter taste and also because
their parents tended to push it so hard.

One American, however, found great
strength in the green miracle vegetable.
Popeye the Sailor Man entered American
culture by way of the newspaper funny
pages in 1929, when he joined the cast of
Elzie Segar's comic strip *Thimble Theatre*.
Popeye was constantly assaulted by villains, but when he needed an extra dose
of strength, he simply turned to his always handy can of spinach. An individual
in fact needs to consume large amounts of
spinach over several weeks to increase the
iron blood level. Moreover, spinach contains iron in a bound form, which is not
as readily absorbed as other natural
sources of iron, such as liver. Adult men
do not need appreciable amounts of iron
in their diets, as children and women do.
These facts, however, did not constrain
Popeye from defending Olive Oyl and
promoting the strength-building properties of the iron-rich vegetable. The message was clear: if you want to be strong,
eat your spinach (fig. 10).

Fig. 10   These first four frames of a 1934 installment of Elzie Segar's *Thimble Theatre* illustrated the strength-giving properties that spinach reputedly contained. © 1934; reprinted with special permission of King Features Syndicate, Inc.

Tonic patent medicines were popular in the rapidly growing United States of the nineteenth century because iron was widely viewed as a panacea. This image of the metal coincided neatly with the prevailing theory of disease, a connection that was continually seized upon by tonic and bitters manufacturers. One mid-1880s trade card for Brown's iron bitters claimed the solution to be "a certain cure for diseases requiring a complete tonic, indigestion, dyspepsia, intermittent fevers, want of appetite, loss of strength, lack of energy, malaria and malarial fevers, &c. Removes all symptoms of decay in liver, kidneys and bowels, assisting to healthy action all functions of these great organs of life, enriches the blood, strengthens the muscles and gives new life to the nerves" (fig. 11). Another implored women to "stop one moment to think" about how they might restore strength to their systems:

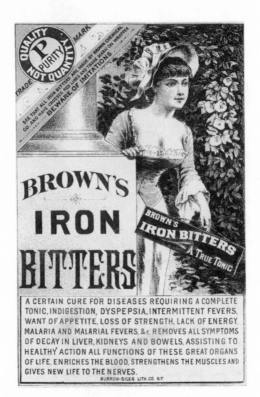

Fig. 11   Trade card for Brown's iron bitters, chromolithograph by Burrow-Giles Lithography Company, New York, about 1885.

> If your blood is too thin and watery, if you are weak and lanquid [*sic*], if you have no appetite and feel debilitated and "all gone," have courage, Brown's Iron Bitters will cure you.
>
> If you feel dizzy, faint and gloomy, broken down and used up, if you are incapable of doing anything without getting worried, if life is becoming a burden, be of good cheer, Brown's Iron Bitters will cure you.
>
> If you, nursing mother, see your baby pining for lack of sufficient food and

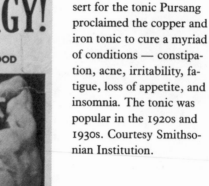

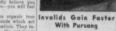

Fig. 12   This package insert for the tonic Pursang proclaimed the copper and iron tonic to cure a myriad of conditions — constipation, acne, irritability, fatigue, loss of appetite, and insomnia. The tonic was popular in the 1920s and 1930s. Courtesy Smithsonian Institution.

strength, if you are weary, despondent and hysterical, you can be cured, Brown's Iron Bitters will do it without fail.[20]

These themes repeat themselves constantly: iron tonics will restore to health and strength the body harmed by the wasting effects of diseases caused by overwork, poor digestion, and old age.

However, as Popeye's example illustrates, iron products were not only promoted for the sick and infirm; they were often endorsed by the nation's physical champions (fig. 12). Nuxated iron, a combination of *nux vomica* (strychnine) and iron, was a blend of the botanical and metal tonic systems (fig. 13). It contained only 4 percent of the iron in the standard iron preparations, but it promised health, strength, even greatness. In 1917, advertisements designed to look like regular newspaper articles showed baseball great Ty Cobb giving credit for his comeback to Nuxated iron. The headline reads, "Ty Cobb Comes Back/Nuxated Iron Makes Him Winner." The copy continues, "Greatest baseball batter of all time says Nuxated Iron filled him with renewed life after he was weakened and all run down. Supplies that 'stay there' strength and vim that makes men of mark and women of power." Ty Cobb did not write the

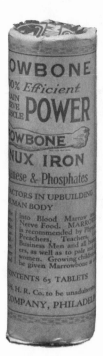

Fig. 13 Package of Nux iron tablets, Munyon's H. H. R. Company, Philadelphia, about 1930. This combination of iron and strychnine used bone marrow instead of the more common beef extract or liver. Nux iron was recommended for brain, muscle, and nerve ailments. Added in a subtoxic dosage, the strychnine acted as a stimulant to the heart. Photograph by Laurie Minor; courtesy Smithsonian Institution.

copy, but he did sign a contract with the Dae Health Laboratories of Detroit, manufacturers of Nuxated iron, to have his name used in endorsing the product. In 1916, the advertising director for Dae Health Laboratories signed the world heavyweight boxing champion Jess Willard to promote Nuxated iron. The advertisement read in part, "I have often taken Nuxated Iron and have particularly advocated the free use of iron by all those who wish to obtain great physical and mental power. Without it I am sure that I should never have been able to whip Jack Johnson so completely and easily as I did, and while training for my fight with Frank Moran, I regularly took Nuxated Iron, and I am certain that it was a most important factor in my winning the fight so easily." In 1919, Willard lost the championship. But Nuxated iron was not defeated, for the new advertisement read, "How Nuxated Iron helped put me in

such superb condition as to enable me to Whip Jess Willard and win the world's championship—Jack Dempsey 'tiger of the ring.' "[21]

The American Medical Association's Committee on Nostrums and Quackery criticized such advertising gimmicks during the later teens. The federal Food and Drug Administration also took note of these exaggerated statements and compelled the company to modify its claims. But the FDA had even more fraudulent iron products to deal with than Nuxated iron. In the 1940s, the manufacturers of Ferrol were claiming that the "tonic and alternative preparation is especially made for the person whose vitality was below normal, or who may be suffering from one of the following disorders: Tuberculosis, anemia, chlorosis, amenorrhea, malnutrition, la grippe, typhoid, malaria, rickets, rheumatism, etc."[22] A similar product, made by the F. T. Park Company of Philadelphia, contained iron, potassium, arsenic, mercury, and hypophosphites of lime soda in the form of an emulsion, which imparted a nonirritating and easily assimilated quality to the drug. Park's product ran into trouble with other agencies of the United States government. After 1918, Prohibition laws brought many medicines with a high alcoholic content under scrutiny. Tonics and bitters had to decrease their alcoholic content from between 40 and 50 percent to between 10 and 12 percent.

One iron combination product that was able to survive this review, and that therefore received widespread use during the Prohibition period, was a combination of beef, iron, and wine (fig. 14). This product simply blended the ancient iron and wine of the Greeks with the addition of extract of beef. The use of extract of beef as a "food" for invalids and a restorative was popular throughout the nineteenth century. By the turn of the century, beef extract companies were aware of the popularity of iron products and began to advertise their natural wine. This blend was so popular during the Prohibition period that the pharmaceutical firm Wyeth and Company transported red wine from California in small tankers through the Panama Canal to the East Coast and from there by railroad car to its plant outside Philadelphia. Wyeth prepared so much beef, iron, and wine that many California vintners owe their survival through the 1930s to this tonic and restorative.[23]

By the late 1940s, the use of iron in tonics, bitters, nerve preparations, and in the once-popular beef, iron, and wine was greatly decreasing. The demand for medicinal alcoholic beverages created by Prohibition was long gone. Medical and nutritional research had by this time fostered a better understanding of the causes of anemia. As knowledge of human physiology increased, stimulating tonics were put aside as archaic; new preparations were being promoted.

The research of the first quarter of the twentieth century produced a series of discoveries that outlined the body's use of and need for vitamins. By the 1930s, combination vitamin preparations were being mass marketed in the United States. The food rationing of World War II increased the need for and the sale of vitamin supplement products. Iron and other minerals were combined with vitamins to form a new tonic for the twentieth century (fig. 15).

The 1940s and 1950s witnessed the

Fig. 14 Bottle of McKesson's Beef, Iron and Wine, McKesson and Robbins, Inc., New York, and Bridgeport, Connecticut, about 1950. McKesson's combined beef extract, ferric ammonium chloride, and sherry. Courtesy McKesson Corporation. Photograph by Laurie Minor; courtesy Smithsonian Institution.

rise of a special subset of vitamin and mineral preparations marketed to women and promoted for general health and the cure of anemia. Several brands of vitamin and iron combinations, such as Geritol (B vitamins and iron) and One-A-Day Plus Iron (multiple vitamins and iron) were particularly successful in reaching women, and they continue to appeal to them today. And, as earlier in the century, skepticism about the marketing of such products has arisen. In 1978, the Consumers Union published a research article entitled, "Do Women Need Iron Supplements?" that castigated the misleading television advertising of several companies:

A recent Geritol ad campaign . . . depicts women who "take good care" of themselves by exercising, eating right—and taking

Fig. 15 Iron and vitamin combinations, 1920–1940. Iron was often combined with B vitamins in tonic, capsule, and tablet forms beginning in the 1920s. Photograph by Laurie Minor; courtesy Smithsonian Institution.

Geritol. Adoring husbands then reward them with a kiss for such healthful habits. Still another Geritol commercial shows a woman who takes the preparation "to look as young as I can." A television commercial for One a Day Plus Iron presents the product as a way to get enough iron without overeating. And a magazine ad for Stresstabs 600 With Iron refers to the mineral as "a touch of womanhood."

Consumers Union went on to warn against the popular tendency to treat one's malaise with iron preparations:

Self-diagnosis . . . is a tricky business. Weakness, listlessness, and the tendency to tire easily can signal a number of conditions other than anemia. Furthermore, all anemias are not due to iron deficiency. Some are caused by red blood cell destruction, bone marrow failure, or deficiencies of other nutrients, such as vitamin B12. Many anemic people are without symptoms and haven't a clue to their anemia until a routine blood test uncovers a low blood count (less hemoglobin and a lower number of red blood cells than normal). People with mild anemia generally don't feel sick and show little or no apparent evidence of harm.[24]

Fig. 16 Advertisement for Timex wristwatch, a plastic and silicone timepiece for "men of iron," published in the May 1986 issue of *Triathalon*. Reprint permission granted by Timex Corporation.

Even with the greatly increased knowledge about iron and its limited role in health maintenance and the cure of certain anemias, it continues to be widely used in vitamins and mineral preparations. Sales of women's vitamins with iron have not decreased. Various health foods and body building supplements promote their iron content as an all-powerful substance. A popular movie of 1985, *Pumping Iron*, capitalized on the association of iron and strength in its glorification of body building. The image and metaphor of iron as a symbol of health continues in this age of titanium and plastic. Advertisements in sports magazines promote a watch by calling it "A Timex for Men of Iron" (fig. 16) or a bicycle by answering the question "Why a man of steel rides a frame of carbon." Despite vast strides in popular understanding of medical knowledge, the metal's public personality remains unsullied. And despite the fact that its ability to cure is limited, it stands in mass culture as a general symbol of health and vitality.

Notes

1   *A Letter to Clergymen on the Preservation of Health and the Use of Peruvian Syrup or Protected Solution of Protoxide of Iron Combined, as Medicinal Agent* (Boston: N. L. Clark and Co., 1858), 9.
2   Trade card for Brown's iron bitters, Brown Chemical Co., Baltimore, printed by Burrow-Giles Lithography Co., New York, ca. 1885.
3   Catalog of the Milwaukee Drug Company, Milwaukee (1907). The Milwaukee Drug Company was a representative full-line wholesaler of the turn-of-the-century United States.
4   Ten of the most often consulted formulary and receipt books, of the 292 nineteenth-century English-language volumes in the National Library of Medicine's history section, were included in this sample. These books listed ingredients and recipes for medicinal preparations, paints, and other products sold in American pharmacies. Some formulary and receipt books, largely used by pharmacists, were also available to the general public.
5   Monographs in *The Pharmacopeia of the United States of America*, 8th ed. (Philadelphia: Lippincott, 1905), and *The National Formulary*, 4th ed. (Washington, D.C.: American Pharmaceutical Association, 1916); catalog of the Milwaukee Drug Company (1907).
6   The 1914 Harrison Narcotic Act limited but did not ban the use of opium (and its derivatives, morphine and heroin) in patent medicines. It was only after continued abuse that Congress in 1924 effectively outlawed all domestic use of heroin. See David T. Courtwright, *Dark Paradise: Opiate Addiction in America before 1940* (Cambridge: Harvard University Press, 1982), 104, 107.
7   Christian Hole, *Encyclopaedia of Superstitions* (London: Hutchinson, 1961), 204–5.
8   John Ayrton Paris, *Pharmacologia* (New York: Collins and Hannay, ca. 1831), 8.
9   Erwin H. Ackerknecht, *A Short History of Medicine* (New York: Ronald Press, 1968), 56.
10   Paris, *Pharmacologia*, 15.
11   William Salmon, *Pharmacopeia Londinensis; or, The New London Dispensatory*, 2d ed. (London: Printed for T. Dawks, T. Basset, J. Wright and R. Chiswell, 1682).
12   J. C. Drummond and Anne Wilbraham, *The Englishman's Food* (London: Jonathan Cape, 1939), 155.
13   Thomas Sydenham, *The Entire Works of Dr. Thomas Sydenham*, comp. John Swan (London: Newbery, ca. 1769), 427, 425.
14   Discussed in Ackerknecht, *Short History of Medicine*. References to opium and alcohol uses are many in medical and pharmaceutical histories such as Charles Joseph Singer and Edgar Ashworth Underwood, *A Short History of Medicine* (Oxford: Oxford University Press, 1962), 341.
15   Descriptions of these botanical products have been taken from *The Dispensatory of the United States of America*, 20th ed. (Philadelphia: J. B. Lippincott, 1918). Virginia snakeroot (996), *Aristolochia serpentaria* roots and rhizome, was a feeble stimulant, also called topas snakeroot. Wild cinnamon (536), *Cinchoniae obtusifolium*, is an aromatic and flavored spice often used as a carminitive, as-

tringent, and stimulant. Wormwood (1224), the leaves and flowers of *Artemisia absinthium*, was a tonic and anthelmintic. The flowers of chamomile (147), *Anthemis nobilis*, act as an aromatic, a tonic, or an emetic. It can also be used as an infusion for skin irritations. The bark of quassia (925), *Picrasma excelsa*, was a bitter-tasting aromatic. The root of ginger (128), *Zingiber officinate*, was an aromatic spice used as a stimulant and carminative. The bark of angostura (1354), *Cuspariac cortex*, is an aromatic stimulant still used today to flavor alcoholic mixed drinks.

16   Harry N. Draper, *Manual of the Medicinal Preparations of Iron* (Dublin: Fannin, 1864).

17   These figures are based on journal sources in the catalog of the National Library of Medicine.

18   *The Dispensatory of the United States of America* (Philadelphia: J. B. Lippincott, 1883), 689.

19   Charles D. F. Phillips, *Materia Medica and Therapeutics* (New York: Wood, 1882), 124.

20   Trade cards for Brown's iron bitters, printed by Burrow-Giles Lithographic Co., New York, ca. 1885.

21   Arthur J. Cramp, *Nostrums and Quackery*, 3 vols. (Chicago: American Medical Association, 1921), 2: 538, 542.

22   Ibid., 542.

23   Ibid.

24   "Do Women Need Iron Supplements?" *Consumer Reports*, September 1978, 502.

Eating to Win

Popular Concepts of Diet,
Strength, and Energy in the Early
Twentieth Century

James C. Whorton

"The period of pills is passing," proclaimed the alliteration-addicted author of
a 1902 editorial in the magazine *Outlook*,
"and diet dawns instead, in hopefully
hygienic hues, upon a welcoming world."
A passion for eating hygienically was indeed beginning to stir the country just
then, suffusing the public imagination
with rosy visions of a citizenry made perfect through diet, and as exalted in mind
and spirit as in body (fig. 1). The editor's
continuation, therefore, tongue-in-cheek
though it was intended to be, had a plau-
sible enough ring for many: "as the college athlete has learned to feed with a
view to the laurels of the field, so the college orator may yet take a special course
of diet for the valedictory—who
knows?"[1] To be sure, where might limits
be set to the rewards of right eating? The
valedictory and nearly anything else are,
after all, implicit in diet, for food pro-
duces muscle and energy, and these in
turn provide the strength and stamina and
vigor needed to do work and do it well.
As the science of nutrition has moved
ahead with ever-quickening step over the
past century and a half, uncovering ever-
deeper layers of complexity in food, so
has the world extended its welcome to the
idea that diet can be designed to bring
forth all the best in a person. Lately, the
welcome has become so warm as to make
a "sports nutrition bible" the number
three best-selling nonfiction book for
1984. Cynics might challenge that classification and insist that fiction is the proper
category for a work that guarantees not
only maximal athletic performance from
its low-protein, high-carbohydrate diet,
but also maintenance of youthful sexual
vigor into the tenth decade of life. The
promise of heightened energy for all life's

General Health commands—

Eat a plate of good, hot soup at least once every day! It will act as the healthiest kind of stimulant to your appetite, nourish you, make you take greater pleasure in all your food, strengthen your digestion and improve your general health.

Campbell's Tomato Soup

has a delightfully tonic, bracing effect on your appetite that you will notice from the very first taste of it. Plump, meaty, full-ripe tomatoes give all their lusciousness to this soup—just the tomato juices and fruity parts in a fine puree, made even richer by velvet creamery butter, tasty herbs and dainty spices.

21 kinds   12 cents a can

Campbell's SOUPS

Fig. 1   As this March 1922 advertisement for Campbell's tomato soup in *Literary Digest* demonstrated, some food companies promoted their products as necessary for good health— and as requisite for those who would be good citizens. Courtesy The Campbell Soup Company.

activities was the secret of the book's popularity, though—that and the sporting of a title that captured all the ambitiousness of nutritional perfectionism in one pointed phrase. *Eat to Win* evokes the images of social dynamism and conquest long resident in athleticism as metaphor. It suggests that careful selection of food allows people to take control of their futures and shape them to their highest aspirations. It virtually paraphrases Brillat-Savarin: "Tell me what you eat," it seems to say; "I will tell you what you will become." The true meaning of *Eat to Win* is

"eat to succeed," and in acknowledgment author Robert Haas has recently sent forth a sequel: *Eat to Succeed.* The editor of *Outlook*, then, has been vindicated, for while he had great fun satirizing the health-food mentality, he ended with a sober reflection: "Is diet a passing fad of the day, or will it survive and dominate the race? The indications seem to point the latter way."[2]

Those indications were clear enough to the close observer of 1902, but they would not become manifest to all until the decade following World War I, when the science of nutrition reached maturity and popular consciousness of diet was raised to unprecedented heights. From the 1840s onward, biochemists had made steady progress in distinguishing the chemical components of foods and clarifying their roles in body functioning. By 1900, nutritionists had not only established the physiological uses of fat, carbohydrates, proteins, and numerous minerals, but had also devised and refined methods for determining the energy values for each type of nutriment, the rates of metabolism of people engaged in different activities, and so much similar data that they were convinced they could now design ideal diets for all ages, sexes, and occupations. With reason, they smugly referred to their science as the "new nutrition."[3]

The more farseeing among their number, however, suspected that the new nutrition was but a phase, that for all its intricacy, nutrition was still only at the threshold of discovery. Wilbur Atwater, the most accomplished student of nutritional science in turn-of-the-century America, predicted more than once that "in its [nutrition's] study we stand upon the borders of a continent of which only a small portion has been explored."[4] He lived long enough to see only the earliest experiments that would begin to open the continent. Between 1900 and 1912, feeding trials conducted in several laboratories made it increasingly evident that something was missing from diets that nutrition theory indicated should be perfect. In 1912, Casimir Funk, a Polish biochemist working in London, isolated a concentrate of thiamine and demonstrated that its absence from the diet was responsible for the disease beriberi. Suspecting that the long-known ailments scurvy, pellagra, and perhaps rickets were likewise due to dietary deficiency, he proposed the term vitamine (for vital amine) to apply to an undetermined number of substances that had to be present in the diet in small quantities for health to be maintained. Thiamine was christened vitamin B, and then, in quick succession, vitamins A, C, D, E, and G were discovered.[5]

The excitement that the vitamins produced among nutrition scientists is difficult to exaggerate. They immediately coined a term—"the newer nutrition"—to set themselves above the Atwater generation, and, from the late 1910s into the 1930s, professional literature fairly reverberated with that phrase. No article or text was considered complete without it, or without the self-flattering reminder that, as one medical editor crowed, "More actual knowledge has been acquired concerning diet in the past twenty-five years than in all the previous centuries of the life of man."[6]

Euphoria over the progress of modern science was an emotion shared by all the other laborers in the vineyards of health maintenance and promotion. The newer nutrition was only a component of the far larger enterprise of "the new public health," generated at the start of the century by the germ theory of infection and an expanded epidemiology of disease transmission. Like other Progressive-era reform campaigns, the new public health was commanded by experts (bacteriologists) who personally led the attack on evil, corruption, and waste with all their skill and energy yet also enlisted an educated laity as foot soldiers. By 1920, the public were veterans of struggles against tuberculosis, venereal disease, and the housefly threat. Once inadequate diet was exposed as still another enemy, nutrition experts immediately rallied the public for the next battle. In truth, mobilization had already been activated by real war, the agricultural devastation of Europe by World War I having provided a moving lesson in the consequences of nutritional deprivation. Fresh from sacrificing to the slogan "Food Will Win the War," Americans entered the twenties prepared to accept nutrition as the renewer of American even more than French and Belgian vitality. A 1922 advertisement for Campbell's tomato soup drew upon this sense of the power of wholesome food: a Campbell's Kid attired as a commanding officer was shown issuing "General Health Commands" to a saluting infantryman Kid. The order of the day was,

We'll limit our arms, build cities and farms,
And flourish in strength and vigor.
For our greatest wealth is our jolly good
    health—
It's the nation's best bet to grow bigger.[7]

The message of the newer nutrition was that more precise orders than eat and grow bigger were needed if jolly good health was to be enjoyed by all. The people had to know exactly what to eat for health and they had to appreciate both the complexity of the body's dietary demands and the need to eat a variety of foods, a balanced diet, to satisfy those demands. Through most of human history, balance had not been a concern. As recently as a century before, selecting an invigorating diet had been simple. The special foods were only three: breakfast, lunch, and dinner. Any and all items that went into those meals were supposed to contribute the same nutritive substance, a universal pabulum that scientists straightforwardly dubbed "aliment."[8] Some foods, meat being a prime example, might be quantitatively more potent, but, qualitatively, one food was the same as any other.

The growth of nutritional science from the 1840s onward, however, had been largely a process of discovering important qualitative differences between foods and recognizing distinct nutritive functions for each dietary class. Public consciousness followed in the train of science, and, by the early twentieth century, American consumers had been induced to look upon eating as, in reality, a rather complicated affair requiring careful selection of a variety of foods. Such, at least, was the theory. Practice was more resistant to change. Elmer McCollum, the most prominent of the newer nutritionists, estimated in the early 1920s that "at least 90 per cent" of the food eaten by most American families was restricted to the old standards of white bread and butter, meat, potatoes, sugar, and coffee. Other experts and dietary surveys agreed that those were the staples of the American table and joined McCollum in calling for nationwide "dietary reform."[9]

The key element in that reform was

educating the public to eat more of what McCollum called the "protective foods," the vegetables, fruits, and dairy products whose vitamins and minerals would compensate for the errors of the traditional diet. So eagerly did nutritionists take on that task that the 1920s became as truly the decade of newer nutrition as of bathtub gin and jazz. Food educators bombarded the public through every medium. They presented the facts of modern nutrition in magazine articles; McCollum's multipart series appeared in 1923 in the very first volume of the American Medical Association's popular magazine *Hygeia*. They dramatized the facts with countless pictures contrasting laboratory rats raised on the older and the newer nutrition, and in cartoons that portrayed rundown children being transformed into budding he-men by nutrition classes and nutrition camps. A typical hero, little Jimmy, was featured in a 1924 *Hygeia* strip (fig. 2). Eight pounds underweight his first day at nutrition camp, he was soon ordering extra servings of spinach, and dreaming of hoisting dumbbells and being looked up to by his peers as "Big League Stuff."[10] The public responded as enthusiastically as Jimmy. The editor of *Hygeia*'s section on health in education, at any rate, asserted that schoolchildren showed greater interest in nutrition than in any other aspect of health, and that assessment seems confirmed by the number of articles in that magazine and others reporting on classroom experiments in feeding. Children in the public schools throughout Texas, for example, ran trials during the mid-1920s that involved monitoring the growth of white rats on five different dietaries: candy, soda pop, coffee, milk, and, of course, chili. One class's experi-

JIMMY'S FIRST DAY IN NUTRITION CAMP

Fig. 2 Nutrition reformers used popular media such as cartoons and colorful posters to interest Americans in improving the diets of school-children. In this cartoon by Edith Ingersoll Bullen, which appeared in *Hygeia* in September 1924, eating spinach and exercising transformed an emaciated little Jimmy into "Big League Stuff."

ence represented all: Buster, the milk rat, outgained all rivals, and was seriously challenged only by the rodent named Chili Bean. Soon, parents noticed, the children were also requesting more milk as well as vegetables. A nutrition education program in Fargo, North Dakota, met with even more remarkable success: by the conclusion of the two-year project, pupils were eating ten times as much spinach as before.[11]

Anyone who has struggled to get a child to give spinach any friendlier reception than E. B. White's "the hell with it" will accept that Fargo trial as conclusive

proof that the newer nutrition did profoundly influence popular notions of diet (fig. 3). Its particular impact, so well represented by that phrase "protective foods," was to encourage consumers to single out specific foodstuffs as especially powerful nutrients. The primary rule for identifying super foods, furthermore, was exactly the one to be expected from a nutritional revolution incited by the discovery of vitamins. It was its vitamin content above all else that won a food public acclaim. The public was simply fascinated with vitamins. Unlike germs or poisons, vitamins produced disease by being ab-

"NOW LET'S GET IT STRAIGHT ABOUT THE SPINACH BEFORE THE GUESTS BEGIN TO ARRIVE!"

Fig. 3   Given the attitude of many children toward spinach, school programs that promoted the vegetable—and showed evidence that children were eating more of it—had a significant effect on beliefs about nutrition and actual dietary habits. Cartoon by Graham Hunter in *Hygeia* (August 1935).

sent, yet their presence in just minuscule amounts prevented such well-known afflictions as rickets and pellagra. By traditional standards, vitamins were incomprehensible, even miraculous; they were what the advertisement for a 1922 text called them: "invisible life-preserving somethings." Another early vitamin primer *Ten Little Lessons on Vitamins* created still deeper awe: "The man in the electric chair, waiting for that mysterious, invisible force to tear asunder the billion cells of his body that nature was years in building up is doomed with no more certainty than the man deprived of those mysterious substances called 'Vitamins.' "[12]

The mystery grew, fed by pharmaceutical companies marketing every imaginable preparation from crude cod liver oil to purified vitamin pills. By the end of the 1930s, an observer of what she called "The Vitamin Follies" could accuse her fellow citizens of being "vitamin-crazy."

> Hypnotized by the latest health fad, they gulp quantities of vitamin pills and capsules to prevent colds, to ward off a long list of dread diseases, to give themselves pep, beauty and strength. The family washes with vitamin soap, and milady may rub vitamin cream into her skin. . . . Children chew vitamin gum. In drug store sales, vitamin preparations have leaped from tenth to third place [behind only laxatives and cold medicines].

Vitamin pills were also available on the breakfast menu at the Waldorf Astoria and were sold alongside cigarettes and cigars at the Stork Club (fig. 4).[13]

Swallowing a pill was one way to get

"CIGARS, CIGARETS AND VITAMIN CAPSULES."

Fig. 4   Drawing by Galbraith in *The New Yorker* (4 June 1938); reprinted in *Hygeia* (November 1938). © 1934, 1962 The New Yorker Magazine, Inc.

vitamins; eating the right foods was another. Popular magazine articles with titles such as "Vegetables as Life Insurance" exhorted the public to eat greens to stave off illness and no doubt contributed to the rise of spinach as a health food in the 1920s. (A leading gastroenterologist summed up the situation at the beginning of the 1930s when he speculated that "the time may even come again when a six-months-old infant can nurse happily at his mother's breast without having to stop to drink orange juice and cod liver oil, and to eat spinach.") Even spinach, however, lagged behind another food in the vitamin derby. In "The School Lunch Room," a one-act play written by Chicago fifth graders in 1929, the anemic child rescued by his classmates had spinach put on his tray to improve his blood, but, friends told him as they added the last item, "we put milk in a class by itself because it does so many things for you" (fig. 5).[14]

Milk had always been in a class by itself as a food for the young, for it was the product nature manufactured for our first nourishment. But it had been presumed that milk could be left behind with infancy as soon as the cutting of teeth made more substantial fare manageable. In the light of the newer nutrition, though, milk took on a more virile appearance. A harmonious mix of fat, carbohydrates, protein, minerals, and virtually all the vitamins, milk was consummate nourishment. As the title of a 1930s book announced to the unending delight of dairy trade organizations, milk was *The Most Nearly Perfect Food*. Anyone who had attended school in the 1920s already knew that, for health classes had adopted "drink milk, and more milk" as their first commandment. Lunch rooms followed that lead, subscribing to a "milk bottle and straw idea" that was promoted nationwide to stimulate milk consumption. The idea took, ob-

Fig. 5 The "Milk Song" was written originally for the Child Health Organization of America, a society of volunteers concerned with the health problems of school-age children. "Milk Song," lyrics by Mrs. Frederick Peterson, music by Gustaf Hagg, published in 1909 by G. Schirmer, Inc., reprinted in *Hygeia* (April 1923).

Fig. 6 School health poster by Irma Ullrich in *Hygeia* (October 1924).

viously, for "Drink More Milk" was the dominant theme in school health poster contests by the mid-twenties, and school health plays revealed the same preoccupation (fig. 6). In 1926, an Alabama school was actually delayed in staging its production because every child wanted the lead role of King Milk, and no one would accept the part of the villain, King Coffee.[15]

The period's health literature for adults also overflowed with the good news of milk. There were reports of orphans doubling their growth rates when given an additional pint of milk a day, accounts of husky steelworkers finding the strength for an afternoon of girder-wrestling in their lunchtime quarts of milk, and assertions that milk was now the prescribed beverage at athletic training tables (fig. 7). Football players rushed for their milk after practice, West Point athletes drank nothing but milk, and Jack Dempsey, Gene Tunney, and Max Schmeling all claimed to train on milk.[16] The "milk bottle and straw" lunch program was extended into industry, generally with favorable, occasionally with striking, results. The superintendent of the Huntington (Indiana) Shoe and Leather Company, for one, was "convinced that the efficiency of our men is increasing by the use of milk." He had in mind moral as well as physical efficiency, for he had also observed that "the men use less tobacco, they no longer sneak down the fire escapes to buy near beer and soda water." Thanks to these

Fig. 7 This photograph in the October 1928 issue of *Hygeia* showed football players running to get post-practice glasses of milk.

mass conversions, milk consumption rose an estimated 30 percent during the 1920s, so that the authors of *The Most Nearly Perfect Food* could conclude, and not entirely without reason, that the "tremendous increase" in milk drinking "has unquestionably been one of the factors in adding to the marked increase in our span of life."[17]

The suggestion that milk drinkers should enjoy an increase in life expectancy, with perhaps a heavyweight championship thrown in, is indicative of an optimistic definition of health that had been unfolding since early century and came into full flower with the newer nutrition. Nineteenth-century health philosophy had placed a premium on reserving power and preventing exhaustion. In its later days, its proponents worried endlessly about

paying the mental and emotional taxes of urban industrial civilization, and despaired all would succumb to neurasthenia. Hygienic thought was ruled by a parsimony of spirit that found satisfaction in simply coping and making ends meet, and that was particularly evident in the realm of nutrition. Nutrition research in the later 1800s consisted in large part of measurements of the calorie contents of various foods. The figures obtained were then given utilitarian meaning by being translated into the quantity of physical labor they would support. The service often given these calculations was to persuade workers that inexpensive foods such as potatoes and beans would actually meet their needs better than more costly chops and joints. The purpose to be served was pecuniary, and the emphasis was on preserving resources: as it was phrased in an article titled "Food and Labor Force," "The stomach is the best savings bank."[18]

At that same time, the stomach was more and more frequently being likened to a boiler that generated the energy to run the human machine. As early as the 1880s, Wilbur Atwater compared brick layers to steam engines, and he explained that the energy released in the metabolism of food was identical to the energy released in the combustion of coal. The machine analogy was attractive and, by 1900, it was commonplace to talk about the human body as a dynamo. Several decades later, the author of a widely read work on nutrition would still describe man as a "steam engine in breeches."[19]

The metaphor of the dynamo signaled the passing from anxious hoarding of limited energy toward exuberant spending of the unbounded energy that scientific eating could generate. Atwater straddled this divide. A favorite theme of his popular writings on nutrition was the wastefulness of working-class expenditures for food. Yet in urging laborers to apply economy to their eating, he also challenged them to make the most of a basic balanced diet. The abundance of food in America, if eaten according to scientific principles, offered opportunities for advancement closed to the workers of the old world. Atwater believed, "To the American workingman is vouchsafed the priceless gift which is denied to most people of the world, namely, the physical conditions, including especially the liberal nourishment, which are essential to large production, high wages, and the highest physical existence, and . . . as a corollary he has a like peculiar opportunity for in-

tellectual and moral development and progress." Thanks in large measure to their diet, American laborers possessed "the vigor, the ambition, the hope for higher things—and . . . their effort leads them to the realization of their hope."[20]

The advent of the newer nutrition only made that message of realization of hope and of personal ambition through dietary rectitude more vibrant. In his foreword to a 1930 nutrition text, American Medical Association leader Morris Fishbein submitted that diet should be understood to have a "constructive" role: "It promises not only additional years of life but additional years of healthfulness and of strength and of achievement." Doctors, and the public, began to think of diet as the foundation of "optimal health" (or what we today call wellness), as opposed to average or ordinary health (fig. 8).[21]

The newer nutritionists' hopes of leading the nation to optimal health were dampened, however, by the public's tendency to wander off after any self-endorsed expert on diet. The motivating assumption of the nutritionists' education work had been that enlightenment would banish gullibility and superstition and be a vaccination against folly. To their exasperation, they discovered education to be an allergen that induced hypersensitivity to folly, the lay grasp of science being the sort of learning Pope warned against. Made familiar with terms but not fully comprehending principles and mechanisms, the people became more vulnerable to being misled by individuals using quasi-scientific arguments to prop up schemes based on preconception or personal experience. Ill equipped to distinguish between authorities sound and spurious, unable to separate the chaff from the whole wheat, the public of the 1920s and 1930s drew much of their understanding of diet from food faddists.

Hence the professional literature's hosannas to the newer nutrition were regularly followed by sighs of despair at the prevalence of dietary mythology among the laity. To illustrate, a 1935 tirade against faddism with the arresting if blunt title *Diet and Die* opened with applause for "the great advance in scientific knowledge which had been characteristic of the modern era," only to acknowledge immediately that science "has also multiplied to a considerable extent the means whereby human ignorance and credulity can be exploited." As a result, it was explained, "no single subject, with the possible exception of religion, has had grown up around it a larger body of error, misinformation, and plain buncombe than has the subject of diet." Other books and articles echoed the lament. "America is a land of food cults," the author of *Eat, Drink and Be Wary* complained; the author of "Spinach—for Others" scoffed at a public lost in "the Wilderness of Fad"; a third writer submitted that the popularity of food faddism was the strongest proof "that U.S. citizens are the most credulous people on earth." *Diet and Die*'s author turned the most telling phrase, though, entitling his chapter three "ODSAA"—or, "One Damn System After Another."[22]

The National Diet and Health Association of America was one of those systems; its president, Paul Bragg, advocated bran bread, laxatives, and aphrodisiacs in roughly equal measure. G. H. Brinkler's program of mucusless diet ("*Remember My Address in the Hour of Approaching Death,*" he enjoined clients of his mail-

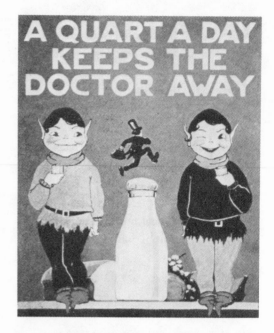

Fig. 8 Followers of popular teachings on nutrition in the 1920s believed that by drinking milk and eating certain natural foods they could raise their level of health above those less conscious of diet. Health poster by Phyllis Shantz in *Hygeia* (November 1924).

order operation) was another. Still another was Eugene Christian's "Course in Scientific Eating," which maintained that cooking destroyed all nutrients; during World War I, Christian made an in-person appeal to the surgeon general to change the army's rations to all raw foods. Actually, he preferred the adjective uncooked to raw, for "foods that have ripened and been brought to a state of maturity by nature cannot consistently be called 'raw.' . . . These things are finished, ready for use; they are perfect, they are not raw, they are done; and when they are cooked they are undone."[23]

By analogy, humankind had been undone by its deviation from nature. Since the late eighteenth century, professional and popular health ideology had fastened on industrial and urban people's estrangement from primitive regimen as the source of all their ills. The development of evolution theory furthered the conviction that the unsophisticated physical life of the savage, the life that had supported the species through virtually its entire evolution, must be more invigorating than the sedentary and pressurized existence of the modern city worker. The late nineteenth-century obsession with neurasthenia was the most developed statement that civilization breeds disease, but nervous agitation was only one unnatural aspect of modern life. Restrictive dress, physical inactivity, and improper diet were others, but, where the nineteenth century saw modern diet as erroneous for its additions (particularly meat and alcohol), by the beginning of the twentieth century the deletions were most deplored. The prevailing trend in civilized diet was the substitution of factory-produced processed foods for natural foodstuffs. Foods were being undone in the factory even more thoroughly than in the kitchen, being refined and concentrated beyond recognition. All food reformers decried the artificiality of industrial diet, and one, Alfred Waterson Mc-Cann, probably the most vociferous antagonist of "depraved food," even held up sugar as a once excellent food now ruined by civilization. In its raw form, he argued, it was "an indispensable element of diet." Refined, however, it was a poison that corroded pancreas, liver, kidneys, and lungs, and laid the nation low with "sugaritis."[24]

An even greater abomination in Mc-Cann's eyes, white bread, was also an important object of attention for the third group of actors in the 1920s nutrition drama, the manufacturers of processed foods. A 1922 advertisement for a popular brand of yeast, for example, seated a fashionably dressed young couple in a posh restaurant, but left them with incongruously lethargic expressions on their faces. Their lassitude was explained by an inset in a lower corner depicting a sinewy caveman plucking a leafy plant to complement the antlered carcass slung over his shoulder. "Primitive man," the caption read, "easily secured the necessary food factors from his fresh meats and green leafy vegetables—modern diet too often lacks these elements."[25]

From that truth followed the moral that nutritionists were also trying to impress upon the public, that—to cite a different ad for the same yeast—"Not what you eat but what you don't eat—is the cause of many troubles." By explaining disease as the result of the absence of simple foods that consumers could select and add to their own diets, manufacturers tapped into the public's growing appreciation of the superiority of prevention. A semi-invalid peering out his window at two ruddy-faced yeast eaters off for a romp on the ice pond was a typical object lesson: "Medicine cannot do this for you—Your strength and vigor depend on what you eat."[26]

That health depended on diet was hardly news, but, by the 1920s, the point to be made by that reminder had changed. Nineteenth-century prophets of better nutrition had renounced the common diet as a congeries of sins of commission and demanded abstention from all stimulating fare, whether alcoholic beverage, flesh food, or spice. Only those inclined toward asceticism, naturally, heeded the call. The newer nutrition's

"IF THERE IS ONE THING an actress must do it is to keep her health and looks at their best—always. To my sorrow I found that when I overtaxed my strength Nature exacted her toll. I became run down, my skin lost its freshness—I was a victim of indigestion. Remedy after remedy—no added relief—no being the mind I longed for. And then, at last, I started on the Yeast diet, taking it in milk or hot water. Wonderful to say, it relieved my indigestion and toned me up in every way."

Edith L. Ransom, New York City

"For Years *I was always tired*"

"I was IRRITABLE, DESPONDENT. Constipation clogged my system with the wastes from my own body; day after day I was literally, slowly poisoning myself. This had gone on for so long that I had begun almost to think my condition was normal.

"I had heard of Fleischmann's Yeast again and again; I had listened to my friends tell what it had done for them. But, until a physician suggested it, I had never thought of trying it myself.

"The doctor told me that intestinal poisons were daily being absorbed into my body. First of all, he said, elimination must be made certain and regular.

"How simple and easy it was! Just three cakes of Fleischmann's Yeast regularly every day, I am alert, full of unconquerable energy. Constipation is gone—forever. My old optimism is on top again."

THOUSANDS of letters like this are received by the Fleischmann Company every year. One person in every three American families is a user of this remarkable food today.

The millions of tiny active Yeast plants in every cake speed up elimination, keep the entire digestive tract clean. They aid digestion, clear the skin. They actually neutralize the poisons of constipation. Unlike weakening, habit-forming cathartics, Fleischmann's Yeast strengthens the intestinal muscles—"trains" them to do their proper work again.

Millions have found relief from their ailments in this sure, natural way. Start eating Fleischmann's Yeast today! Buy two or three days' supply at a time and keep in a cool dry place.

Write for the latest booklet on Yeast for Health. Address—Health Research Dept. A-94, The Fleischmann Company, 701 Washington Street, New York.

AT LEFT
FOR A LONG TIME Miss Alice Cowart was as tired and discouraged as even the wretchest swimming in Hawaii was spoiled for her. "I was despondent," she writes. "My complexion was poor, I did not enjoy my meals." She did not know how to remedy the trouble. But a friend of hers who had been eating Fleischmann's Yeast suggested that she try it also. She says, "For the last six weeks I have averaged two cakes a day. Now I never feel tired out. I go surfing and swimming almost daily. And my complexion is better than ever before."

Alice Cowart, Honolulu, Hawaii

AT RIGHT
Michael I. Pupin, Inventor; President, American Association for the Advancement of Science; Professor in Columbia University.

"I HAVE LONG KNOWN the therapeutic value of fresh Yeast. I myself have sometimes felt the need of special diet to counteract the fatigue and strain of my work and have successfully used Yeast for that purpose. My experience justifies my belief that Yeast is a wise addition to the daily diet under modern living conditions."

M. I. Pupin, New York City

The New Easy Way to keep well

Eat three cakes of Fleischmann's Yeast regularly every day, one before each meal: just plain in small pieces, or on crackers, in fruit juice, water or milk. For constipation physicians say to dissolve one cake in hot water (not scalding) before meals and before going to bed. (Be sure that a regular time for evacuation is made habitual.) Dangerous cathartics will gradually become unnecessary.

Fig. 9 With the help of testimonials from celebrities such as actress Edith L. Ransom and scientist M. I. Pupin proclaiming yeast's superiority for imparting strength and vitality, as well as for relieving constipation, Fleischmann's stepped up sales of its mundane product. Advertisement in *Literary Digest* (5 March 1927).

preoccupation with completeness, though, made dietetic error a sin of omission and shifted attention away from the possible dangers of whiskey or sirloin. As long as each of the newly discovered nutrients was included in every day's menu, the optimist could reason, any potentially injurious foods would be buffered, and full health might be enjoyed without sacrifice; antidote was as preferable to abstinence as it is for the smoker who switches to filtered cigarettes rather than stop the habit. The pain-free gospel of nutrition was even more joyfully received by the food industry. Abstinence was not a product, but a preparation of vitamins or minerals, even if unappetizing, could be sold as a preventive medicine. People would eat their yeast cake if they could have steak too (fig. 9).

If yeast manufacturers had been the only ones trumpeting their products' virtues, the public would have been kept busy enough trying to identify the best dietary supplement. Health was too alluring, though; only the most spiritless of copywriters could overlook its charms, while those who gave in sired in their cynical passion a numberless progeny of health-affirming commercial notices. The product did not have to be edible. Perhaps the most indisputable evidence that the ideal of health had become embedded in the popular psyche is the unashamed scrambling of many advertisers to discover some—any—health potential in their wares. An editorialist complained in 1931 that in recent years, "There has come a veritable avalanche of advertising filled with health claims for this and that, and the other. Quite obviously, the thing has been overdone. Many an advertiser has been 'bitten by the health bug' and has forthwith found himself persuaded that his product was destined to save the entire human race."[27]

Such was the claim of the manufacturer of Kitchen Craft waterless cookers, ads for which featured a football player whose heft had been built by the water-soluble vitamins preserved by that pot; "Build a Vigorous Body," the legend implored. Baseball star Lou Gehrig was hired a few years later by a cigarette company to attest that his postprandial smoke was "the best part of eating," and not just because it eased tension; it "speeds up the flow of digestive fluid" as well, so that "smoking Camels and eating go together naturally." Even an advertisement for pajamas placed health above appearance and comfort. Its satisfied customer was presented not immobilized in sleep but smilingly running in place with a dumbbell in each hand (fig. 10).[28]

Only exercise equipment could rival food products in the plausibility of its claims for health building, but in sheer number of advertisements neither that industry nor any other could compare with food manufacturing. The processing of

Fig. 10 Healthfulness, not comfort or appearance, was used to sell Faultless pajamas. Advertisement in *Literary Digest* (18 March 1922).

foods had become so massive and competitive a business by the 1920s that bold and persuasive advertising was critical to survival. Impelled by the profit motive, manufacturers might employ any distortion of scientific or faddist idea if it promised increased sales. To be fair, many were conscientious and advanced nothing more than the truth that a product was rich in this vitamin or that mineral. But many others stretched the truth to its limits, then beyond, and stamped the fabrication indelibly on the public mind with saturation advertising. "Wherever we turn," a physician grumbled in 1931, "our retinas are scorched by the vitamin claims of some bread, milk or 'sunkissed' orange.

Gigantic signboards proclaim the therapeutic advantage of this or that. The air is filled with radio messages in song or verse, extolling the special health giving virtues of one food or another, ad nauseam." When at the end of the 1920s Robert and Helen Lynd assessed the impact of advertising on life in the quintessential American Middletown, one context they chose was its influence on food selection. "Modern advertising," they wrote, "pounds away at the habits of the Middletown housewife. Whole industries mobilize to impress a new dietary habit upon her."[29]

What was a housewife to do to deal intelligently with this advertising Babel? Were Quaker oats really "the food of foods"? Or were Diamond walnuts? Both laid claim to the title, Diamond reinforcing its case by describing the low-moisture nuts as "over 96% pure nutrition." That kind of embellishment eventually brought the American Medical Association to the housewife's rescue. The association had been active in exposing health quackery since the beginning of the century, concentrating through its Council on Pharmacy and Chemistry on the grossly misleading advertisements for popular over-the-counter nostrums. Hence when the food industry made clear its determination to imitate the excesses of patent medicine manufacturers, it was just an extension of duty for the AMA to step in and, it hoped, prevent "the sinking of the modern food market in a morass of hokum such as engulfed the drug industry in its developing stages." In 1930, the association announced the formation of a Committee on Foods assigned to evaluate advertisements submitted by food man-

ufacturers claiming special nutritional values for their wares. Submission of advertising copy was voluntary, but satisfaction of the committee's standards of scientific accuracy earned a product official recognition as an "accepted" food, and a seal of approval—a badge with the legend "Accepted, American Medical Association Committee on Foods"—that could be displayed in advertisements and encourage consumer confidence.[30]

Many companies had to make do without the committee's badge, and some did quite well, especially those catering to the overriding popular health bogey of the time—constipation. The philosopher who recognized that the more things change the more they remain the same may well have had in mind the human race's fixation on its bowels. Surely no other part of the body has been so persistently suspected of being the seedbed of disease. But then, where else is there such impurity, such putrefying foulness remindful of the organic decay of death? Little wonder that, through all the fluctuations of medical theory over the centuries, the stools held fast as a supposed *materia peccans*, and purgation ruled as therapy, physic being at once a synonym for medicine and for a cathartic. The oldest "book" in existence, the *Papyrus Ebers*, set the tone in the sixteenth century B.C. Its collection of pharmaceutical recipes opened with three incantations to enhance the efficacy of any therapy, the first two addressed to gods, the third to the medication: "Come remedy! Come thou who expellest (evil) things in this my stomach." That the ancient Egyptians understood "remedy" as most of all a gastrointestinal evacuant is verified by the specific recipes that followed the incantations, the first three being for diseases in the belly, the next thirty-odd for the intestines and their "noxious excrements" and "purulency." Three millennia later, the *Cottage Physician and Family Advisor* of 1830 would still be making *Every Man His Own Doctor* by giving him formulas for cathartic cures for ailments as diverse as scurvy and canine rabies. Of his "Strengthening Pills for the Weak"—a salvo of calomel, antimony sulfide, and guaiac—author William Buchan wrote, "We know nothing better," for they would "carry off, by stool, the obstructions in the stomach, the liver, and the bowels, and . . . sweeten the blood, and invigorate the body and nerves." Comparable health insurance was available to readers of *The People's Medical Lighthouse*, for its author offered, at only twenty-five cents a box, his renowned Anti-Bilious pills, "the *ne plus ultra* of all purifying medicines," "the most beneficial discovery for mankind that ever was made." If every family purchased a box, he predicted, "the *whole country would be freed from all disorders.*"[31]

Less profit-oriented domestic guides observed that antibilious and other pills would not be necessary if costiveness were prevented in the first place by proper diet and obedience to nature's urgings. The most respected and reprinted of all popular works on health maintenance, the medieval *Salernitan Regimen of Health*, made that point in its opening lines and peppered its commentary on diet with references to the laxative effects of various foods. An 1861 Paris edition of *Regimen* added the advice to urinate at least six times a day,

And twice or thrice all alvine calls obey,
Nor pause should e'en the King pass by that
    way.[32]

Most authors of health manuals were content to suggest only one daily movement and, while they acknowledged that a small minority of people seemed to stay healthy on a still less frequent schedule, the bulk of humankind, they warned, courted illness and death by doing so. "Beyond this period" of two days, wrote John King in *The American Family Physician* in 1860, "it is unsafe for anyone to allow the bowels to remain unmoved." The reason, he explained, was that the intestines held "those refuse and worn-out particles of matter, which are not only of no further utility to the system, but which are actually pernicious when retained."[33]

King was merely legitimating in technical language what anyone might fear to be true, that feces contained or generated poisons that could penetrate to the rest of the body. Thus Anti-Bilious pill vendor Harmon Knox tried to set off a stampede for his product by decreeing that,

> *Daily Evacuation of the Bowels* is of the utmost importance in the maintenance of health. Without attention to this the entire system will becomes [*sic*] deranged and corrupted. Beauty of person as well as health depends in no small degree upon regular evacuations; and a diseased stomach, bad breath, sallow complexion, enlarged and diseased liver, rush of blood to the head, loss of memory, headache, heart diseases, bleeding at the lungs, a thick, coarse skin, loaded and contaminated blood and bile, falling of the womb, dyspepsia, piles, hectic fever, consumption, and confirmed costiveness, are induced by neglect of this matter.[34]

Although the damage could be specified, the mechanism by which corruption of feces could become systemic remained nebulous until the 1880s. During that decade, laboratory scientists isolated several substances produced in the intestinal tract through the putrefaction of protein residues. The compounds were determined to be toxic when injected directly into the blood stream of animals and were given the class name of ptomaines, from the Greek for corpse. So ominous a name encouraged the easy jump from there to the conclusion that the ptomaines were absorbed into the human bloodstream from the colon and produced a kind of self-poisoning, or intestinal autointoxication (fig. 11). Although it lacked any solid scientific foundation (early experimental studies having indicated that ptomaines were not absorbed from the colon in appreciable amounts), autointoxication was welcomed by many rank-and-file physicians. Since the ptomaines were produced by the intestinal flora, autointoxication seemed an extension of medical bacteriology, the science that had early twentieth-century medicine so flushed with excitement that some researchers actually reported the discovery of germs they believed to be the cause of beriberi and other diseases now recognized as non-infectious. Some physicians of the time were particularly agitated over sewer gas, the malodorous fumes from toilet drains that, it was feared, might convey diphtheria and other germs into the home when they leaked back through faulty plumbing. Autointoxication was the microcosmic equivalent of sewer gas: "One cannot live over a cesspit in good health," a physical educator wrote. "How much more difficult to remain well if we carry our cesspit about inside us—especially when, as so often happens, the cesspit is unpleasantly full."[35]

In addition, autointoxication was a useful diagnosis. Constipation (the retention of ptomaine-releasing feces) was accompanied by an array of symptoms, including mental and physical lethargy, poor appetite, headache, and coated tongue. Constipation was also a frequent complaint of patients presenting no definite pathology, those exasperating unfortunates who in earlier times would have been diagnosed as hypochondriacs or neurasthenics. Now they became sufferers of gastrointestinal autointoxication. The plausibility and usefulness of autointoxication outweighed, for many physicians, its lack of experimental or clinical documentation. The leaders of the medical profession during the 1910s and 1920s had to admonish their colleagues repeatedly for using autointoxication "as a convenient cloak for ignorance."[36] "Time and again," a San Francisco practitioner complained, "I have been put to the embarrassment of having to point out to some brother physician that his beautiful case of 'autointoxication' was really an aortic regurgitation, a chronic nephritis, a myxedema, a high blood pressure, tuberculosis, or some other well-known disease." The renowned Logan Clendening was less diplomatic, dismissing the medical literature on autointoxication as "mad, maudlin, jumbled, mystic, undigested," and "sophomoric."[37]

The literature was also widely circulated and unsettling. The author of *The Culture of the Abdomen*, for instance, implied that nearly all adults were afflicted with intestinal stasis and characterized the typical constipated person as a man with a

Fig. 11 "Auto-intoxication," a health scare of the teens and twenties, was said to drain energy and dull the senses. In this advertisement from *Literary Digest* (18 September 1928), the maker of Sal Hepatica recommended the laxative for those "off days."

"stagnant morass . . . fermenting in his belly. His digestion is a mockery, gurgling and groaning in hopeless disability, his breath reminiscent of a Limburger cheese, and his general outlook upon life a pessimistic wail." An athletic trainer of the 1920s issued a similar warning to young sportsmen, advising them not to overeat because excess food "becomes a burden, fermenting, decomposing, putrefying, filling the body with poisonous substances, which are taken up by the bloodstream and this sewer-like blood flows all over the body, bent upon its mission of nourishing the bodily tissues. The result is inevitable—we have the inception of some of the numberless forms of disease."[38]

The public of the 1920s were inundated with such comparisons of their bodies with sewers. Walter Alvarez, a gastroenterologist who waged a lifelong battle against the autointoxication scare, objected that the American citizen

can hardly escape. No sooner does he begin going to school than there appears the school nurse who is likely to hold up to him the bogey of autointoxication. Later his doctor will ascribe many of his complaints, large and small, to intestinal poisoning; and every newspaper and magazine which he picks up will tell him of the terrible results that will follow if he fails to buy so and so's laxative pills, patented syringes, paraffin oil, yeast, sour milk, agar or bran.[39]

Alvarez's condemnation is striking for laying as much blame on nurses and doctors as on commercial interests. The newer nutrition, a medical observer noted, had not found much room in the crowded medical school curriculum: "The education of physicians in nutrition is thus scarcely better than that of laymen. It comes largely from such interested sources as the circulars of commercial houses and the propaganda of purveyors of food." As a result, he was convinced, "physicians are more guilty than dietitians for the whole-wheat craze." It indeed appears that many medical professionals were so caught up in the national alarm over bowel residues as to allow their better medical judgment to be overwhelmed. Alvarez maintained that physicians regularly diagnosed autointoxication in patients and prescribed a diet high in roughage to cleanse their bowels. If the doctors failed to do so, dietitians often corrected the oversight. All too frequently, Alvarez said, he had called on patients recovering from gastric surgery "and have found on the luncheon tray salad, raw fruit, bran muffins, and, I need hardly add, spinach." He also repeatedly told with morbid fondness the story of the colon cancer patient who died from the irritation of the lettuce given him by the hospital dietitian.[40]

The coarse, anti-autointoxication diet was no good for healthy stomachs either. Medical journals of the period were replete with reports of intestinal irritation and injuries induced by too heavy loads of roughage. Abdominal pain and flatulence were said to be common, and worse things could happen. One patient with an obstructed bowel had an egg-sized ball of bran removed surgically, and another was found to be clogged with "a mass composed of celery fibers, prune and raisin skins and other residue that could not be digested." There were, one only half-facetious commentary submitted, "minor epidemics of colitis, with occasional perforated ulcers, in regions addicted with particular credulity to the tirades of diet quacks interested in selling whole wheat products." "The craze for roughage," Alvarez quipped, "is worth $300 a month to any good stomach specialist."[41]

There surely seems justification for the sneering observation of another physician that Americans had set off on a "stampede for rabbit food." In truth, however, a certain amount of rabbit food was needed. The traditional low-vegetable diet was a binding one, costiveness had been a common complaint for centuries, and, at the outset of the twenties, constipation was still, in McCollum's words, "the heavy burden of many adult Americans." The Metropolitan Life Insurance Company gave mathematical precision to that estimate. Its 1921 survey of more than 16,000 men found that nearly half were guilty of some major error in diet and hygiene, and that 39.7 percent suffered with constipation. They and their female counterparts paid a bill of more than fifty million dollars annually for laxatives. Under the threat of autointoxication, in fact, the nation had become what critics derided as "Cathartic-Conscious America." "Things have almost reached such a point in these United States," began the author of "A Purgation of Purgatives," that "it is impossible to look anywhere without seeing an advertisement for a laxative. It is also impossible to listen to the radio more than a few minutes without being implored to attend to your bowels." Americans had become, consequently, "the most liberally purged people on the globe."[42]

Laxative manufacturers created this bonanza for themselves by raising autointoxication as the threat of the age. The producers of Sal Hepatica called it "the most common ailment of these hurried times," "the most common Twentieth Century ailment." A 1924 advertisement in the *Saturday Evening Post* for Nujol, an intestinal lubricant, was more graphic: "Your health will eventually break down. Your mind will lose its keenness. Your ambition will be dulled. Others will win the reward you strive for." Worse yet— you will die. That was the threat posed by the Nujol ad that asked, "How long will you live?" and then estimated that constipation-induced toxemia was responsible for more than three-quarters of all disease.[43]

Yet precious little gratitude for the laxatives' work of lifesaving was shown by the medical profession. Charging that the repeated use of such stimulants at best caused the bowel to lose its tone and become permanently constipated, and at worst killed (when taken by victims of acute appendicitis), doctors bemoaned the creation of the "cathartic addict" and "colonic cripples—life-long slaves to pills." Like nutrition, those warnings were a form of popularized medical science that could be exploited by food manufacturers (fig. 12). Presenting their prod-

ucts as a safe, more natural alternative to laxatives, these manufacturers used this strategy to make their fortunes with more than one food product in the age of autointoxication. Even manufacturers of sauerkraut, a food in less demand than ever in the aftermath of the war, tried to help consumers acquire its taste by telling them that its lactic ferments would counteract the bacteria responsible for intestinal putrefaction.[44]

Sauerkraut, more than likely, was one of the less favored preventives of autointoxication. Most favored, it appears, were the breakfast cereals, and fittingly so, because the foremost promulgator of autointoxication, John Harvey Kellogg, director of the Battle Creek (Michigan) Sanitarium, had made an even deeper impression on American culture as the founder of the breakfast food industry. His first cereal, prophetically named Granola, was introduced in the 1870s and was followed by a parade of toasted, flaked, puffed, and otherwise reformed grains, all pronounced to be health foods. Kellogg's essentially philanthropic nature restrained him from aggressive promotion of his products through advertising, but restraint was not a virtue of his brother Will Kellogg (who would establish the modern Kellogg's cereal company), nor of former sanitarium patient C. W. Post, nor of many others in the veritable horde of entrepreneurs who rushed to Battle Creek once John Harvey Kellogg had struck gold in the breakfast cereal market. By 1903, Battle Creek cereal magnates were investing ten million dollars a year in advertising and had so buried consumers in drivel that one had to cry out that he "cannot pick up a magazine, or ride in a streetcar, or walk down a street, without

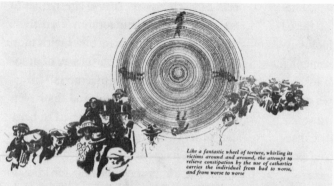

Like a fantastic wheel of torture, whirling its victims around and around, the attempt to relieve constipation by the use of cathartics carries the individual from bad to worse, and from worse to worse

The "vicious circle"
that is wrecking the health of millions

MORE than half of the American people are sufferers from constipation today! Wrecked bodies and ruined health—a host of other diseases that start from this one—the total cost to human happiness can never be fully known.

We do know that many millions of dollars are spent every year *for cathartics and purgatives alone!*

Yet medical science says that drugs not only fail to cure—they actually *increase* the trouble. Regular use of them leads to what doctors call a "vicious circle."

How constipation starts

Our whole mode of life is unnatural today. We take less and less physical exercise. We work under constant nervous strain.

And instead of the raw foods of the forest for which our bodies were built, modern civilization demands a more delicate, concentrated diet which gives our *intestinal muscles* no real work to do.

It is these muscles which, by contracting one after another like a set of powerful clamps, keep the waste products moving.

Nature intended our food to stimulate and exercise these muscles regularly—instead, our modern diet lets them get soft and flabby. They fail to act. Day by day poisons flood our system.

How the "vicious circle" begins

Then we start taking drugs and cathartics. These blast a way through at first, but they weaken the intestinal muscles still more, and so you have to take larger and larger doses. Thus the "vicious circle" is established: the more drugs you take, the more constipated you get—the more constipated you get, the more drugs you must take.

What this does to the muscles of your arm, Fleischmann's Yeast does to the muscles of your intestines — gives them normal healthy exercise

And at last the intestines, jaded and weakened by this constant purging, refuse to respond at all!

The simple food that is restoring health to thousands

Nothing can permanently cure constipation which does not build up these muscles by gently encouraging them to act for themselves.

Everywhere physicians and hospitals are prescribing Fleischmann's Yeast today—not as a medicine, but as a fresh corrective food which gives the intestinal muscles regular, natural exercise.

Every cake of Fleischmann's fresh yeast consists of *millions of tiny living plants,* which mix with the waste products in the colon, softening them, and increasing the bulk of the waste. This greater bulk gently encourages the muscles to act, and at the same time *strengthens* them by offering just the resistance they need.

Your own physician will heartily endorse this principle of regularly exercising the intestinal muscles as *the only way* to relieve constipation and all its evils.

Fleischmann's Yeast is in no sense a purgative and does not produce immediate violent action.

It must be *eaten regularly* to secure lasting results.

Eat at least 2 or 3 cakes a day—plain, or dissolved in water, milk, or fruit juices—preferably before a meal, or the last thing at night. If you eat it plain, follow with a glass of water. Get several cakes at a time—they will keep in a cool, dry place for several days. Be sure you get Fleischmann's Yeast. All grocers have it.

Send today for this free booklet!

THE FLEISCHMANN COMPANY, Dept.12, 701 Washington St., New York, N.Y.

Please send me free booklet, "The New Found Value of Fleischmann's Yeast in Building Health."

Name ....

Street ....

City .... State ....

Fig. 12 The makers of Fleischmann's yeast, as well as a number of cereal manufacturers, capitalized on consumers' fears of falling into the "vicious circle" of laxative abuse. Advertisement in *Literary Digest* (10 February 1923).

having the merits of some new cereal food brought before his eye."[45]

The dominant theme in all that advertising was the original Kellogg's assertion of the extraordinary healthfulness of cereal foods, buttressed not simply by vegetarian faith but with revelations of the protein, carbohydrate, and mineral content of grain. In truth, cereals could be legitimately touted as uncommonly well-balanced food able to satisfy nearly all the body's needs. Early advertisements for Grape Nuts described it as "a universal food," "quickly absorbed into the blood and tissues, certain parts of it going directly to building and nourishing the brain and nerve centers." Other ads resounded with testimonials to the therapeutic powers of Grape Nuts, miracle cures being reported across the spectrum of pathology from paralysis to flatulence. A competitor, Wheatlet, identified itself as "the ideal breakfast food," with power to feed the brain, strengthen muscle, and harden bones, while Quaker oats promised to contribute "a wholesome sturdiness, a rugged health, a splendid ambition and conquering strength." Shredded wheat's version of the conquering strength motif reflected the prejudices of the times with the exhibition of a marching Japanese soldier, fresh from annihilating the Russians at Tsushima, alongside the statement that "the Plucky Little Jap illustrates the triumph of cereal foods in the building of a sturdy and industrious race."[46]

Digestibility and flavor were other emphases in cereal advertisements, and, on into the 1920s, Armour's toasted corn flakes could ignore nutritional value in favor of "You'll Like the Taste," and Puffed Rice could describe itself in no more robust terms than "Flimsy, Flavory Bubble Grains." For most producers, though, healthfulness was the pitch more than ever, for the newer nutrition meant new science to manipulate and a new level of consumer food awareness to take advantage of. Grape Nuts was still a universal food, but now the buyer was taught why: "It is rich in tissue-building elements, and in the mineral salts that nourish nerves, provide iron for the blood, and furnish phosphates for the teeth and bones."[47]

Cereals were similarly modest in admitting their vitamin content, yet even those fabulous "life-preserving somethings" were outshone in advertisements by bran, the indigestible coat of the wheat kernel, a health food of repute ever since Sylvester Graham's 1830s advocacy of unbolted flour. His rationale for bran as a health food was only tangentially related to fear of constipation, however, and bran never attracted widespread popular respect until its late nineteenth-century glorification by Kellogg. A dedicated veg-etarian, Kellogg saw in autointoxication the most powerful argument yet for the superiority of meatless diet. Vegetable food being lower in protein than flesh food, he observed, it was less likely to produce autointoxication. The standard meat diet was also too concentrated, with insufficient bulk and roughage to stimulate the bowels to action; its sluggish passage through the gut gave putrefactive bacteria time to convert all unabsorbed protein to ptomaines. In the meat eater's rancid bowels, Kellogg believed, lay "the secret of nine-tenths of all the chronic ills from which civilized human beings suffer," including "national inefficiency and physical unpreparedness" as well as "not a small part of our moral and social maladies." His life goal was to establish for society the "sensitive colon conscience" necessary to rescue civilization from the "race-destroying effects of universal constipation and world-wide autointoxication."[48]

But, Kellogg realized, abstaining from meat was not enough to prevent autointoxication, for vegetable protein too could undergo intestinal degradation and release ptomaines. He therefore recommended the liberal use of bran to flush the intestines of unabsorbed food. Bowel regularity was in fact an obsession with him, and, though few others could keep up with his busy agenda of five movements daily, the more manageable standard of at least one evacuation per day did become associated in the public mind with freedom from autointoxication and with maintenance of general well-being. The nutritional consciousness of the 1920s lifted bran's popularity still higher, until it became, doctors disparaged, "The National Mania." It was, at least, a mania based on a kind of logic. If bread is the staff of life, and therefore the food most essential to protect from refining and denaturing, then bran, the major ingredient removed by processing, is ipso facto a health food. And if autointoxication—warned about for decades but now confronting a newly enlightened, nutritionally aware citizenry—is produced by bowel irregularity, then bran, a laxative food par excellence, might be the very salvation of the race. Manufacturers of bran cereals were perhaps marginally less hyperbolic in their proclamations. One calculated odds of nine to one that a random consumer needed bran, presenting constipation as the neurasthenia of the new century. An ad for Post bran flakes placed a ten-foot-tall menu card in the dock, flanked by burly policemen: "Indicted! The menu is charged with being responsible for a high percentage of ill health due to a definite lack of bulk food" (fig. 13). Inactive bowels resulted from the same hurry and pressure and inattention to nature that had formerly caused neurasthenia as well as from too little dietary bulk. "The pace is fast in today's world; everything is abbreviated. The very food you eat is concentrated." It was a "Tabloid Life," and "tabloid diet" would not do; only bran would. The ads for Pettijohn's were even more ominous: "Dullness, headaches, irritability, intestinal auto intoxication. Are you one of the army who suffer from the great unnecessary handicap?"[49]

Although identification of autointoxication as the great handicap flew in the face of authoritative medical opinion, cereal producers eagerly joined hands with the authorities on a related point, the danger of laxatives. Laxative preparations

Fig. 13 In this advertisement for Post bran flakes in *Literary Digest* (31 March 1928), a menu of unhealthful foods is "indicted" for causing constipation, "one of the underlying causes of ill health." Courtesy General Foods Corporation.

were bran's direct competitors in the battle for consumers, so it was good business as well as truthful for Pettijohn's to say that its bran could provide a "complete release from laxatives," Post to state that its bran flakes "make drug laxatives unnecessary," and Kellogg to certify that All-Bran "eliminates the evil of harmful, habit-forming patent pills." "Kellogg's ALL-BRAN follows Nature's laws."[50]

Bran was not habit forming, but, nevertheless, Post bran flakes insisted, it should be "included in your diet every day." That was a wholesome, voluntary habit, though to get people to adopt it took more than the free health booklets (*Feeding the Child from Crib to College*, *The Road to Wellville*) many manufacturers offered, or even the free and edible "Ounce of Prevention" samples supplied by Post bran flakes. Bran was not, after all, in its natural and unrefined state, an epicure's fantasy. The smiling family shown seated around the festive board laden with fig bran flakes had not always been so happy: "Like many people," the text related, "they gagged on straight bran." The different styles of flaking and baking employed by various manufacturers were all aimed at making bran palatable, at making, as Post bran flakes cleverly phrased it, "partners of your health and appetite." (In the laxative market, incidentally, another manufacturer named Kellogg perfected a "tasteless castor oil" for the very same reason.) Such was the ingenuity of food chemists that bran could be made tasty in any strength—all the way up to Kellogg's All-Bran or Post's whole bran, introduced in 1931 as a more potent mate to bran flakes: "Full strength bran for stubborn cases of constipation," whole bran was also "a triumph of taste."[51]

By other standards, pure bran might be judged a failure. Separated from the mother grain, it was just as much a refined food as white flour. So makers of

Wheatena, a whole grain cereal, argued: "Wheatena . . . brings you—at no extra cost—all the strength, growth and energy materials of the whole wheat, Not just the bran!" "Served with milk," another Wheatena blurb declared, "it provides the most nearly perfect food known to science." In retort, advertisements were soon asserting that bran cereal contained vitamins and iron as well as roughage. A manufacturer of bran cereal even dragged in wonder-monger Ripley to astound the public with the food's diversity: "The bodies of 10 men contain less iron than there is in a ten-penny nail. Yet without this tiny amount of iron you could not live—Believe it or Not." Those who believed surely dashed to the grocer for some 40% Bran Flakes.[52]

The ploys devised by bran promoters were innumerable. What ultimately mattered, though, was the net effect, and that was the apotheosis of bran as a preventive panacea. Fishbein recalled in 1937 that "not so many years ago a craze for bran— 'the horse food'—swept the country. Newspapers and magazines were full of recipes for making bran biscuits, bran muffins, bran gems, bran patties and otherwise disguising this coarse and, to many people, unappetizing material." A rural Georgia schoolteacher even concocted a bran lemonade, the recipe for which he sent to *Hygeia* in the hope children could be enticed to substitute it for soft drinks and thus improve their health. The attitude of many other laymen was characterized by the editor of the American Dietetic Association's *Journal* as a "hopeful feeling that eventually coarse, wheaty, nut-flavored muffins may stop the crime wave."[53] The bran wagon clearly was loaded with grain foods other than breakfast cereals. Flour to be used for Pillsbury Health Bran muffins was guaranteed to "conquer constipation" and "safeguard [one's] health" ("A muffin a day is the natural way"). A Chicago firm advertised its whole grain wheat food as a cure for tuberculosis, diabetes, cancer, and bed-wetting, in addition to constipation. The wonder food was pushed through newspaper advertisements, pamphlets, a company monthly called *The Motive*, and a front organization known as the American Educational Food Council which sponsored nutrition clinics in towns around the country. Another "natural laxative food" distilled all this bran worship into its vulgarly expressive name: DinaMite. There was even an Uncle Sam's laxative cereal to suggest that dynamiting the bowels was a patriotic duty.[54]

Bran became the national mania in part because it was a convenient addition to the diet that might absolve nutritional sins by flushing them away. It could even be substituted for more irksome health duties. After Walter Camp's "daily dozen" setting-up exercises became a ritual many Americans aspired to practice (and a few did), Post bran flakes began to urge the consumer to "help your daily dozen with a teaspoon." The point was that everyone should exercise but did not always have the time or will: "if you do 'cheat' on your exercise," the ad proposed knowingly, "it's all the more important that you get a full quota of bulk in your food." Given the choice of pushups or a bowl of cereal, most would opt for the latter, so a health magazine editor was perhaps not excessive in mourning the death of "the sportsman," who had "been reduced to a braneater."[55]

Cereal manufacturers told the tale in reverse, maintaining that bran eaters were being elevated to sportsmen. Well before Wheaties began to bill itself as the breakfast of champions in the early 1930s, other breakfast cereal producers built upon the postwar explosion of popular interest in sports and reverence for sports heroes and the understanding that muscle and energy were derived from food. Time and again the bran eaters of copywriters' imagining were shown charging through defensive lines or taking Ruthian cuts at the baseball. Yet if buyers did sometimes fantasize about athletic glory, they were more seriously concerned with victory in the economic arena, and the chief use of athletic iconography in advertisements was to make sport an allegory for the game of life. The Grape Nuts depiction of a straining runner just edging ahead of a rival at the tape featured the headline, "That extra ounce of energy is the ounce you need to win" and asserted that the extra ounce was as necessary "in business . . . as in athletics." The proposition that health was vital to occupational success became a commonplace in 1920s advertising, the portrait of the healthy and therefore prosperous businessman at his desk being used for products as different as chewing gum and X-ray film. But nowhere did he appear with more regularity than in bran cereal ads. That constipation could undermine the efficiency necessary for getting ahead in business did, after all, make sense to a populace conditioned to think of productivity in assembly-line terms. Food that had been processed had to pass smoothly through the body; if the intestinal conveyor stalled, the resultant backup was sure to play havoc with all the other departments of the body factory. Thus Pillsbury Health Bran could raise the banner of "Health—Your *best* Business Partner." Post's bran flakes could describe the corporate struggle as "The Survival of the Fittest": "One of the most important allies of success is health. Guard it well, if you have your eyes fixed on the top rung of the ladder of success." According to another Post cereal advertisement, fifteen hundred business and professional men agreed that "what a man eats when he's twenty five is more than likely to influence what he earns when he's fifty." "If you hope for success eat for success!" Kellogg's All-Bran explained what happened to those who ignored that advice, putting a slouching, colorless man in a business suit beside the announcement that he had "Lost . . . another big order . . . the fourth defeat that day. All because he didn't have the energy to fight when his prospect said 'No'. Something had blunted his senses and stolen his strength. . . . That something was constipation, the world's most universal disease."[56]

The most commonly used image in this advertising genre was that of the husband setting off to work with new spring in his step, waving to his wife in the doorway, she beaming with pride at having sent hubby off with clean bowels. "What does HIS health mean to you?" the largest packager of prunes asked women. "It means everything to you. It is the very foundation of your home, your happiness, your security." As a cereal ad that used a strikingly similar picture elaborated, in telling women "How you can help him WIN!": "A wife, in a sense, is custodian of her husband's health. The food she selects can help him in his daily battle for success."[57]

Woman was custodian of her own

health too, but, in her quest for success, beauty was far more important than energy and efficiency. Beauty was also, according to cereal manufacturers, more than skin deep; it reached down to the intestines, where lurked, Post bran flakes warned, "cargoes of digestive waste. . . . the common foe of . . . beauty." "Constipation wrecks health and happiness for thousands of women," All-Bran insisted. "Some women," such as the one slumped in a chair watching two others play golf, "age so young." They may have started "out in life radiantly fresh and alive," but "almost before you know it—their bloom and freshness have gone." Another sufferer "always just missed romance and marriage" because of dulled eyes, wrinkled skin, and listlessness. Finally, after receiving another rejection in "The Bouquet that broke her Heart," she sought advice from a friend, was directed to All-Bran, and presumably found happiness at last. Bran flakes were still more remarkable, giving women the drive, in addition to the charm, to succeed in a man's world. In one episode of the "real life movie" series of ads of the early 1930s, Jane Talbot got off to a fast start in the fashion industry only to be halted suddenly by constipation. A "sharp reprimand" from her boss followed, but, in the nick of time, Nurse Betty Lane diagnosed her problem, prescribed bran flakes, and enabled Jane to realize her dream of success.[58]

Such "continued objectionable advertising" of bran cereals, by one firm in particular, finally proved too much for the American Medical Association. In 1936, its Committee on Foods agreed "that acceptance of all products of the Kellogg Company be rescinded." (All-Bran seems to have had an especially odious reputation; the most comprehensive exposé of food and cosmetic abuses in the 1930s, Kallet and Schlink's *100,000,000 Guinea Pigs*, gave All-Bran as its very first example of items that "are not only worthless, but are actually dangerous.") Bran products generally drew increasing fire from professional and lay consumer champions by the early 1930s, both for their advertisers' hints that bran was a panacea and for excessive claims of vitamin B content. One observer felt the public had been so thoroughly seduced that "a great truth that should be announced in the street car advertisements is this: vitamins and roughage are not inseparable."[59]

This advertising revision might have been stretched to state that yeast and vitamins were not inseparable either. One of the most widespread follies established by advertising in the 1920s was the eating of yeast for health. An estimate made in the mid-1930s, in fact, stated that "in recent years no food product has received more extensive advertising in the lay press and on the air than has yeast." When the author of *Diet and Die* selected products that had manipulated science for profit, the first he identified was Kellogg's All-Bran; the second was Fleischmann's yeast. The Committee on Foods agreed that Fleischmann's advertisements stood apart from those for other yeasts for their "grossly exaggerated or unwarranted claims"; indeed, for exaggeration, Fleischmann's had few challengers from any sector of the food industry. The product had served for half a century in the humble capacity of leavener when around 1920 the company sensed the public's newer nutrition gullibility and began to publicize the findings of experimenters in "the country's

greatest laboratories" in "The New Importance of Yeast in Diet," a free booklet offered in an advertisement for the product. Vitamins, "the new mysterious factor in food," had been discovered in "the familiar foil-wrapped cake"; in fact, "the richest source of this life-giving vitamine . . . is—yeast!" In time, it became apparent that yeast was a storehouse of vitamins: its vitamin A prevented colds, its B strengthened bowels, its D straightened legs, and its G promoted growth. It was "the only natural food that furnishes such a rich supply of all 4 of these vitamins at once." Taken in the three cakes recommended as the daily allotment, Fleischmann's generated the power that energized athletic standouts such as the Yankees' Red Rolfe.[60]

An equally significant element in yeast's new importance was its laxative effect (brewer's yeast had long been a folk remedy for costiveness among the northern French). Constipation, "the greatest enemy of mankind today," "the curse of present day civilization," was best treated with yeast, which was not habit-forming like cathartics or irritating like bran. It was instead a natural substance that when mixed with the concentrated foods of modern diet softened and increased their bulk and thereby stimulated the intestinal muscles, strengthening them through exercise as a dumbbell strengthened biceps. Finally, yeast "by increasing the white corpuscles in the blood acts as a powerful agent in clearing the complexion of many skin disorders."[61]

In the summer of 1923, Fleischmann's announced a contest for the best letter on "What Fleischmann's Yeast has done for you." So many thousands of entries were submitted that the judges, "swamped with work," had to postpone determination of the winner for several weeks. The wait was worth it, though, for Mrs. Lillian Ramsey's one thousand dollar prize letter could not have been a better condensation of yeast's virtues had it been written in the Fleischmann offices. A "Frenzied Medicator" who had abused herself with cathartics for years, she finally yielded to her husband's plea to take "food, not dope." In just two months of munching two "yeast sandwiches" a day, she cured her chronic constipation, her complexion cleared, she no longer had colds, and afternoon drowsiness became a thing of the past. That, in short, was the "story of one woman's triumph over a universal menace."[62]

The triumph supposedly could not have been achieved with any other yeast, any "so-called yeast preparations." Yet the market was so large that so-called yeasts could carve out a share. The makers of Yeast Foam tablets seem to have taken the largest slice after Fleischmann's, and perhaps they deserved more, for they provided all the same benefits to skin and bowels, plus "they don't cause gas!" Eventually manufacturers of both yeasts realized that the product possessed another potent nutrient—iron. Iron's function in hemoglobin production had long before built its reputation as a blood builder. Its metallic imagery—hard, strong, tempered through a trial by fire, the material from which steel and the dynamos that powered industry were wrought—made it seem a critical food for constructing the human dynamo as well. As nutrition consciousness rose, the 1920s became, in the judgment of the leading dietetic journal, the "iron age of nutrition."[63] Any food, no matter how lowly, could win favor if it contained iron. The 1927 discovery that liver could cure the deadly disease pernicious anemia, for example, immediately transformed that bit of offal into "the aristocrat of viscera." "Today," a contributor to *Good Housekeeping* warned, "the unsuspecting individual who fails to observe the prices on the menu suddenly wakes up to find his order of liver and bacon has jumped into the luxury class of dietary articles, and the reason for it is that the world is now eating liver as blood insurance." In New York, another joked, "It is now almost necessary to make a reservation for your liver as you do for a popular play sold out weeks ahead."[64]

A formerly despised vegetable also ascended to the dietary aristocracy on the basis of its iron content. Spinach won its inflated status as a nearly perfect food during the 1920s, partly for its vitamins, more for its iron. A lesson in nutrition presented to Chicago schoolchildren in the mid-twenties, for instance, vividly demonstrated the importance of iron for healthy blood by adding varying amounts of iron oxide to test tubes of water. The students, who had started the experiment by gladly proclaiming that they "all detested spinach," were so impressed by the intensity of the iron salt's redness that "they were ready when asked as a climax to the lesson what vegetables they would like to have for their next lunch to chorus, 'Spinach!' to their own surprise, as well as to that of their teacher." So hungry was the rest of the public for spinach that even dried preparations of the vegetable could be successfully marketed—in fact, one such product, Spintrate, was the second product given "Accepted" recognition by the AMA's Committee on Foods.[65]

Still another item that became a delicacy during the iron age was raisins, especially Sun-Maid raisins. "Have You Had Your Iron Today?" was a familiar slogan by the end of 1921, associated in consumers' minds with long-jumpers hurtling toward records, women "with the bloom of youth" in their cheeks, and well-dressed men commanding the conference table: "Energize—Ironize!" Recipes for raisin pie and raisin bread were circulated through the press, and then "LITTLE Sun-Maids," five-cent packages to be used as afternoon snacks, were introduced "to counteract brain fag, lassitude and letdown which come to millions at 3 o'clock." One witness reported that every secretary in the country adopted the habit, and perhaps their bosses would too, if they read ads such as the one featuring two ski jumpers soaring above a text that read, "Raisins fit you to make 'the long jumps' in business and land right side up with the big orders and well-turned deals."[66]

By the mid-1920s, however, the secretaries "have forgotten raisins and cultivate yeast gardens in their stomachs." Yeast's staying power was assured by still another nutritional service it could provide: relief from acidosis. Although there is a genuine medical condition known as acidosis, it occurs only rarely, and only in serious diseases. The term refers to a lowering of the blood's normal alkalinity, not a positively acidic condition, but much of the public of the twenties had been schooled in the century's earlier uric acid scare, the monistic pathology of Alexander Haig that presumed a wide variability in blood pH. Uricacidemia was a disappearing fear by the 1920s, but it was leaving a heritage of popular belief that the body could become highly acidic, and that sour stomach, heartburn, and gas were signs of acidification. More serious problems, such as loss of vitality and lowered resistance to disease, might result if the condition were allowed to continue. Interpreters of the newer nutrition nurtured the belief with discussions of acid-ash and alkaline-ash foods, foods that produced an acid or an alkaline reaction in the body, and soon, one dietary authority reported, "that terrible condition known as 'acidosis' became psychically pandemic." A colleague in health journalism elaborated:

> The whole world, it would seem, is suffering from "too much acid." The public has become acid-conscious. Full-page magazine advertisements scream at us to "alkalize." Billboards and train placards shout warnings of dire consequences from acidosis. Citrus fruit promoters swell the chorus, while, alas, even health periodicals join the refrain. It would seem that alkalid and alkali-forming foods without stint constitute a panacea for whatever ails you—from Spanish influenza to housemaid's knee, from high blood pressure to hemorrhoids. Little wonder, then, that so many fear their brains, blood and body tissues are being excoriated by the blistering acids which so relentlessly pursue them.[67]

Citrus growers were the first to come to the rescue of the acid-pursued masses. At the beginning of the 1920s, both Sunkist and Sealdsweet fruits were heavily promoted for their vitamin content, as well as for their calories, "concentrated sunshine," "germ-repelling" skins, and, inevitably, "mild laxative effect."[68] And as late as 1923, the acids of citrus fruits were being praised as aids to digestion. As acid acquired negative connotations, however, citrus fruits began to be advertised as alkaline-ash foods (despite their organic acids, they do indeed have an alkaline reaction in the body). Sunkist repeatedly explained this "Orange-Lemon Paradox" ("although *acid* in *taste*, [they] are two of the most potent correctives of Acidosis") in urging consumers to "start your daily fight against Acidosis" with breakfast juice.[69] Sunkist's free booklet, "Telling Fortunes with Foods," foretold business success, beauty, and energy for those who adopted the citrus habit; other ads maintained lemons relieved morning sickness or brought laurels to such champions as Jack Dempsey, Charley Paddock, and Duke Kahanamoku. "But it isn't athletes alone who have found the benefit in lemons. Scores of thousands in the business world take lemon juice . . . as a tonic."[70] Even the inclusion of lemon juice in salad dressing was presented as a secret of how to succeed in business. While the body of the ad touted lemon dressing as "a measure of protection against Acidosis," the ad's upper left corner displayed another business failure:

> "*I don't know why that fellow doesn't get ahead,*" said the president. "He seems to have a good brain and he works. He just lacks the 'punch,' somehow." The manager replied, "I believe he is suffering from the same condition that took my pep. The doctors call it Acidosis. Oranges and lemons would do him a world of good."[71]

Another Sunkist advertisement clarified the fact that oranges would do a world of good, because they too were an alkaline-ash food and so would relieve the chronic fatigue and mental dullness of acidosis and clear the road to success (fig. 14).

Fig. 14   Acidosis, or low blood alkalinity, was a genuine but rare medical condition that was said to produce fatigue and mental dullness—symptoms that Sunkist promised its oranges would cure. Advertisement in *Literary Digest* (10 August 1929).

Producers of other citrus fruits capitalized on acidosis, and even cranberries, a fruit that texts identified as acid-ash, were sold with guarantees of acidosis-prevention. So were Camel cigarettes, by whose use "alkalinity is increased."[72]

Fruit and cigarettes were not the only answer; there was also Hay. All commentators from the 1930s agreed that the Hay diet was that decade's most widespread fad, so popular as to persuade many restaurants to add Hay dishes to their menus. Those were not plates of grass intended to raise the roughage level to new heights, however, but victuals carefully prepared to the specifications of William Howard Hay, the *chef de cuisine* of acidosis. Hay was a doctor gone astray, a graduate of a New York medical school and a licensed practitioner in Pennsylvania who discovered that food promoted health better than drugs. A man with a punishing sense of humor, Hay early made a specialty of using diet and rest to treat hay fever, and later, in 1932, opened a health resort in Pennsylvania's Poconos that he called the Pocono Hay-ven. His notoriety, though, came from his advocacy of what Fishbein ridiculed as "haywire diets." In *Health via Food*, his 1929 best-seller, Hay elaborated a theory of the dietetic origins of disease that took the country by storm: the antifaddist who wrote an essay entitled "Gullible's Travels" identified Hay as "the dietary hurricane with the most victims in recent years."[73]

"Victims" may seem a harsh term, until one considers the sacrifices Hay's followers had to make. The central precept of the Hay system was that because the digestion of starch is initiated by the alkaline saliva of the mouth, and the digestion of protein begins with the action of the acid pepsin in the stomach, carbohydrates and proteins cannot be eaten together. The alkali needed by the first class of food, he reasoned, will be neutralized by the acid attracted by the sec-

ond class. Starches would thus have their digestion arrested halfway and be left in the stomach to undergo a fermentation that would release acid by-products to be absorbed into the bloodstream. Acidosis would result and eventually precipitate any of countless diseases. The consumption of acidic fruits with starchy foods could have the same effect, so health required the practice of "compatible eating," the separation of conflicting foods into separate meals.[74]

Accomplishing such a separation was a considerable feat, because the large majority of foods are naturally a mix of some carbohydrate with some protein. Hay overlooked that inconvenient fact, as well as several others related to the physiology of digestion, and blithely assured disciples that as long as they divided their meat and potatoes into separate meals, all would be well, if not perfect. Compatible eating would eradicate disease—mental, moral, and social, as well as physical—from the world. And for those who fell short of perfection due to addiction to incompatible eating there was a form of consolation in Hay's warning that the gastric fermentation of carbohydrate produced alcohol as well as acids. When Hay first presented his system, Prohibition was still in effect, and his caveat that one "can get up a very sizable jag from the alcohol generated in the stomach" may have had just the opposite effect from what he intended. Even after repeal, one nutritionist laughed that it would be cheaper but just as effective to serve guests corned beef hash instead of cocktails.[75]

Hay was usually taken more seriously, indeed had to be, for he drew a sizable following. The American Medical Association reported in 1933 that in the last year or two it had received hundreds of inquiries about the Hay diet from physicians around the country. Letters to *Hygeia* showed a similar curiosity among laypeople, and a physician was quoted in the American Medical Association's *Journal* to the effect that patients often attributed their flatulence and eructations to the fermentation of incompatible foods: "It is most difficult," he added, "to convince these patients they are laboring under a misapprehension." A professor of medicine found even medical students frequently suffered from that misunderstanding. So entrenched was the fear of promiscuity in diet that a physician, Martin Rehfuss, conducted an elaborate experimental study to prove once and for all the obvious, that human beings could digest meat and potatoes at the same meal and could do so without injury to health.[76]

Rehfuss's demonstration seems to have done little to alleviate acidosis anxiety, in part, perhaps, because Hay preached that acidosis could result just as surely from retention of any food residues in the intestines more than twenty-four hours. Faddism thus folded back on itself, returning to an emphasis on bowel regularity, roughage, and yeast. It was truly (and continues to be) one damn system after another, and identification of the many systems remaining would overly belabor the point that in industrial society the ancient pursuit of health has been made a far more taxing endeavor. With science continually discovering facts and devising theories beyond the ken of the laity, and faddists and businesspeople bombarding the public with selective and self-serving interpretations of science, the consumer has been put in the unenviable position of having more choices and less wisdom. The likelihood of going astray would thus seem greater, yet perhaps because they were beset on all sides by foods of every classification, the most impressionable consumers of the 1920s may actually have had well-balanced diets. Others survived on common sense. Clarence DeMar, the great distance runner who ruled the Boston Marathon in the 1920s, was representative, one would like to think, of a majority who muddled through on native wit. DeMar's first trainers advised lots of meat. He obeyed, but after some early victories, he was contacted in 1911 by John Harvey Kellogg, who persuaded him to eliminate meat from his diet (except, the runner insisted, on Thanksgiving). Before the Brockton Marathon in 1911, DeMar forced down Kellogg's recommended breakfast of one dozen oranges, a quarter pound of pine nuts, and one pound of caramels, and though "it took nearly the whole morning to eat all this stuff," he not only managed somehow to run the whole race; he won. DeMar was so heartened by the outcome he remained on the diet for a year but then abandoned it after losing the marathon at the Stockholm Olympics of 1912. He returned to an ordinary regimen until the 1930s, when he went on the alkaline diet long enough to win three marathons. Nevertheless, he seemed to feel its greatest benefit had been the strengthening of his teeth, and by the mid-thirties, he had decided that too much bother was being made over the value of special diets for athletes. His experience had convinced him that "very likely the balance is there in a simple diet, so well that if we fussed with it we wouldn't make the proportion much better and we might take all the joy out of eating."[77] In lay terms, that was approximately the lesson the newer nutrition had been trying to teach all along.

Notes

1 "The Spectator," *Outlook* 70 (1902): 612, 614.

2 Robert Haas, *Eat to Win: The Sports Nutrition Bible* (New York: Rawson Associates, 1983), 167; Haas, *Eat to Succeed* (New York: Rawson Associates, 1986). Sales figures for *Eat to Win* are to be found in Julia Moore, *The Bowker Annual of Library and Book Trade Information*, 13th ed. (New York: Bowker, 1985), 591; "The Spectator," 614.

3 Elmer McCollum, *A History of Nutrition* (Boston: Houghton Mifflin, 1957), 115–56.

4 Wilbur Atwater, "What the Coming Man Will Eat," *Forum* 13 (1892): 498.

5 McCollum, *History of Nutrition*, 201–376.

6 "The Facts about Proprietary Foods," *Hygeia*, August 1933, 682.

7 Advertisement for Campbell's tomato soup in *Literary Digest*, 25 March 1922, 37.

8 McCollum, *History of Nutrition*, 63.

9 McCollum, "Scientific Nutrition and Public Health," *Hygeia*, July 1923, 234–35. See also Lovell Langstroth, "Relation of American Dietary to Degenerative Disease," *Journal of the American Medical Association* 93 (1929): 1607 (hereafter cited as *JAMA*); Willard Stone, "Dietary Facts, Fads and Fancies," *JAMA* 95 (1930): 709; Robert Lynd and Helen Lynd, *Middletown: A Study in American Culture* (New York: Harcourt and Brace, 1929), 158; United States Department of Agriculture, *Food and Life* (Washington, D.C., 1929), 128–29.

10 McCollum, "Scientific Nutrition," 93–95, 175–78, 233–36, 301–4; cartoon of nutrition camp in *Hygeia*, September 1924, 596.

11 "Teaching Nutrition in the Grades," *Hygeia*, August 1933, 742; Kathryn Maddrey, "Lessons of Food and Growth from White Rats," ibid., April 1926, 210–12; "Spinach," *Scientific American* 139 (January 1928): 39; "Experiment Succeeds in Child Health Work," *New York Times*, 24 September 1927, 17. See also "The Dietary Defense of Spinach," *JAMA* 89 (1927): 1336; and Ernest Clowes, "We Like Greens," *Hygeia*, April 1927, 169–71.

12 Advertisement for C. Houston Goudias, *Eating Vitamins*, in *Literary Digest*, 16 December 1922, 60; Eugene Christian, *Ten Little Lessons on Vitamins* (Westfield, Mass.: Vitamin Research Association, 1922), 8.

13 Lois Miller, "The Vitamin Follies," *Hygeia*, September 1938, 1004; Rima Apple, "'They Need It Now': Advertising and Vitamins, 1925–1940" (Paper delivered before the American Institute of the History of Pharmacy, San Francisco, 17 March 1986), 16.

14 "Vegetables as Life Insurance," *Literary Digest*, 5 April 1924, 75–77; Walter Alvarez, "Opinions of 470 Physicians in Regard to the Advantages of Using Bran and Roughage," *Minnesota Medicine* 14 (1931): 300; "The School Lunch Room," *Hygeia*, September 1929, 923.

15 Samuel Crumbine and James Tobey, *The Most Nearly Perfect Food: The Story of Milk* (Baltimore: Williams and Wilkins, 1930); "More Prize Winners in the Health Poster Contest," *Hygeia*, November 1924, 573–76; "King Coffee Unpopular in Play," ibid., November 1926, 659.

16 "Daily Pint of Milk Doubles Gain," *Hygeia*, December 1926, 718; William Woods, "The Modern 'Milksop,'" ibid., November 1935, 971; Alfred Parker, "Training for Athletics and Health," ibid., October 1933, 984; James Tobey, "Some Famous Milk Addicts," ibid., October 1931, 935.

17 M.W., "Milk for Working Men," *Hygeia*, November 1926, 281; Crumbine and Tobey, *Most Nearly Perfect Food*, 12.

18 "Food and Labor Force," *Review of Reviews* 13 (1896): 600.

19 Wilbur Atwater, "The Potential Energy of Food," *The Century* 34 (1887–88): 398; Carl Malmberg, *Diet and Die* (New York: Hillman, Curl, 1935).

20 Atwater, "What the Coming Man Will Eat," 497–98.

21 Morris Fishbein, Foreword to Katharine Blunt and Ruth Cowen, *Ultraviolet Light and Vitamin D in Nutrition* (Chicago: University of Chicago Press, 1930), vii.

22 Malmberg, *Diet and Die*, 10; F. J. Schlink, *Eat, Drink and Be Wary* (New York: Covici, Friede, 1935), 56; T. Swann Harding, "Spinach—for Others," *North American Review* 226 (1928): 559; "The Wonders of Diet," *Fortune* 13 (May 1936): 88; Malmberg, *Diet and Die*, xx. For other examples of the period's concern for food fadism, see "Too Much Acid," *Journal of the American Dietetic Association* 9 (1933–34): 498; Marion Farren, "Food Fads and Faddists," *Hygeia*, December 1924, 885–87; and "Rational Dietary Advice," *JAMA* 103 (1934): 190.

23 "Prof. Paul C. Bragg," *JAMA* 96 (1931): 288–89; G. H. Brinkler, quoted in "Modern Magic—Some Freaks and Fallacies of the Food Faddists," part 3 of "Exploiting the Health Interest," *Hygeia*, January 1925, 16–21; John Murlin, "Some Controverted Questions in Nutrition," *Journal of the American Dietetic Association* 6 (1930–31): 300; Mr. and Mrs. Eugene Christian, *Uncooked Foods and How to Use Them* (New York: Health Culture Co., 1904), 35–36.

24 Alfred McCann, *The Science of Eating* (New York: George H. Doran Co., 1918), 19, 30, 39, 117–18, 291, 293.

25 Advertisement for Fleischmann's yeast in *Literary Digest*, 10 June 1922, 67.

26 Advertisements for Fleischmann's yeast in *Literary Digest*, 8 July 1922, 57, and 8 February 1922, 55.

27 Charles Mohler, "Health Claims in Advertising," *Hygeia*, August 1931, 690.

28 Advertisement for the Kitchen Craft waterless cooker in *Hygeia*, November 1928, 32; advertisement for Camel cigarettes in *Life*, 26 April 1937, 98; *Literary Digest*, 18 March 1922, 58.

29 Russell Wilder, "The Significance of Diet in Treatment," *JAMA* 97 (1931): 435; Lynd and Lynd, *Middletown*, 158.

30 Advertisement for Quaker oats in *Literary Digest*, 19 February 1921, 67; advertisement

for Diamond walnuts in ibid., 17 December 1921, 1; James Burrow, *AMA, Voice of American Medicine* (Baltimore: Johns Hopkins University Press, 1963), 71–75; "The Committee on Foods," *JAMA* 94 (1930): 415; Council on Foods, *Accepted Foods and Their Nutritional Significance* (Chicago: American Medical Association, 1939).

31 B. Ebbell, trans., *The Papyrus Ebers* (Copenhagen: Levin and Munksgaard, 1937), 30–32; William Buchan, ed., *The Cottage Physician and Family Advisor; or, Every Man His Own Doctor*, 3d ed. (London: John Anderson, 1830), 10; Harmon Knox Root, *The People's Medical Lighthouse* (New York: Ranney, 1856), 395–96.

32 John Ordronaux, trans., *Regimen Sanitatis Salernitanum* (Philadelphia: Lippincott, 1871), 47, 132–33, 163. "Alvine calls" refers to the need to empty one's bowels.

33 John King, *The American Family Physician* (Indianapolis: Streight and Adams, 1860), 150.

34 Root, *People's Medical Lighthouse*, 114.

35 James Whorton, *Crusaders for Fitness: The History of American Health Reformers* (Princeton: Princeton University Press, 1982), 216–24; F. A. Hornibrook, *The Culture of the Abdomen* (Garden City, N.Y.: Doubleday, Doran, 1934), 9.

36 Wilder, "The Significance of Diet in Treatment," 435–36; Walter Alvarez, "Intestinal Autointoxication," *Physiological Reviews* 4 (1924): 353.

37 Alvarez, "Origins of the So-Called Autointoxication Symptoms," *JAMA* 72 (1919): 8; Logan Clendening, "A Review of the Subject of Chronic Intestinal Stasis," *Interstate Medical Journal* 22 (1915): 1192–93.

38 Hornibrook, *Culture of the Abdomen*, 11; S. E. Bilik, *The Trainer's Bible* (New York: Athletic Trainers Supply Company, 1928), 86.

39 Alvarez, "Intestinal Autointoxication," 352.

40 Alvarez quoted in T. Swann Harding, "Diet and Common-Sense," *Journal of the American Dietetic Association* 6 (1930–31): 196–97.

41 "The Nutritional Significance of Bran," *JAMA* 107 (1936): 877; Murray Davis, "Intes-

tinal Obstruction from Eating Bran," *JAMA*
97 (1931): 24–25; Morris Fishbein, "Indigestible Vegetables," *Hygeia*, September 1926,
531; Harding, "Diet and Common-Sense,"
202; Alvarez quoted in Malmberg, *Diet and
Die*, 13.

42 Harding, "Diet and Common-Sense,"
197; McCollum, "Scientific Nutrition," 302;
Metropolitan Life Insurance Company survey
in Louis Dublin, Eugene Fisk, and Edwin
Kopf, "Physical Defects as Revealed by Peri-
odic Health Examinations," *American Journal
of Medical Sciences* 170 (1925): 576–94; Elmer
McCollum and Nina Simmonds, *Food, Nutrition and Health* (Baltimore: Published by the
authors, 1925), 84. See also Victor Levine,
"Should Whole Wheat Products Displace the
Refined Products?" *Archive of Pediatrics* 46
(1929): 293; Lemuel McGee, "Cathartic-
Conscious America," *Hygeia*, August 1937,
731–34; T. Swann Harding, "A Purgation of
Purgatives," *Scientific American* 157 (October
1937): 222.

43 Advertisement for Sal Hepatica in *Literary
Digest*, 18 September 1926, 61; advertisement
for Nujol in *Saturday Evening Post*, 8 November 1924, 171.

44 McGee, "Cathartic-Conscious America,"
733; Bernard Fantus, *Useful Cathartics* (Chicago: American Medical Association, 1920),
107.

45 Richard Schwarz, *John Harvey Kellogg,
M.D.* (Nashville, Tenn.: Southern Publishing
Association, 1970); Gerald Carson, *Cornflake
Crusade* (New York: Rinehart, 1957); Horace
Powell, *The Original Has This Signature—W.
K. Kellogg* (Englewood Cliffs, N.J.: Prentice-
Hall, 1956); Frank Fayant, "The Great Break-
fast-Food Industry," *Review of Reviews* 27
(1903): 613.

46 Advertisements for Grape Nuts in *Collier's
Weekly*, 28 September 1901, 22, and 28 December 1901, 23; advertisement for Wheatlet
in ibid., 20 October 1900, 19; advertisement
for Quaker oats in ibid., 7 April 1906, 32; advertisement for shredded wheat in ibid., 26
May 1906, 32.

47 Advertisement for Armour's toasted corn
in *Literary Digest*, 4 June 1921, 71; advertisement for Puffed Rice in ibid., 16 April 1921,

49; advertisement for Grape Nuts in ibid., 71,
22 October 1921, 41.

48 John Harvey Kellogg, *The Itinerary of a
Breakfast* (Battle Creek, Mich.: Modern Medicine Publishing, 1919), 87, 93, 99.

49 Whorton, *Crusaders for Fitness*, 223–24;
"The National Mania," *Hygeia*, January 1924,
53–54; advertisement for Post bran flakes in
ibid., August 1931, 783, and ibid., May 1929,
534; advertisement for Pettijohn's bran in *Literary Digest*, 31 March 1928, 57.

50 Advertisement for Pettijohn's bran in
Hygeia, April 1931, 390; advertisement for
Post bran flakes in ibid., April 1926, 13; advertisements for Kellogg's All-Bran in ibid., June
1931, 592, 791.

51 Advertisement for Post bran flakes in
Hygeia, January 1927, 17; advertisement for
fig bran flakes in ibid., April 1931, 385; advertisement for Post bran flakes in ibid., November 1926, 17; advertisement for Kellogg's
Tasteless Castor Oil in ibid., February 1925,
15; advertisement for Post's whole bran in
ibid., May 1931, 504.

52 Advertisement for Wheatena in *Hygeia*,
September 1928, 23; advertisement for Wheatena in ibid., January 1929, 85; advertisement
for 40% Bran Flakes in ibid., February 1938,
102. Bran's vitamin and iron content were
publicized from the early 1920s onward; for an
example, see *Literary Digest*, 8 December
1923, 71.

53 Morris Fishbein, *Your Diet and Your
Health* (New York: Whittlesey House, 1937),
36; F.C.M., "Bran Lemonade," *Hygeia*, May
1927, 269; "Diet-Minded Laymen," *Journal
of the American Dietetic Association* 5 (1929–
30): 50.

54 "Whole Grain Wheat, Quackery in the
Food Field," *JAMA* 84 (1925): 1441–43;
"Committee on Foods," ibid. 104 (1935):
1605–6; advertisement for DinaMite in *Hy-
geia*, March 1925, 15; advertisement for Uncle
Sam's laxative cereal in *JAMA* 4 (1926): 17.

55 Advertisement for Post bran flakes in
Hygeia, November 1931, 1078; ibid., January
1924, 54.

56 Advertisement for Grape Nuts in *Physical
Culture* 53 (June 1925): 73, 77; advertisement
for Beeman's chewing gum in *Literary Digest*,

25 June 1921, 52; advertisement for Post bran flakes in *Hygeia*, November 1930, 1063; advertisement for Pillsbury Health Bran in *Literary Digest*, 16 February 1924, 52; advertisements for Post bran flakes in *Saturday Evening Post*, 3 July 1926, 32, and 6 November 1926, 42; advertisement for Kellogg's All-Bran in ibid., 9 October 1926, 46.

57   Advertisement for Sunsweet prunes in *Literary Digest*, 28 April 1928, 55.

58   Advertisement for Post bran flakes in *Hygeia*, February 1926, 15; advertisement for All-Bran in *Physical Culture* 77 (May 1937): 65; advertisement for Post bran flakes in *Hygeia*, December 1932, 1152.

59   "Kellogg's All Bran Omitted from the List of Accepted Foods," *JAMA* 107 (1936): 1303; "The Nutritional Significance of Bran," 877; Arthur Kallet and F. J. Schlink, *100,000,000 Guinea Pigs* (New York: Grosset and Dunlap, 1933), 3–4; Harding, "Spinach—for Others," 560.

60   Florence Brown et al., "A Study of the Therapeutic Value of Yeast," *Journal of the American Dietetic Association* 10 (1934–35): 29; Malmberg, *Diet and Die*, 12–14; "Fleischmann's Yeast Not Eligible for the List of Accepted Foods," *JAMA* 109 (1937): 277; a booklet entitled "The New Importance of Yeast in Diet" was offered in an advertisement for Fleischmann's yeast in *Literary Digest*, 18 November 1922, 55.

61   John Murlin and Henry Mattill, "The Laxative Action of Yeast," *American Journal of Physiology* 64 (1923): 75–96; advertisements for Fleischmann's yeast in *Literary Digest*, 10 March 1923, 65; 12 May 1923, 49; 10 February 1923, 67; 28 April 1923, 61; and 18 November 1922, 55.

62   Advertisements for Fleischmann's contest in *Literary Digest*, 14 July 1923, 71; 8 September 1923, 57; and 20 October 1923, 87.

63   Advertisements for Yeast Foam Tablets in *Literary Digest*, 23 September 1922, 70; 7 October 1922, 56; and *Physical Culture* 77 (May 1937): 75; "Too Much Acid," 499.

64   Clarence Lieb, "The 'Compatible Eating' Fad," *Hygeia*, August 1936, 685; Walter Eddy, "Must We All Eat Liver?" *Good Housekeeping*, November 1928, 96; Mrs. Christine M.

Frederick, *Selling Mrs. Consumer* (New York: The Business Bourse, 1929), quoted in Apple, " 'They Need It Now,' " 2.

65   Lydia Roberts, "Teaching Children to Like Wholesome Foods," *Hygeia*, March 1924, 141; "Importance of Spinach in Ordinary Diets," ibid., June 1933, 567; "The Wonders of Diet," 123; "Committee on Foods," *JAMA* 94 (1930): 411.

66   Advertisements for Sun Maid raisins in *Literary Digest*, 30 July 1941, 43; 21 October 1922, 1; 11 June 1921, 51; 11 February 1922, 77; 21 October 1922, 1; 16 July 1921, 45; and 27 January 1923, 1.

67   Harry Gauss, "Food Fads," *Hygeia*, March 1935, 212; "Too Much Acid," 499; James Short, "The 'Alkalize' Notion," *Hygeia*, March 1939, 244. See also Stone, "Dietary Facts," 711.

68   Advertisements for Sealdsweet oranges in *Literary Digest*, 7 January 1922, 71, and 22 January 1921, 62, 47; advertisement for Sunkist oranges in ibid., 2 December 1922, 1.

69   Advertisement for Sunkist oranges in *Literary Digest*, 24 November 1923, 74; discussion of "Orange-Lemon Paradox" in advertisement for Sunkist oranges in ibid., 21 November 1925, 78.

70   *Telling Fortunes with Foods* was a booklet offered to readers in an advertisement for Sunkist oranges in *Literary Digest*, 7 June 1928, 41; advertisement for Sunkist lemons in *Literary Digest*, 15 June 1929, 2; advertisement for Sunkist oranges in *Saturday Evening Post*, 7 August 1926, back cover.

71   Advertisement for Sunkist lemons in *Literary Digest*, 7 June 1928, 41.

72   Advertisement for Sunkist oranges in *Literary Digest*, 10 August 1929, 3; advertisement for Eatmoor cranberries in *Hygeia*, October 1936, 955; advertisement for Camel cigarettes in *Life*, 26 April 1937, 98.

73   C. C. Furnas and S. M. Furnas, "Gullible's Travels," in *Man, Bread and Destiny* (New York: Reynal and Hitchcock, 1937), 225; Lewis Wolfberg, "The Hay Food Fantasy," *Hygeia*, April 1938, 311–13, 372; Morris Fishbein, "Modern Medical Charlatans," ibid., February 1938, 113–15, 172, 182–83; "William Howard Hay and His

'Corny Dietetics,'" *JAMA* 112 (1939): 762–63; "William Howard Hay," ibid. 100 (1933): 595–97; Ruth Wadsworth, "Eat It Any Time," *Reader's Digest*, May 1933, 27–29.

74 Malmberg, *Diet and Die*, 65–77.

75 Ibid., 74–75.

76 "William Howard Hay," 595; W.P.A., letter to *Hygeia*, January 1925, 60; H. B., letter to ibid., July 1932, 664; R.E.J., letter to ibid., September 1933, 851; Martin Rehfuss, "Proteins Versus the Carbohydrates," *JAMA* 103 (1934): 1600–605.

77 Clarence DeMar, *Marathon* (Brattleboro, Vt.: Stephen Daye, 1937), 33, 50, 57–58, 112, 140–41, 152.

O' for a touch of the Olympic games rather than this pallid effeminacy! O' for a return to the simple Persian elements of telling the truth, and hurling the javelin, instead of the bloodless cheeks, and lifeless limbs, and throbbing brains of our first scholars in Harvard, Yale, or Princeton! . . . How much more sound and beautiful would the masterpieces of literature have been, had they proceeded from hearty minds in healthy bodies.

Rev. A. A. Livermore,
"Gymnastics," *North American Review*
(July 1855)

Healthy, Moral, and Strong

Educational Views of Exercise and Athletics in Nineteenth-Century America

Roberta J. Park

Americans have been preoccupied, if not at times obsessed, with images of the man who embodies health, strength, and moral rectitude (fig. 1). While the attributes that defined such a man shifted during the course of the nation's history, the belief persisted that these qualities were inextricably bound together. To a considerable extent, it was through exercise, athletics, and physical culture that all three were to be developed and displayed. What had begun in the early 1800s as moderate efforts to engender interest in "physical education," "gymnastics" and out-of-door pursuits had become a veritable craze for physical training and athletics by the 1880s and 1890s.[1] By the end of the nineteenth century, American fascination with notions of the healthy, strong, and moral male had become closely bound to an enthusiasm for physical training and competitive athletics.

While physical training and athletics have a number of elements in common—the most obvious being that both provide the body with exercise—there are also important differences. At the turn of the

Fig. 1 This engraving from S. D. Kehoe, *The Indian Club Exercise* (1866), illustrates not only one particular exercise but also the proportions of the ideal male at the time of the Civil War. Kehoe's book was published by Peck and Snyder, a New York City athletic equipment manufacturer.

gued, that the much-valued attribute of *character* was formed.

The majority of nonprofessional commentators, numerous physicians, and virtually every athlete and coach were convinced that games and sports provided the superior form of exercise. Many professional physical educators were also willing to admit by the early 1900s that most students preferred to take their exercise in the more diverting form of games and sports than in routine and often monotonous gymnastic and calisthenic drills. The shift in emphasis was also prompted by the rise of the "child-study movement," developments in psychology, and the belief that through play the child recapitulated the evolutionary stages of the race. By 1906, the new emphasis found expression in the formation of organizations such as the Playground Association of America. For those who subscribed to the belief that play was a vital developmental medium, athletics were an expression of its "highest" and most mature form.

Nineteenth-Century American Views of "Healthy, Moral, and Strong"

In 1897, the Reverend John Bigham contributed an article to the *DePauw Palladium* in which he declared football to be a "game of so much service as to render it a legitimate, valuable, and necessary equipment in all our higher institutions." In less than thirty-five hundred words, Bigham aptly summarized late nineteenth-century American attitudes. Citing the "great annual games," the revival of the Olympics, recent athletic meetings between American and British universities, the newly popular bicycle, the emergence of sporting journals such as *Outing*,

century, there was fairly broad agreement that both physical training and athletics could lead to improved organic health and muscular strength. Those who identified themselves as "physical educators," as well as many physicians, contended that gymnastic and calisthenic programs designed in accordance with the dictates of the structures and functions of the body's systems were more "scientific." Advocates of athletics, on the other hand, maintained that games and sports were more social in nature, required participants to make quick judgments, and called for such qualities as courage, cooperation, and self-reliance. It was in the crucible of athletic competition, they ar-

rapidly expanding athletic columns in *Harper's Weekly* and other periodicals, and "the chronic and incurable enthusiasm for athletics in our educational institutions," he proclaimed vigorous exercise and sports to be of the greatest value to "all who recognize the importance of robust, physical manhood in a modern commonwealth."[2]

For Bigham and many other Americans at the turn of the century, football was the supreme game (fig. 2). It required superior skill, strength, endurance, regular habits, suppleness, scrupulous care in diet, intelligent practice, obedience, self-control, mental alertness, and the ability to act cooperatively. Vital as were the contributions that the game could make to a man's physical development, however, its contributions to his mental and moral development were deemed to be even more important. In fact, Bigham held, "as played by college men the game involves some beautiful and even spiritual elements." A decade later, Fielding Yost, football coach at the University of Michigan, asserted, "Football not only requires keen minded men to play it but it makes its players still keener of mind. . . . Along with the mental benefits of football comes the moral development."[3]

It is, perhaps, not surprising that a man of the cloth would invoke religious and biblical phrases and passages in his enthusiastic endorsements: "The great apostle to the Gentiles appreciated athletics, and used them as illustrations of spiritual struggles. . . . Foot-ball and Christianity have some common factors." Although he was aware that the game had caused injuries and deaths, Bigham was convinced that the evils of football had been grossly exaggerated. Railroad acci-

A RUN AROUND THE END.

Fig. 2 "A Run around the End," front-ispiece in Walter Camp, *Walter Camp's Book of College Sports* (1893).

dents, bicycle injuries, and excessive study were far more harmful to young men. Allegations that the use of signals and infringements of the rules posed moral dangers were also exaggerated; in fact, this ordained minister and professor of philosophy concluded, "The ethics of foot-ball, as now played, seems to me above reproach."[4]

Bigham claimed nine years of close association with football during his student days (four at Amherst, three at Yale, two at Harvard), as well as experience while a faculty member at the University of Michigan and at Indiana's DePauw University. He had known Amos Alonzo Stagg, Charley Gill, W. W. "Pudge"

Fig. 3 William W. "Pudge" Heffelfinger and Thomas "Bum" McClung, photograph by Pach Brothers, New Haven, Connecticut, 1891. Courtesy Yale University Archives, Yale University Library.

Heffelfinger, Thomas "Bum" McClung, Frank Hinkey, Frank Butterworth, and numerous other collegiate players (fig. 3). He also claimed familiarity with such major statements as A. A. Stagg and H. C. Williams's *Treatise on American Football* (1894) and Walter Camp's *American Football* (1893), crediting the "conscientious labors" of Yale's football coach with eliminating professionalism and giving the game a more "wholesome character than ever before." Football, Bigham asserted, was the preeminent game for preparing men for "tackling heavy responsibilities on foreign mission fields, in church work,

in professional and business enterprises, with the same undaunted vim and self-control that won our applause on the grid-iron field."[5]

Many commentators in the late 1800s proclaimed that little—or nothing—could match football for making men healthy, moral, and strong. Although most were not as rhapsodic as Bigham—at least in so few pages—paeans to athletic sport issued from countless books, journals, and periodicals. Walter Camp, who would repeatedly stress the value of athletics in developing men who possessed pluck, courage, and "sand," wrote in the *New Englander and Yale Review* in 1885, "It is during school and college days, before life's burdens feel heavy upon his shoulders, that a man should increase his biceps and expand his chest." Camp urged college faculties to take a more positive view of athletics and aid in their extension, noting that exercise advocates such as Archibald MacLaren and William Blaikie were equally busy trying to make physical culture attractive to professionals and businessmen.[6] For more than three decades, the man who has been called the great "architect" of American intercollegiate football wrote about, directed, coached, and served as an arbiter of sport (fig. 4).[7]

Football (1896), which Camp wrote with Lorin Deland, noted that the "effects of the game on the players" served two great ends: physical and moral. A man in training for football was likely to have three and a half "times the strength and endurance of the student who does not take vigorous bodily exercise." Diet and habits of training, it was assumed, usually made the athlete more healthy than the average man, and the need to

Fig. 4 Walter Camp, photograph by C. W. Pach, New Haven, Connecticut, 1880. Courtesy Yale University Archives, Yale University Library.

think quickly trained his intelligence and fostered self-reliance and restraint. What was more, football taught both moral and physical courage, two qualities that were intimately related. The Civil War, Camp (and others) insisted, had shown that "the men of best morals were the best fighters"; football required both qualities in abundance (fig. 5).[8]

Walter Camp's Book of College Sports (1889) had provided readers with the latest information about the four sports that comprised the main focus of late nineteenth-century college athletics: track, rowing, football, and baseball. The reader was admonished to preserve the standards of amateur sports and act at all times like a gentleman. A gentleman was always courageous—morally and phys-

ically.[9] In *Football Facts and Figures* (1894), a compilation of expert opinion on the game's place in American athletics, Camp and scores of other commentators found football players to be superior to the average student in height, weight, and lung capacity—and the game to be without peers for teaching self-control, quickness of mind, and courage.[10]

It was also in 1889 that Charles Kendall Adams, president of Cornell University, devoted one-third of a paper entitled "Moral Aspects of College Life" to a discussion of the merits of athletics and regularly prescribed gymnasium work. Rejecting the notion that the only function of physical exercise was strengthening and invigorating the body, Adams held "the moral import of college athletics" to be equally valuable. Indeed, he considered gymnastic training to be so important in the development of both physical vigor and "moral power" that he would have two years of regularly prescribed physical exercise made a requirement for every student. "The sermon I would here preach, if there were time and space," Adams declared, "would be devoted simply to the moral uses of the gymnasium and of the athletic field." The amount of moral benefit was proportional to the vigor of the physical training. Football, in particular, called "into active effort the mental and moral, no less than the bodily, faculties of the players" and demanded self-restraint and subordination of the individual will to the greater good of the whole.[11] C. A. Young agreed. In playing organized games, a youth received "many impressive lessons in prompt decision, quick obedience, manliness, self-control, and self-sacrifice. The discipline of a well-managed ball nine or foot-ball team is by

Fig. 5 Walter Camp is shown standing third from left in this photograph of the 1876 Yale College football team. Courtesy Yale University Archives, Yale University Library.

no means to be despised in the making of a man" (fig. 6). Benjamin Garno, former editor of the *New York Clipper*, likewise held physical exercise that "toned the nerves" to be "the basis of a deeper morality than even the spiritual catechism."[12]

While Adams, Young, Garno, and scores of other late nineteenth-century commentators acknowledged that gymnasium work was valuable for making the body symmetrical, the biceps larger, and the chest fuller, they also believed that gymnastics could not provide the exhilaration of rowing, tennis, lacrosse, baseball, football, and other outdoor sports.[13] The young reader of the *Book of Athletics and Out-of-Door Sports* (1895), edited by Norman Bingham, captain of the 1895 Harvard track team, was instructed to set for himself a high standard of manhood and remember that because "strength and power [are] the results of temperance and right living," the boy who developed physical, moral, and intellectual force was "doing his share toward the realization of a race of stronger men and more beautiful women." Bingham called upon fellow col-

lege athletes John Graham (the athletic manager of the Boston Athletic Association), Kirk Munroe (founder of the League of American Wheelmen), and numerous other authorities to discuss more than a dozen sports and gymnastics. A decade later, many of the contributors to *Sports, Pastimes and Physical Culture*, the sixth volume of *Draper's Self Culture* series (edited by Andrew Sloan Draper, commissioner of education for the state of New York), offered similar observations and advice. J. W. Page, director of the Department of Physical Culture at Ohio Wesleyan University, for example, noted the effects of physical struggle on the evolution of body and mind and called for both systematic gymnastic training and sports and games to develop "our ideal perfect man."[14]

Like most turn-of-the-century physical educators, Page believed that gymnastic exercises were more systematic than athletics and resulted in better all-around development, yet he, too, was captivated by games such as football, baseball, and hockey. "Oh! the exhilarating effects of a good football game!" he proclaimed.

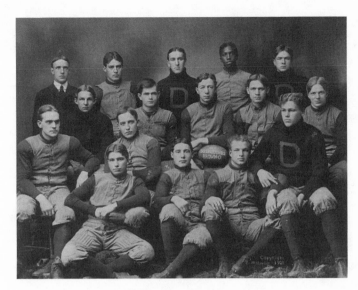

Fig. 6   The Dartmouth College football team of 1902, photograph by H.H.H. Langill, Hanover, New Hampshire. Courtesy Dartmouth College.

"How strong and healthy one feels throughout the season, and throughout the year as a result of the season." As for the small number of "chronic grumblers" who were finding fault with college sport, Page found the "social and national unity" that these games provided to be of wonderful value. The advantages of athletics far exceeded their "evils."[15] Such "evils" were usually seen to be professionalism, commercialism, excessive travel schedules, gambling, the use of "tramp athletes," and an inordinate desire to win, which resulted in transgressions of both written rules and unwritten "moral codes." When such excesses occurred, the otherwise highly beneficial contributions of athletics could be lost. Much worse, athletics might actually teach young men to be unethical. For the last one hundred years, commentators have repeatedly proclaimed that college athletics are "too good to lose," while at the same time observing that they must be changed to eliminate moral evils.[16]

The Emergence of "Professional" Physical Education: The American Association for the Advancement of Physical Education, 1885

In the same year that the *DePauw Palladium* published Rev. John Bigham's article in praise of college football, the American Association for the Advancement of Physical Education (AAAPE) was preparing to hold its first *national* convention. The Association for the Advancement of Physical Education had been founded on November 27, 1885, "to disseminate knowledge concerning physical education, to improve the methods, and by meetings of the members to bring those interested in the subject into closer relation to each other." By 1897, the AAAPE had held ten annual meetings, formed a national council, and established committees on anthropometry and vital statistics, bibliography, and the theory and practice of gymnastics; it had also initiated a journal, the *American Physical Education Review*.

Several local and district societies had been founded, especially in the Northeast, but the association had yet to hold a convention that had been designated as "national."[17]

During its first two decades, the AAAPE registered a singular lack of interest in athletic sports. Formal gymnastics in the form of various types of calisthenic exercises, German "gymnastics," Swedish "gymnastics," and various indigenous forms such as those that Dudley Allen Sargent had developed at Harvard were the preferred exercise modes (figs. 7 and 8). Gymnastics were believed to provide more thorough, scientific, and all-round exercise than games. To a group anxious to establish its legitimacy as a profession, this was an important consideration.[18]

No annual AAAPE meeting was held in 1889, but members of the new organization joined with doctors, theologians, educators, social reformers, and hundreds of others who were interested in health and the physical, intellectual, and moral development of children and youth to attend "the largest and most notable Conference on Physical Training ever held in the United States." The Conference in the Interest of Physical Training, held at Massachusetts Institute of Technology, was made possible through the efforts of Miss Amy Morris Homans and of Mrs. Mary Hemenway, the Boston philanthropist whose largess had also made possible the founding of the Boston Normal School of Gymnastics (later the Department of Hygiene and Physical Education of Wellesley College). The call for the 1889 conference had been signed by John W. Dickinson, secretary of the Massachusetts Board of Education, E. P. Seaver, superintendent of the Boston Public

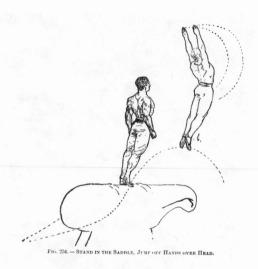

FIG. 234. — STAND IN THE SADDLE, JUMP OFF HANDS OVER HEAD.

Figs. 7 and 8   Swedish gymnast Baron Nils Posse, who founded a gymnasium named for himself in Boston, also published several books about the Swedish system including *The Special Kinesiology of Educational Gymnastics* (1894), in which these illustrations appeared. Posse dedicated the volume to his gymnasium pupils and to all those who encouraged his "work for gymnastics as a liberal art, as a cosmopolitan science, and as a universal truth."

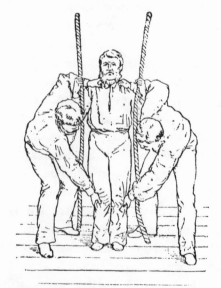

FIG. 94 *a*. — SOMERSAULT WITH ASSISTANCE.

Schools, Francis Amasa Walker, president of MIT, the presidents of Boston University and Wellesley College, and a large number of Boston physicians and educators.[19]

Opening the conference, William Torrey Harris called upon participants to avoid all narrow interpretations of the subject. The United States commissioner of education then acknowledged the several impulses that coalesced in late nineteenth-century beliefs about "physical education." These drew on older notions of reciprocal action of body and mind, newer discoveries in experimental physiology (especially those that involved the nervous system), and recent theories of evolution. He pointed to the importance of the involuntary system (lungs, heart, digestive organs) in the maintenance of health and noted that the quality of the involuntary functions depended upon the strength and action of the voluntary system (muscles and nerves). Harris also noted the importance of "habit" and commented on recent views regarding the function of "play" in "the development of individuality through spontaneity."[20]

The first major address was given by Dr. Edward M. Hartwell, director of the gymnasium at Johns Hopkins University, who presented a medically and scientifically informed paper on the physiological and evolutionary aspects of exercise (fig. 9). Hartwell acknowledged the value of out-of-door sports and athletics but insisted that gymnastics were "more comprehensive in their aims, more formal, elaborate, and systematic in their methods, and . . . productive of more solid and considerable results." These views contrasted rather sharply with those of advocates of athletics such as Walter

Fig. 9   Edward M. Hartwell, photograph in Fred E. Leonard, *Pioneers of Modern Physical Training* (1915). Courtesy Association Press.

Camp. In the introduction to his *Book of College Sports*, Camp ridiculed the enthusiasm of "the new Professor Dumbbell, who drags you willy-nilly through a complex system of chest-measurement and pulley-prescriptions."[21]

The papers and discussions of the Boston conference dealt with gymnastics, especially the German and Swedish systems and the Sargent system; brief remarks were also made about the gymnasium work that Edward Hitchcock had initiated at Amherst College in the 1860s, about Dio Lewis's light gymnastics, and about physical training for young criminals at New York's State Reformatory at Elmira. When Baron Pierre de Coubertin, secretary of the French Educational Re-

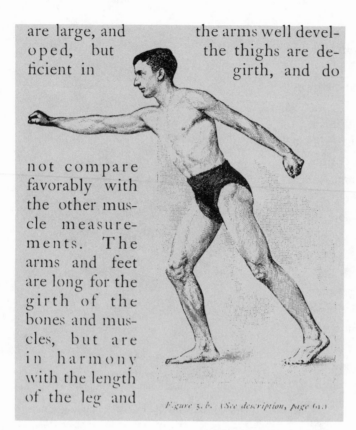

are large, and oped, but deficient in the arms well developed, but the thighs are deficient in girth, and do

not compare favorably with the other muscle measurements. The arms and feet are long for the girth of the bones and muscles, but are in harmony with the length of the leg and

Figure 5, b. (See description, page 61.)

Figs. 10 and 11   In his essay "The Physical Proportions of the Typical Man," Dudley Sargent included engravings and detailed descriptions of college athletes to illustrate a statistical analysis of the effect of sport on physique. "Figure 5,b" was in the Harvard class of 1890, weighed a little more than 142 pounds, and held the intercollegiate record for running three miles; Sargent pointed out that he "has raced but one season, but has practised much in the gymnasium." "Figure 6,a" was an eighteen-year-old Yale student who weighed 150 pounds and held the one-mile intercollegiate record.

form Association, staunch advocate of English public-school sport, and "renovator" of the Olympic games, addressed the conference, the audience heard the only direct appeal for "the wonderful influence of athletic sports on the moral and social qualities of boys." Lauding educational reforms that had been initiated by Thomas Arnold at Rugby School, Coubertin declared that the training of a youth's *will* was more important than the training of his body and brain.[22]

In his opening paper, Hartwell had referred to the action of nerve cells in muscular contraction, the sarcolemma, the irritability of muscle, the gray matter of the forebrain, "centres of motor ideation," and similar topics. These subjects may have been of interest to some of the

doctors and physiologists who were in the audience, but most listeners were probably more intrigued by statements such as this one:

The aim of any and all human training is to . . . develop power. . . . Power when developed takes the form of some action or exercise due to muscular contractions. Viewed thus, muscular exercise is at once a means and an end of mental, and moral, as well as of physical training . . . ; muscular exercise . . . when properly chosen, regulated, and guided . . . may make a boy into a better man . . . and enable him to transmit to his progeny a veritable aptitude for better thoughts and actions. Herein lies the power of the race for self-improvement, and the evolution of a higher type of man upon the earth.[23]

them a scientific patina, enjoyed a remarkable persistence in spite of experimental work in physiology and psychology that had begun to call some of them into question. (Late twentieth-century "theories" of exercise still retain much of this mingling of "health reform" and modern medical science.)

Whereas before the Civil War individual redemption and regeneration had been seen as fundamental to the reform of society, reform efforts after 1865 were increasingly focused through organizations like the American Social Science Association (ASSA) (1865) and the Playground Association of America, two of the many agencies that devoted at least some attention to physical education, play, games, and/or sports. Hartwell, Sargent, and others who would soon become members of the AAAPE addressed annual meetings of the ASSA in the 1870s and 1880s.[24] By the late 1890s, sports were an important— even dominating—part of the college extracurriculum, and departments of physical culture were rapidly being formed at colleges and universities across the United States. Presidents' reports, like that of Cornell's Charles Kendall Adams in 1888, spoke of the improved health, strength, vigor, and even scholarship that athletics and exercise had wrought among the student body (figs. 10 and 11). Acting professor of physical culture Edward Hitchcock, Jr., proudly proclaimed that even weak students who had engaged in regular gymnasium work soon exceeded the anatomical and physiological measurements of students at other institutions, and that members of Cornell athletic teams were found to be at the seventy-sixth percentile in a variety of anatomical and functional tests.[25]

Hartwell had a Ph.D. in biology as well as a medical degree, and his scientific training prevented him from making some of the extravagant claims that others made about the potential of physical education. He nonetheless considered physical education to be one of the most important subjects of the curriculum for the benefits it could bestow upon the individual and the race.

Late nineteenth-century notions of how exercise and athletics could make a man strong, healthy, and moral incorporated many of the millenarian attitudes of the early part of the century. Strengthening the body, it was assumed, would also strengthen the "will." The older views, often thinly disguised in rhetoric that gave

The Background of Late Nineteenth-Century American Attitudes toward Physical Education and Athletics, 1800–1865

American interest in health, exercise, calisthenics, and "physical education" had arisen early in the nineteenth century. Perhaps the first effort to make physical education a regular part of the school curriculum occurred in 1809 when Joseph Neef, an Alsatian ex-Napoleonic soldier, established a school near the falls of Schuylkill. Neef had taught music, French, and gymnastics at the Burgdorf school of the famous Swiss educator Heinrich Pestalozzi after wounds had forced his retirement from military service.[26] The intense interest in educational reform that swept western Europe at the close of the eighteenth century attracted the attention of several Americans, one of whom was William Maclure. Upon leaving his native Scotland, Maclure settled in Philadelphia, completed the nation's first full-scale geological survey, and became president of the American Geological Society. Having observed Pestalozzi's innovative work on a trip to Yverdun, he was convinced that it offered the type of democratic and practical learning that his adopted country needed. Maclure contacted Neef, who was then teaching in Paris, and arranged for him to come to America in 1806. Within three years, Neef had established a school for about one hundred pupils, including the sons of some of the best Philadelphia families. Here he instituted an extensive program of exercises and simple games. A former pupil recalled, "We were encouraged in all athletic sports, were great swimmers and skaters, walkers and gymnasts."[27]

Neef's ideas regarding education were set forth in his *Sketch of a Plan and Method of Education Founded on an Analysis of the Human Faculties and Natural Reason Suitable for the Offspring of a Free People and for All Rational Beings* (1808). In the section devoted to gymnastics and exercise, he criticized traditional conceptions of teaching and learning for being in conflict with nature and insisted upon the absolute necessity of the play element in education.[28] (Apparently he spent a great deal of time exercising with his students and considered this to be an important way to teach them valuable lessons.) Although his school at the falls of Schuylkill was short-lived, Neef's ideas regarding physical education and developmental play were given a broader hearing when he joined Maclure and Robert Owen, the noted British social reformer, in an effort to establish a "communitarian" settlement at New Harmony, Indiana, in 1826.

Between 1826 and the Civil War, scores of secular utopian communities were established in America, although most of them lasted only a few years. The most famous are generally considered to have been the Owenite community at New Harmony, Indiana; the Fourierist Phalanxes; Brook Farm in West Roxbury, Massachusetts, which was founded in 1841 by the Unitarian minister George Ripley; and the Oneida Community of Perfectionists at Kenwood and Sherrill in upstate New York. Most of these sought to offer both children and adults opportunities for healthful and pleasant physical exercise and elevating recreations. The *New Harmony Gazette* included numerous commentaries on gymnastics, and the *New Harmony Disseminator* declared that physical exercises ought to proceed on a par with moral instruction at all ages, with gymnastic exercises preceding moral instruction during the early period of childhood. Exercise and recreation were also encouraged at Brook Farm, where Horace Greeley, editor of the *New York Tribune*, Horace Mann, "father" of the common school movement, and Ralph Waldo Emerson spent considerable time in the early 1840s.[29]

Emerson believed that a sound body was prerequisite to individual perfection, and that because everything tended toward its highest manifestation, "bodily vigor [became] mental and moral vigor." He urged parents and teachers to provide for the physical education of children and spoke favorably of games such as cricket and "football" (which before the Civil War was a loosely structured soccerlike game). Such sports helped boys develop self-reliance, a quality that Emerson considered to be of the utmost importance. He also extolled the virtues of walking and exercise for adults, noting that in the English universities men trained daily in boat clubs and at other vigorous pursuits. Fellow New Englander Henry David Thoreau sought health in harmonious relationships with nature and filled his journals with notations of swimming, sailing, skating, and paddling his boat; he was not, however, enthusiastic about calisthenics or contrived exercises. Bronson Alcott, father of the author of *Little Women* and peripatetic educator who became superintendent of schools in Concord, Massachusetts, in 1859, considered *play* to be an indispensable aid to intellectual, moral, and physical progress and happiness; in his various short-lived schools, he endeavored to provide playful physical activities for all children.[30]

Other American educators had preceded Alcott, Emerson, and their contemporaries in devoting considerable and more sustained attention to play and "physical education." In January 1826, editor William Russell introduced the first issue of the *American Journal of Education* by stating, "In many plans of education, which are in other respects excellent, the fact seems to have been overlooked that man possesses an animal, and a moral, as well as an intellectual constitution. . . . We shall give to *physical education* that proportion of our attention which seems due to its importance to form habits and stamp the character."[31] Indeed, in the first volume alone, the "conductors" of the *Journal* talked about gymnastics at New Harmony, the new gymnasium that had opened at Harvard, one that was about to open in Boston, and the work of Charles Beck at the Round Hill School in Northampton, Massachusetts. Several European treatises on gymnastics were reviewed as were the affairs of the London Gymnastic Society and of the school that the expatriate Francisco Amoros had established in Paris. Readers were also referred to various articles on physical culture and health that had recently appeared in the *Boston Medical Intelligencer*.[32]

The following year, the *American Journal of Education* included a lengthy article based on the Glasgow physician James Kennedy's *Instructions to Mothers and Nurses on the Management of Children in Health and Disease* (1825) which reminded readers of the intimate relationships that existed between the "internal functions" (e.g., digestion, circulation) and the "voluntary operations" of the muscles, nerves, and brain. Exercises and simple games were advocated for their physiological benefits to strength and health as well as for their contributions to the "benevolence and firmness of the character."[33]

The belief that mind and body are reciprocally related can be traced to classical antiquity. In the seventeenth and eighteenth centuries, relationships between the physical, mental, and moral functions had begun to receive renewed attention. Readers of the *North American Review* were reminded in 1818 that "the influences of mind and body are so perfectly reciprocal, that it would be hardly possible to say, which exerted the most power." All men, but especially those engaged in literary and professional pursuits, needed "free, careless exercise in the open air." A few years later, the reviewers of Charles Beck's 1828 translation of Friedrich Ludwig Jahn's *Die Deutsche Turnkunst* (1816) used the occasion to discourse on the history of gymnastics and athletics. Observing that men needed to take regular exercise in forms where the mind "may be occupied at the same time as the body," the reviewers noted that pedestrian excursions, running, climbing, jumping, exercises on the horizontal and parallel bars, wrestling, skating, swimming, the use of dumbbells, and dancing were appropriate for men until they reached the ages of sixteen or seventeen. Older men needed activities such as vaulting, fencing, riding, boxing, and driving. Although they stated that they did not wish to discuss "the intimate connexion subsisting between soundness of body and of mind," the authors insisted that "the best performers in the gymnasium were almost uniformly the best scholars."[34]

The intimate relationship between physical culture and moral development was explicitly made by the Boston physician Dr. John Jeffries in an 1833 article for the *American Quarterly Observer*. Relying heavily on biblical scripture and John Sinclair's *Code of Health* (1807), he advocated cultivation of the powers of the body because of its connection with mind, spirit, and "eternity." Drawing upon an analogy that has had a remarkable persistence, Jeffries declared, "One of the prominent laws of the animal economy is . . . that the strength of an organ is increased by use"; the strength of the blacksmith's arm and of the pedestrian's limbs, the strength and swiftness of the athlete, and the "prodigious feats of the gymnasium" were all examples of this law. (The example of "the blacksmith's arm" would recur repeatedly in treatises on exercise and athletics well into the twentieth century, as would the belief that proper mental and moral development depended upon a healthy and strong body.)[35]

Many others in the 1820s and 1830s sought to extend knowledge of physical health and its relationship to moral development to their fellow Americans. John Stuart Skinner's *American Farmer* characterized sport as "possessing the power to promote good health and prevent disease, produce sound and respectable morals, create a reputable character, and encourage pleasure and enjoyment." The *Journal of Health, Conducted by an Association of* [Philadelphia] *Physicians* stated its intention to devote due attention to, "air, food, exercise, the reciprocal operation of mind and body, climate and localities, clothing, and the physical education of children."[36] Introducing his small volume, *Thoughts on Physical Education* (1834), Dr. Charles Caldwell declared that because the sound and vigorous operations of the mind depend upon the sound and vigorous condition of the body, physical education provided "that scheme of training, which contributes most effectively to the development, health, and perfection of living matter." Physical education was, in fact, "tantamount to an entire system of Hygiene." Dr. John Bell's *Health and Beauty: An Explanation of the Laws of Growth and Exercise . . .* (1838) urged readers to value exercise by means of both sports in the open air and systematic gymnastics. The cause of both health and sound ethics, Bell insisted, required mind and body to be reciprocally influenced, "the one aiding and giving vigor to the other."[37]

In the early 1830s, William Woodbridge became editor of Russell's *Journal*, renaming it *American Annals of Education and Instruction and Journal of Literary Institutions*. A continued interest in reciprocal influences among mind, body, and morals was evident from articles such as "Sketches of Hofwyl, Letter XIII: Influence of Physical Education on the Mind and Character," which appeared in April 1831. In 1836, Dr. William Andrus Alcott assumed the editorship from Woodbridge, whom he had assisted since 1831. Alcott used *Annals of Education* to discourse on his favorite topics—human physiology, health, and physical education. He had already prepared a series of articles designed to instruct children in human anatomy and physiology for the *Juvenile Rambler*; these were printed in serial form in *Annals of Education* and appeared as a book entitled *The House I Live In* in 1837.[38]

As James Whorton and Harvey Green have shown, Alcott was a staunch antebellum devotee of both "Christian physiology" and health reform. In *The Library of Health and Teacher on the Human Constitution* (1838), which was also drawn from articles that had appeared in *Annals of Education*, Alcott declared, "He who would educate successfully, must first know how to keep his pupils healthy" and provide them with ample exercise in the open air in all weather. In *The Laws of Health* (1839) and many other books, he stressed the advantages of pleasurable out-of-door exercises that actively engaged the mind—for example, running, fencing, swimming, and ball games—over routine gymnastic exercises.[39]

Many of the numerous health reform journals that appeared in the 1840s and 1850s included excerpts from or references to Alcott's writings. The *Water Cure Journal*, which Dr. Russell T. Trall had established in 1845, referred readers to Alcott's comments on "healthy children," to Walter Channing's article "On Physical Education" (which had appeared in the *Journal of Health*), and to numerous other contemporary sources. The *Health Journal and Advocate of Physiological Reform* included excerpts on physical education drawn from Caldwell's *Thoughts on Physical Education*, from Alcott's books, from the *New England Farmer*, from Sylvester Graham, proponent of vegetarianism and dietary reform—and founder of the *Graham Journal of Health and Longevity*—as well as from the writings of Dr. Andrew Combe.[40]

Andrew Combe, brother of the phrenologist George Combe, was an Edinburgh physician who had studied medicine at Paris and Edinburgh. His *Principles of Physiology Applied to the Preservation of Health and to the Improvement of Physical and Mental Education . . .* was written for the use of the intelligent layman. This well-informed text on the body and its mechanisms was extensively reviewed in *Annals of Education* and subsequently published as number 55 of the Harper's Family Library Series. The *Boston Medical and Surgical Journal* also commented favorably upon Combe's book and urged its readers to "study it." (By 1854, it had gone to a sixteenth American printing and was considered to be one of the most useful and authoritative books available to the reading public.) Although Combe was careful to distinguish between "mind" and "brain," he observed that because both were "inseparably associated during life," those laws of exercise that pertain to the body also pertain to the mind. He held sports to be superior to "mere measured movements," such as walking and calisthenics, because sports were more active and social and brought "the nervous impulse" into fuller and more harmonious operation.[41]

Numerous American medical journals throughout the nineteenth century paid at least some attention to physical education. From its founding in 1823, the *Boston Medical Intelligencer* included articles on the types of gymnastics taught in the schools of Germany, Sweden, Denmark, and France, as well as commentaries on English sport. In 1826 a series of lectures by editor Dr. John G. Coffin on "Physical Education in Connection with Intellectual and Moral Culture" was announced; also in 1826, William Bentley Fowle reported developments at the Boston Monitorial School. Fowle considered walking and household labors— activities that many of his contemporaries recommended—to be entirely inadequate substitutes for gymnastics. Having installed a variety of calisthenic and gymnastic activities for both boys and girls at his school, he concluded that "the effect of the exercises on the character and conduct" of the children had been most salubrious.[42]

The author of a letter to the editor of the *Boston Medical Intelligencer* in 1827 was of the opinion that the work that Charles Follen had instituted at the Boston Gymnasium had proven to be so beneficial to bodily health and vigor that it was "likely to prove a national benefit." Upon Follen's resignation, the work was taken over by his countryman Francis Lieber, who also opened a swimming school. Follen, Lieber, and Charles Beck had all had experience with the forms of gymnastics that Friedrich Ludwig Jahn had developed in Prussia after Napoleon's victory at Jena in 1806. Having fled the reactionary policies of the Holy Alliance, the three men settled in the Boston area. Follen became the first instructor of German at Harvard University in 1826, where he also introduced students to gymnastics.[43] Beck taught Latin and gymnastics at the new Round Hill School that Joseph Cogswell and George Bancroft had established in 1823. Both Cogswell and Bancroft had studied at Göttingen after graduation from Harvard. While in Europe, they became interested in educational innovations that were underway, and they visited, among other places, Pestalozzi's schools. The 1823 prospectus for the Round Hill School stipulated that a portion of each day would be devoted to healthful sports and gymnastic exercises, and a 1826 school circular stressed the "necessity of uniting physical with moral education." Beck was chosen to fulfill these goals. (Bruce Bennett maintains that gymnastics were actually subordinate to games, and that many types of sports were provided: swimming, ice-skating, sledding, archery, a type of baseball, "pitching the bar," hiking, and camping.) Beset by financial problems, the Round Hill School closed in 1834.[44]

During the 1830s, American efforts to establish public elementary, or common, school education intensified. By the 1850s, at least two dozen—mostly short-lived—educational journals had been started.[45] The first issue of the *Common School Journal* (1838) included comments on "physical education" and "playgrounds." The *Massachusetts Teacher* for March 1850 observed that the Greek practice of preceding moral and intellectual culture with physical culture "coincides so exactly with that which Nature seems to have marked out, that we are surprised that any should deviate from it. . . . Physical health is the condition and groundwork of all perfect moral and intellectual health." The *Massachusetts Teacher* and other educational journals repeatedly pressed for the teaching of physiology and "the laws of health" in schools. Teachers were urged to improve their own health by devoting "a portion of each day to *vigorous* exercise, if possible, in the open air" and were told that they must qualify themselves to teach physical education, physiology, and health. Unless physiques were strengthened, boys were apt to become sickly and effeminate men, and girls would not become fit mothers.[46] The latter concern became even greater after the publication of Charles Darwin's *On the Origin of Species* (1859) and, especially, *The Descent of Man and Selection in Relation to Sex* (1871).

In 1855, the *Massachusetts Teacher* carried an extract entitled "Neglect of Physical Training" from Catharine Beecher's *Letters to the People on Health and Happiness* (1855). For decades, the energetic Beecher had been organizing schools for girls and instructing Americans on the benefits of health, hygiene, and exercise. As early as 1829, she had lamented that "the health of the body, the personal habits and manners, the mental defects, the moral feelings and character have not been considered worthy of the *special* care of anyone." Because parents and teachers had neglected their physical education, the bodies of American children were becoming "feeble, sickly, and ugly." Instead of playing in the snow and ice as children had once done, they were now wrapped up and kept indoors. She contrasted the declining health of the population to "the superior health and activity of our ancestors" and drew unfavorable comparisons between the health and strength of Americans and Europeans. As a first step in remedying this deplorable situation, parents, teachers, and the children themselves needed to understand the construction of the human body and its various physiological functions.[47]

Beecher had no medical training, yet her *Physiology and Calisthenics for Schools and Families* (1856) is a remarkably accurate account of the structures and functions of the body as these were understood in the 1850s. Although phrases appear such as "Our Creator has given us no faculties of action or feeling which he did not design to have duly exercised in securing enjoyment to ourselves and to our fellow-beings," descriptions of such things as the nature of the circulation, the digestive system, the brain and nerves,

Fig. 12   An engraving entitled "Physiology of Playfulness" served as frontispiece for Russell T. Trall's *Illustrated Family Gymnasium* (1857).

PHYSIOLOGY OF PLAYFULNESS.

and the effects of "carbonic acid" on the lungs are factually accurate. (It would not be until the end of the century that the chemistry of respiration would be understood in modern terms.) Beecher implied that she had some familiarity with the gymnastic system designed by Sweden's Per Henrik Ling, which had recently appeared in the United States as the "movement cure" and was receiving attention in health establishments as a cure for disease and deformities. It would not be until the 1880s, however, that the "educational"—as opposed to the "therapeutic"—form of Swedish gymnastics would become popular in the United States.[48]

The year after Harper and Brothers published Beecher's extremely influential treatise, Fowler and Wells published Dr. Russell T. Trall's *Illustrated Family Gymnasium . . .* , one of the more popular of the spate of health manuals that appeared in the middle decades of the nineteenth century (fig. 12). Trall had been chairman of the board of the American Hydropathic Society and was currently associated with New York City's Hygieo-Therapeutic Institute. As did so many of his contemporaries, Trall drew from every conceivable source to present a plethora of observations about the influence of exercise on the body and its organs. (This was a procedure that many American authors and journals used until the enactment of the international copyright law in the 1890s finally put a stop to such wholesale adoptions.) Donald Walker's *British Manly Exercises*, first published in 1834, provided several illustrations. Trall did, however, acknowledge Beecher's recent work and that of Ling and the Royal Central Gymnastic Institute.[49]

Like most of their contemporaries who wrote exercise manuals and health guides in the 1850s and 1860s, Beecher and Trall were concerned with calisthenic exercises, not athletic sports. Large compendiums such as John C. Gunn's twelve-hundred-page *New Family Physician; or Home Book of Health . . .* (1867) and W. W. Hall's *Guide-Board to Health, Peace and Competence; or, The Road to Happy Old Age* (1869) provided their readers with commentaries on every conceivable aspect of diet, rest, disease, sexual hygiene, exercise, and much more; a section on calisthenics was frequently appended to such works. Small manuals prepared for teachers such as Samuel W. Mason's *Manual of Gymnastic Exercises for Schools and Families* (1863), James H. Smart's *Manual of Free Gymnastic and Dumb-Bell Exercises for the School-Room and Parlor* (1864), J. Madison Watson's *Watson's Manual of Calisthenics: A Systematic Drill-Book without Apparatus, for Schools, Families, and Gymnasiums* (1864) and his considerably more extensive *Hand-Book of Calisthenics and Gymnastics: A Complete Drill-Book for Schools, Families, and Gymnasiums* (1864) endeavored to give ill-prepared teachers some help by providing diagrams and descriptions of scores of exercises, both without and with such equipment as dumbbells, wands, or Indian clubs.[50]

In the absence of anything approach-ing professional training for teaching exercise and physical education, such efforts were probably helpful. However, few teachers knew anything about the structures and functions of the body; hence, such calisthenic drills as might have been given to children (and to adults) were likely to be little more than routine, stylized movements, often improperly executed. Teachers of German ancestry who were familiar with the Turner forms of exercise were likely to be among the few who were able to provide anything like systematic instruction.[51] Among the few Americans who before the 1880s established anything like a successful school for training teachers of physical education was Dioclesian Lewis, health reformer, temperance advocate, author of *The New Gymnastics for Men, Women and Children* (1862) and *Our Digestion: Or My Jolly Friend's Secret* (1872), and originator and editor of *New Gymnastics for Ladies, Gentlemen, and Children* and *Boston Journal of Physical Culture*. Lewis was in great demand for years as a speaker at teachers' association meetings, lyceums, and normal schools (fig. 13). The holder of an honorary medical degree from the Homeopathic Hospital College of Cleveland, he combined evangelical zeal with astute entrepreneurial acumen. His Institute of Physical Education, which opened in 1861, prepared 421 gymnastics instructors in its seven years of existence. Other business ventures were opened in various locations, for example O. W. and J. E. Powers's Chicago Northwestern Normal Institute for Physical Education, which in the 1860s offered "full courses" of eight weeks to prepare teachers of "Light Gymnastics," at a cost of sixty-five dollars.[52]

These commercial ventures were a

Fig. 13 Dioclesian Lewis, engraving in Fred E. Leonard, *Pioneers of Modern Physical Training* (1915). Courtesy Association Press.

far cry from the types of scientifically based programs that professional physical educators endeavored to establish in the last two decades of the nineteenth century. However, in the 1860s, the only collegiate physical education department was at Amherst College. This, like many of the departments of physical training that were established in the late nineteenth and early twentieth centuries, was headed by a physician, Edward Hitchcock, who had earned his medical degree from Harvard Medical School in 1853. In establishing the new professorship of hygiene and physical education, the president and trustees of Amherst declared, "Gym-

nasiums may be founded, provisions may be made for ball and cricket playing, as well as other games, and even hours may be set apart for those exercises, but unless they are reduced to some regular system" the true objects of exercise cannot be attained. Books expounding the laws of health, diet, ventilation, sleep, bathing, and exercise, they noted, were not sufficient; only carefully organized programs conducted under the direction of a physician who understood exercise could provide a proper physical education.[53]

As director of Barrett Gymnasium, Hitchcock, the new professor of hygiene and physical education, initiated a series of lectures on health and a program of "light gymnastics," probably based upon those of Dio Lewis. Students could also engage in exercises with "heavy apparatus" or in sports, which Hitchcock considered a valuable adjunct to the regularly prescribed exercises. Because a proper exercise program needed to be designed with the special needs of each student in mind, it was necessary to determine what these needs were; therefore, each student was given a thorough physical examination. Hitchcock also devised an extensive program of anthropometric measurements and even went to England to look into the work in which the English biometrician Francis Galton was engaged. With H. H. Seelye, Hitchcock published the widely used *Anthropometric Manual, Giving the Average and Mean Physical Measurements and Tests of Male College Students . . .* (1888), and, in his capacity as the first president of the Association for the Advancement of Physical Education in 1885, Hitchcock helped to make anthropometric measurement a major preoccupation of the new profession.[54] Until the appointment of Dr. Dudley Allen Sargent as assistant professor of physical training and director of the Hemenway Gymnasium at Harvard in 1879, Amherst College had the only organized department headed by a medically qualified director in the United States.

The fact that Hitchcock, Sargent (a graduate of Yale's medical school), and many other men and women who became directors of the new departments of physical training held medical degrees did not ensure the development of "scientific" physical education. In "Divided We Stand: Physiologists and Clinicians in the American Context," Gerald Geison has argued that research physiologists and medical doctors have persistently held different views of the human body. Moreover, before 1910, few American physicians had much experience with experimental science—and most of those who had such experience had studied abroad, either in Vienna or at one of the German universities. It was not until the 1870s that Henry Pickering Bowditch began to incorporate experimental physiology in the medical curriculum at Harvard. H. Newell Martin, considered by a majority of historians of medicine to be the most accomplished of nineteenth-century American biological scientists, did not arrive at Johns Hopkins until 1876.[55] As a consequence, American physical education was slow to develop a strong "scientific" orientation in spite of the fact that countless articles in the *Boston Surgical and Medical Journal* (from the 1880s through World War I), the *Journal of the American Medical Association*, *Science*, and elsewhere urged such development.[56]

The Emergence of "Modern" Sports in the Community and in the Colleges, 1860s to 1906

Although, as Adelman has shown, the characteristics associated with "modern" athletics emerged well before the Civil War, the decade of the 1860s was significant in the transformation of American sporting practices. In the introduction to his *Hand-Book of Calisthenics and Gymnastics*, J. Madison Watson had acknowledged an indebtedness to the proprietor of Wood's Gymnasium in New York City. Three years later, in 1867, William Wood published *Manual of Physical Exercises*, a three-hundred-page book that included extensive information about rowing, skating, fencing, cricket, sailing, swimming, sparring, and baseball, as well as calisthenics and gymnastics. Wood, who claimed that he had been instructing many of the first families of New York in both gymnastics and athletics for several years, observed that institutions for physical education were springing up all over the country—and that college presidents and boards were beginning to appreciate and support such work. In a statement that possibly reflected the influence of recent debates about evolution, Wood noted that it was increasingly recognized that "the strength and character of future generations depend upon the more frequent use of Gymnastic and Out-door Exercises."[57]

Wood's *Manual of Physical Exercises* is significant for several reasons. It reflected new American attitudes toward athletic sport that had begun to emerge around the middle of the century. The inclusion of sections devoted to various sports anticipated the types of athletic manuals that Camp, Bingham, Stagg, and scores of others would write in the 1890s and early 1900s. "Every year," Wood accurately noted, "brings with it an increased interest in the great national game of Base Ball. . . . Every college in the country has its ball clubs." The growth of sport in the last third of the century was, indeed, meteoric. Harvard had met Yale in what has been described as the "first" intercollegiate contest in 1852. In 1869, *The Nation* observed, "The taste for athletic sports in America is not over fifteen years old. It is only within the last ten or twelve years that it can be said to have found a firm foothold in the colleges." In bringing young men from many regions into close contact, the war facilitated the spread of baseball. The Cincinnati Red Stockings, the first team to sign outright all its players to professional contracts, traveled as far west as San Francisco on a historic barnstorming tour in 1869.[58]

By the late 1860s, a variety of manuals provided Americans with information about an increasing number of sports. *Athletic Sports for Boys*, published by Dick and Fitzgerald in 1866, was loosely fashioned after such English works as *The Boy's Own Book: A Complete Encyclopedia of All the Diversions, Athletic, Scientific, and Recreative of Boyhood and Youth*, which was already in a twelfth edition in 1837. Charles Peverelly's *Book of American Pastimes*, also published in 1866, included brief histories of all principal baseball, cricket, rowing, and yachting clubs in the United States. San Francisco's Olympic Club was organized in 1866; the New York Athletic Club (NYAC), which quickly became the most influential and important club of its kind, was founded in

1868. According to club historians Considine and Jarvis, by 1870 NYAC members were assembling at Wood's Gymnasium on Twenty-eighth Street—an exclusive sporting retreat, with pictures of the "Astors, Roosevelts, Oelrichses, and other muscular dandies" on the walls. Contemporary photographs of NYAC members and other athletes from the last three decades of the nineteenth century endlessly portray lithe runners, more muscular oarsmen and gymnasts, and brawny baseball and football players adorned with the uniforms and emblems that defined their particular sports. There was no mistaking the new emphasis on the icon of the muscular, "active," male body.[59]

Throughout the remaining decades of the nineteenth century, these city-based athletic clubs, along with the country clubs that emerged in the 1880s, the *Turnvereine* that had perpetuated German-style gymnastics since the late 1840s, and the Scottish Caledonia clubs, performed an important role in the extension of athletics. The last was particularly influential in the development of track and field and the eventual formation of the Amateur Athletic Union (AAU) in 1888. As the clubs expanded in number and size, so did a variety of support systems dedicated to athletics. One new industry was the production of guides, manuals, and rule books that covered every phase of sports. George Benedict, manager of the Chicago Olympic Club, discussed boxing, fencing, wrestling, club swinging, swimming, track, and gymnastics in *Hand-Book of Manly Sports* (1883), published by Spalding and Brothers. By the 1890s, Albert Goodwell Spalding and his American Sports Publishing Company were issuing guides of rules, records, and "the Science" of innumerable sports, substantially as promotional devices for the astonishing assortment of sporting equipment that Spalding manufactured. Such noted authorities as James E. Sullivan, secretary of the AAU, wrote guides. Yale's athletic director Michael Murphy (who would become one of the nation's authorities on "training") wrote *College Athletics* in 1894, while Harry Cornish, "professor" of athletics at the Chicago Athletic Association, wrote *All-Around Athletics* in the following year for Spalding's Athletic Library. It is significant that this small publication was influenced by the anthropometry craze that was currently popular among physical educators, for it contained descriptions of the "average dimensions" (for example, height, weight, girth of chest, girth of calf) of "all-around athletes" of four different heights. By the last three decades of the nineteenth century, an athletic fervor had penetrated many diverse aspects of American society. It was the rise of intercollegiate athletics, however, that insinuated the new craze into every crevice of the nation's consciousness.[60]

There were many reasons for the intense and somewhat abrupt enthusiasm for athletics. Urbanization, industrialization, and improved technologies (such as the expansion of the railroads and the telegraph) certainly affected the growth of sport. So did a shorter work week, new patterns of employment, and changing ideas about work. The extension of higher education to larger numbers of Americans resulted in young men assembling together away from the constraints of home and fostered a "student culture" that came to devote exceptional emphasis to athletics.[61] The activities of the student-initiated extracurriculum offered pleasant diversions and contrasts to the formal curriculum. They also served as devices for unifying student body, alumni (the extended student body), and faculty—and for individual and, probably more important, collective status seeking. It is significant that each college or university rapidly identified an arch rival—an "equal" institution against which it could compare its relative worth in agonistic contests. Public "ranking" behaviors also occurred in other contexts, as for example, in "intercollegiate debating," which emulated athletics at the turn of the century at Harvard, Yale, and Princeton.[62]

It was in the sports contests, with their focus on the icon of the male body, that the most salient cultural values of late nineteenth- and twentieth-century American college life have been, quite literally, "acted out." As early as 1876, George W. Green proclaimed that the skillful athlete and the man who aspired to the leadership of his class were doing the same thing—striving for excellence and success. A decade later in *Lippincott's Monthly Magazine*, the physician J. William White concluded that competitive athletics and physical training were generally conducive to "the highest degree of usefulness to mankind."[63]

Developments in "the life sciences"—especially the physiology of the nervous system and evolutionary biology—intensified the interest in both physical education and athletics that was present before *The Origin of Species* and *The Descent of Man* appeared in print. By the latter part of the century, the body had become a symbol and metaphor for expressing—and quite possibly reinforcing—a host of cultural concerns and aspirations. Middle-class Americans, in particular, continued to worry about their health, especially about neurasthenia, feebleness, impotence, and "self-abuse" (masturbation); up to the end of the century, a surprising number lamented that Americans—both men and women—were both physically and morally inferior to the British. To a considerable extent, both organized physical training and athletics were seen as important ways to alter this trend.

Efforts to Achieve a Distinctive American "Physical Education"

From the early 1800s, American periodicals had repeatedly commented on the physical superiority of British men and women who, it was presumed, spent more time than Americans in vigorous out-of-door pursuits. At the close of the Civil War, *Hours at Home* found American education to be no match for "the public schools of England, which have done so much toward making England the power that she is. An English lad is a trained boxer, a cricketer, an oarsman, and so learns muscular control and mastery." *Lippincott's Magazine* wrote in 1868 that the great schools and universities of England provided "a training toward true manliness . . . and a superb physical development." G. S. Young asked in 1872, "Are Americans Less Healthy Than Europeans?" and concluded that they were. Dr. T. M. Coan attributed the differences to the greater "*cerebral* or nervous temperament" of Americans and an insufficient "physical basis of protoplasm and of muscular cells." Much of this deficiency, according to Coan, was due to the limited liquid intake in the American diet. Other

observers—and a very large number—cast their lot with commentators like John Hutchinson, who found Americans overly preoccupied with business pursuits and neglectful of "the school of muscular Christianity, of which Mr. Charles Kingsley is so great a prophet" (figs. 14 and 15).[64]

Commentaries regarding the "muscular Christianity" attributed to Kingsley (a term that he abhorred) appeared frequently in both the British and American press. In 1855, the *North American Review* published a lengthy review of Kingsley's *Westward Ho!* replete with such overtones. The same volume also included an article entitled "Gymnastics" in which Abel A. Livermore, Unitarian clergyman and president of the Meadville (Pennsylvania) Theological School, discoursed at length on contemporary American attitudes toward health, exercise, and vigorous manhood. He maintained that hunting, woodcraft, hardy rural pursuits, and the Indian, French, and Revolutionary wars had been the early American's "Olympic Games," the ramparts against disease and "the effemination of a whole race of men": by the mid-1800s, the growth of cities, indulgent attitudes, and an all-consuming preoccupation with business had begun to threaten the vitality of men and the nation. He called upon the colleges to devote more attention to physical education and provide, as rapidly as possible, programs that would strengthen Americans morally and physically as well as intellectually.[65]

Writing in the late 1850s, Oliver Wendell Holmes also warned his contemporaries of the dire consequences of inadequate physical vigor, declaring, "Such a set of black-coated, paste-complexioned

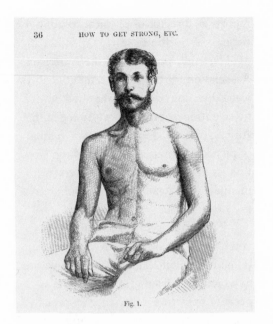

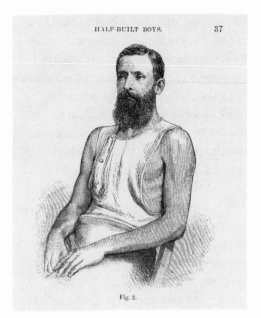

Fig. 1.

Fig. 2.

Figs. 14 and 15   William Blaikie included two depictions of "half-built boys" in his 1879 volume *How to Get Strong and How to Stay So*. Blaikie called readers' attention to "the flat and slab-sided, almost hollow, look about the upper chest and front shoulder" of his first two figures, both professional oarsmen whose exclusive interest in rowing had caused them to neglect the "harmonious" development of their bodies. Blaikie suggested that the oarsmen were not as likely as a better-developed man "to so carry that chest as to ward off tendencies to throat and lung troubles."

youth as we can boast in our Atlantic cities never before sprang from the loins of Anglo-Saxon lineage." His young friend and fellow New Englander Thomas Wentworth Higginson urged his contemporaries to unite the best of German gymnastics with the best of English sports. Happily, Higginson believed, Americans were beginning to appreciate the type of "athletic virtue" attributed to Kingsley and popularized in Thomas Hughes's *Tom Brown's Schooldays* (1857). Hughes's stories of the schoolboy hero at Rugby and Oxford received positive acclaim in America as well as in Britain, were still among the best-sellers in the 1890s, and served as models for the various American student-athlete stories that began to appear in the late 1800s. Higginson called upon his

countrymen to devise a scientifically informed system of physical education, one superior to both English sport and continental gymnastics. Referring to the anthropometric work of the Belgian mathematician Adolphe Quetelet, comparative height-weight-strength tables reported in the *Journal of the London Statistical Society*, and dynamometer tests recently given to students, he concluded that because few physiologists had any practical knowledge of gymnastics, the subject had not yet attained the recognition it merited. What was needed was a unique system of "American" physical education that would produce the type of individual who would ensure that the American nation would fulfill its destiny.[66]

Commentators might differ considerably on just what this system should be, but on one point there was nearly unanimous agreement: Americans worked too hard and were too preoccupied with financial gain. Although hard work might bring success—to the individual and to the nation—it now threatened to debilitate the population. Walter Wells proclaimed in 1868, "The great social or industrial sin of our American people is that they habitually do too much . . . a general habit of amusement is unknown." Nervous diseases, dyspepsia, constipation, and uterine difficulties were believed to be rampant; Americans even "worked" young men and women at their "gymnastic duties." H. C. Williston observed that in spite of all the attention that had been given to gymnastics in recent years, Americans had not yet developed a theory of exercise. The closest to an "American system" were Dio Lewis's "light gymnastics" and George Windship's "heavy lifting," but neither was a complete system. The reason for this, Williston sarcastically observed, was that the only "professors(!) of gymnastics" in the United States were pugilists; exercise programs were indiscriminately advocated by ill-informed health seekers or the "brainless athletes who so frequently manage the gymnasiums." Improved systems of exercise, he insisted, could only be achieved by calling upon the findings of physiology.[67]

It would be several decades, however, before concerted efforts were made to base exercise systems on a sound physiological understanding of the human body. (In fact, given the plethora of "theories" of exercise that exist in the 1980s, one can doubt if this goal has yet been achieved!) Writing the first of his annual reports as director of physical training for the city of Boston in 1891, Dr. Edward M. Hartwell, president of the American Association for the Advancement of Physical Education, declared that he knew of no scientific or practical physiologist in America who had ever written a manual of physical exercises, in spite of the fact that an enormous number of exercise manuals were available to the public by the 1890s.[68]

The point is significant. Rooted in antebellum "health reform" and educational movements of a millenarian nature, to which have been grafted selected aspects of experimental science (especially from physiology, psychology, and evolutionary biology), professional physical education has vacillated between all-encompassing utopian attitudes toward individual redemption and efforts to achieve a rigorously scientific understanding of the human organism. Although a few nineteenth-century experimental scientists paid some slight attention to "exercise" (for example, the German nerve physiologist Emil DuBois-Reymond)—and the subject of "the athlete's heart" received a great deal of attention—it was medical doctors, health seekers, entrepreneurs, and idealists of various persuasions who were more likely to have written articles, manuals, and treatises on exercise. In the absence of licensing laws, there was little to deter anyone from becoming an exercise "expert." Hartwell himself was an example of the very point he had made. In 1881, he received a Ph.D. in biology from Johns Hopkins University (where he had studied under H. Newell Martin) and an M.D. from Cincinnati's Miami Medical College. Hartwell wrote many impor-

BROOM DRILL.

Fig. 16 "Broom Drill," engraving in Alfred M. A. Beale, *Calisthenics and Light Gymnastics for Home and School* (1888).

tant reports on physical training, but it does not appear that he ever wrote a manual of physical exercises.[69]

The amount of literature on the subject of health, exercise, physical education, and athletics that was produced in the last two decades of the nineteenth century was, as Hartwell had observed, truly astounding. In 1905, James H. McCurdy, a doctor and an instructor in the physiology of exercise, gymnastics, and athletics at the International YMCA Training School at Springfield, Massachusetts, published *A Bibliography of Physical Training*. Some four thousand books,

monographs, articles, and journals were cited dealing with gymnastics, athletics, calisthenics, the "science" of physical training, exercise physiology, anthropometry, hygiene, the construction of gymnasia, playgrounds, and athletic fields, organizations devoted to these subjects, and similar topics.[70] Moreover, as McCurdy acknowledged in his preface, much more material remained uncataloged. There were handbooks such as Beale's *Calisthenics and Light Gymnastics for Home and School* (1888) (fig. 16), modeled along the lines of Smart's 1864 *Manual of Free Gymnastic and Dumb-bell Exercises*, which was revised in 1893. Mrs. J. A. Stebbins cautioned against the asymmetry caused by athletics and advocated instead the relaxing and energizing exercises of the Delsarte system. Handbooks on good breeding and refined manners included sections of "physical culture" and home gymnasia. The YMCA initiated its own journal, *Physical Education* (1892–1896), and prepared numerous manuals and books dealing with both exercise and games. Chapter 25 of the *Young Man's Christian Association Handbook*, for example, set the three great aims of the YMCA Physical Education Department as physical health, physical recreation, and physical education. The goals of physical education were to achieve symmetry of the body, muscular strength, endurance, agility, grace, muscular control, physical judgment (described as a kind of "psychic trigonometry"), physical courage, self-possession, and expression (that is, gesture and elocution).[71]

In 1883, Dr. George H. Taylor, consulting physician to the Improved Movement Cure Institute and author of several works on health and therapeutics, issued a new edition of *Health by Exercise* (1879). Taylor was an advocate of the Swedish "movement-cure," a planned program of active and passive (partner-assisted) movements designed to alleviate such conditions as nervousness, scrofula, consumption, constipation, diarrhea, piles, deformities of the spine, and female complaints. An 1853 edition of Mathias Roth's *Gymnastic Free Exercises of P. H. Ling* had brought the "movement cure" and Ling's system of Swedish gymnastics to the attention of the American public. Roth, like Ling, criticized the tour-de-force nature of heavy gymnastics (for example, hanging, climbing, and swinging) and preferred carefully prescribed movements designed by a teacher who had the necessary knowledge of human anatomy and physiology. Homeopathic doctors and health reformers were especially attracted to the therapeutic aspects of the "movement cure," and it was often used in association with the water cure and mechanical orthopedics. In schools and colleges, the more active form, usually known as the Swedish System of Educational Gymnastics, predominated. According to its most ardent spokesman, Baron Nils Posse, only Swedish gymnastics could be considered a rational system because only the Swedish system was based on body mechanics, anatomy, physiology, and psychology and had "survived the scrutiny of scientists all over the world."[72]

This somewhat extravagant claim was criticized by advocates of other forms of calisthenic and gymnastic exercises. Throughout the second half of the nineteenth century, repeated and often acrimonious battles had raged in several European countries over the relative merits of German-style and Swedish-style gymnastics. From the 1880s through the first decade of the twentieth century, a "Battle of the Systems" was also waged in the United States, with the American Association for the Advancement of Physical Education serving as the stage for many of the most protracted debates. Hartvig Nissen's *A.B.C. of the Swedish System of Educational Gymnastics: A Practical Handbook for School Teachers and the Home* (1891) and Posse's *Special Kinesiology of Educational Gymnastics* (1891) are but two of the many books that were rapidly pro-

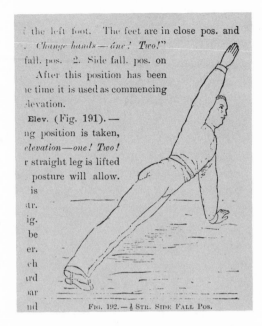

i the left foot. The feet are in close pos. and
. *Change hands — ône! Two!*"
fall. pos. 2. Side fall. pos. on
After this position has been
ne time it is used as commencing
elevation.
Elev. (Fig. 191). —
ng position is taken,
elevation — one! Two!
r straight leg is lifted
posture will allow.
is
str.
ig.
be
er.
ch
urd
yar
nd
Fig. 192. — ⅓ Str. Side Fall Pos.

Fig. 17   Illustration in Baron Nils Posse, *Special Kinesiology of Educational Gymnastics* (1894).

duced (fig. 17). When Mary Hemenway (with the aid of Amy Morris Homans) provided the resources to introduce the Swedish system into the Boston schools, Ling's gymnastics gained a strong position in American physical education, especially but by no means exclusively in women's colleges and in programs for girls and women (figs. 18 and 19).[73]

German Americans also pressed vigorously for their form of gymnastics in the public schools and colleges. Numerous manuals in both German and English were published, ranging from Beck's 1828 translation of Jahn's *Die Deutsche Turnkunst* to the *Turn-Taflen of the Nordamerikanischen Turnerbundes* and *Gymnastics: A Text-Book of the German-American System of Gymnastics, Specially Adapted to the Use of Teachers and Pupils in Public and Pri-*

vate Schools and Gymnasiums (1895), edited by William A. Stecher, secretary of the Committee on Physical Training of the North American Gymnastic Union. Although German gymnastics had been practiced in the United States since the 1820s, it was the arrival of émigrés fleeing the political repercussions of the revolution of 1848 that popularized the Turner form of gymnastics in the last half of the century. The Cincinnati *Turnverein* (gymnastic society) was established in 1848 by Friedrich Hecker, popular hero of the republican uprisings in South Germany, and other "Forty-eighters." In 1865, fifty-eight *Turner* societies met at Washington, D.C., to found the *Nordamerikanischer Turnerbund* (North American Gymnastic Union). The next year, the Normal School of the North American Gymnastic Union was opened in New York City. For more than half a century, the North American Gymnastic Union performed an important role in perpetuating German gymnastics and training teachers for clubs, public schools, and college programs. As late as 1905, the Normal School of the North American Gymnastic Union and the Boston Normal School of Gymnastics still trained the large majority of public school physical education teachers.[74]

The third major contender in the turn-of-the-century "Battle of the Systems" was the program that had been designed by Dudley Allen Sargent (fig. 20). While attending Yale's medical school, Sargent had served as instructor of gymnastics. According to his biographer Bruce Bennett, Sargent also had been a circus gymnast as a youth and had directed gymnastics at Bowdoin while still an undergraduate. Having earned a medical degree and anxious to establish a "rational" program of physical education in a college or university, he was not able to find a job. In 1878, with the support of physical fitness enthusiast and New York lawyer William Blaikie, Sargent opened his own Hygienic Institute and School of Physical Culture in New York City. The next year, he was appointed assistant professor of physical training and director of Harvard's new Hemenway Gymnasium.[75]

Sargent devised numerous pieces of gymnasium equipment (called "developing appliances") that were sold throughout the country for considerable sums of money. He also established an extensive program of physical and anthropometric examinations for all Harvard students, compiled anthropometric charts of "ideal" body measurements for various heights, and wrote numerous articles on these subjects. Three of his articles, which dealt with the physical development of the typical man, of women, and of male athletes, appeared in *Scribner's Magazine* in the late 1880s (fig. 21). In his capacity as president of the AAAPE from 1890 to 1891 and again from 1892 to 1894 and as director of the Harvard Summer School and the Sargent School of Physical Education—both of which trained considerable numbers of teachers—Sargent exerted a major influence on the field of physical education. Draper's *Self Culture* (1907) accurately reported, "If the work of Dr. D. A. Sargent . . . were expunged from the field of gymnastics it would be found that America's original contributions to the cause of physical training have been, until recent years, few." With Sargent, American physical education had taken on a distinctive "national character."[76]

HOME CALISTHENICS.   45

86. Seize the rings and turn them, bending the arms and lifting the body. (Fig. 49.)

Fig. 49.   Fig. 50.

87. Grasp the rings. Step back as far as possible. With a

Fig. 51.

spring, lifting the feet forward, swing backward and forward.

Can Athletics Be "Educational"? The Incorporation of Sports in the Physical Education Curriculum

William Blaikie, who became the second president of the AAAPE in 1887, had dedicated his treatise on exercise, *How to Get Strong and How to Stay So* (1879), to Archibald MacLaren, director of the Oxford Gymnasium. According to Blaikie, MacLaren had done more than almost "any one else now living" to point out "the benefits resulting from rational physical exercise." He also had warm words for Sargent. Blaikie dedicated the 1902 edition of his book to William Ewart Gladstone, "The Greatest Englishman Since Cromwell . . . who daily so intelligently trained his body also that he was able to maintain a true equilibrium between mind and body," and opened the first chapter

Fig. 42.   Fig. 43.

Figs. 18 and 19   These engravings from *Ladies' Home Calisthenics: A Guide to Health for Women and Children* (1890) show fully clothed, even corseted, women and girls performing various calisthenic exercises.

with the tribute to the manly "athletic feats" and robust courage of Nathan Hale.[77]

The 1902 edition of *How to Get Strong and How to Stay So* reflected much that had occurred in both physical education and sport in the two decades since the first edition. In the 1902 volume, Blaikie inserted references to numerous collegiate physical education directors, particularly Sargent, Amherst's Edward Hitchcock, and William G. Anderson, then at Yale. The intensity and diversity of the interest was also manifest in the much wider range of topics that were included. Blaikie referred to Robert Jeffries Roberts, former physical director of the Boston YMCA, who had abandoned heavy weights in favor of "light" work; the noted Philadelphia physician S. Weir

Mitchell (author of books such as *Wear and Tear* [1883]); the Boston clergyman Charles Wesley Emerson, an active member of the AAAPE and an author of popular exercise manuals (fig. 22); and Edwin Checkley, who was more interested in breathing and stretching exercises for the average man than "muscle-building and athletic performance."[78] Blaikie had surprisingly little to say, however, about the several scientifically informed papers that had been published by Edward M. Hartwell, who had become secretary of Boston's new Department of Municipal Statistics in 1897.

In 1887, Hartwell had published "On the Physiology of Exercise," one of the most scientifically informed English-language statements on the subject until the twentieth century, in the *Boston Medi-*

Fig. 20   Dudley Allen Sargent, photograph in Fred E. Leonard, *Pioneers of Modern Physical Training* (1915). Courtesy Association Press.

cal and Surgical Journal. In this article, as well as in "The Nature of Physical Training and the Best Means of Securing Its Ends" (prepared for the 1889 Boston Conference on Physical Training) and elsewhere, Hartwell drew upon work by Mitchell, the British neurologist David Ferrier, Ross's *Diseases of the Nervous System*, and other contemporary authorities. He concluded that the most comprehensive and useful definition of exercise to date had been provided by Emil DuBois-Reymond, professor of physiology at the University of Berlin, and that Archibald MacLaren's definition of exercise as "muscular movement" and "the destruction and renovation of tissue" was the best to be found in the English language.

Although it was not yet a well-known fact, Hartwell continued, active physical exercises were more than "merely exercises of the muscular system . . . such bodily exercises as gymnastics, fencing, swimming, riding, dancing, and skating [were] much more exercises of the central nervous system, of the brain and spinal marrow."[79] Physical education was concerned, then, not only with organic health, but with the sensory and motor nerves, and, hence, the brain as well.

These words, taken directly from the published writings of DuBois-Reymond, gave a kind of "scientific" legitimacy to the long-standing belief that body and mind—or "will"—exerted reciprocal actions, one on the other. Although Hartwell was too well trained in science to revel in the facile connections between "strong muscles" and "sound morals" that many of his contemporaries made, he too was convinced that a proper physical education was the indispensable basis for the full development of the individual and the evolution of the race. The two great ends of physical education were the *hygienic* and the *educative*. The first had as its aim the promotion of health and was largely a physiological concern; the latter was concerned with the formation of proper habits and was both a physiological (that is, neuromuscular) and a psychological concern.[80] Moreover, because habit was closely allied to "conduct"— and conduct implied action in accordance with the standards of a social group— physical education was also a social science. And as a social science, it was concerned with *play* and *athletics* (the mature form of play).

Like most of his colleagues, Hartwell considered gymnastics to be a form of ex-

Fig. 21 Engraving for Sargent's essay "The Physical Proportions of the Typical Man," published in *Athletic Sports* (1897), a volume in the Scribner's series "The Out of Door Library."

ercise superior to athletic sports. By 1896, when he addressed the Boston Medical Improvement Society on the subject "Physical Training, Its Function and Place in Education," however, he was willing to concede that "the predilection of collegiate youth for athletic sports and contests may be justified as natural and fitting by the teachings of neurology and psychology, if once it can be admitted that the development of mind and character, as well as brain and muscles, is subject to the laws of evolution." By the 1890s, a growing interest in "play" as a developmental activity—stimulated by recent theories of heredity and environment and recapitulation, as well as by Karl Groos's *Die Spiele der Tiere* (1895) and the "child-study movement" initiated by G. Stanley Hall at Clark University—was moving physical education closer to an emphasis on play, games, and sports (fig. 23).[81]

The two decades that separated the 1879 and 1902 editions of Blaikie's *How to*

Fig. 22   Cover of Charles Wesley Emerson's book *Physical Culture of the Emerson College of Oratory*, in its fifth edition in 1891.

Get Strong and How to Stay So also reflected the rapidity with which athletic sports—both in the broader society and within the colleges and universities—had become a dominant force in American society. "Twenty years ago," Blaikie wrote, "there was hardly a good gymnasium in this country. Now there are many good ones, and a few great ones." He praised the lengthy athletic career of William B. "Father Bill" Curtis, a cofounder of the New York Athletic Club, and was optimistic that recent meets between English and American crews at Henley would lead to more contests and greater participation among American college youth. "These same friendly trials of speed, and strength, and stay—qualities every Englishman loves," he held—had gone a long way "to breed a friendly feeling between the two nations."[82]

These were somewhat optimistic words, however, for by 1901, after a visit by a crew from the University of Pennsylvania, the Henley stewards served notice that the Americans would henceforth have to leave their "salaried" instructors at home. Reporting on different attitudes—at least "official" attitudes—toward sport in the two countries, Ralph D. Paine, a major contributor to Casper Whitney's *Outing Magazine*, observed, "Our army of professional coaches and trainers, and the almost incredible cost of intercollegiate sport, have helped to feed the suspicions of the British onlooker."[83] From the European side of the Atlantic, the *Quarterly Review* expressed alarm that American Rhodes scholars were tainting British amateur sport with their single-minded desire to win and attendant professional attitudes:

A subtle influence from abroad will shortly be felt in one of these ancient strongholds of fair-play. . . . Mr. Eugene L. Lehmann of New York City, who graduated from Yale in 1902, was chosen as a Rhodes scholar for Oxford at the age of twenty-two. . . . Already American athletes have proved their value as Oxford undergraduates at the Queen's Club meeting. It is not unlikely that several of the Rhodes scholars will be first-rate athletes too. Shall we see future Oxonian teams taking up the methods which American universities consider essential to success? Shall we have to congratulate an English Cambridge on standing unaided in the encounter, or to discount her rival's victories by the fact of alien assistance?[84]

By the turn of the century, a growing number of Americans were also becoming concerned about the excesses they saw in their intercollegiate sport: commercialism

"Playgrounds ought to include water deep enough for swimming," for girls quite as much as for boys.

Fig. 23 The 1908 volume *American Playgrounds: Their Construction, Equipment, Maintenance and Utility* emphasized a less rigorous approach to physical education when it recommended that all playgrounds include " 'water deep enough for swimming,' for girls quite as much as for boys."

and professionalism were the two major culprits under which just about every other undesirable feature could be subsumed. At a time when many hoped that exercise and athletics truly could make a man healthy, moral, and strong, there were indications that athletics might actually be inimical to the first two! President Francis Amasa Walker of MIT gave voice to this anxiety in his 1893 Harvard Phi Beta Kappa address. While he was entirely willing to admit that athletics called forth "courage, coolness, steadiness of nerve, quickness of apprehension, resourcefulness, self-knowledge, self-reliance . . . , the ability to work with others . . . , [and] subordinat[ion] of selfish impulses," Walker was somewhat

troubled by the excesses that were already apparent.[85]

While most commentators were content to speculate about the moral, intellectual, and physical benefits of exercise and athletics on the American male, a few saw the need to subject such questions to scientific investigation. In 1894, U.S. Naval surgeon Henry G. Beyer, recipient of both an M.D. and a Ph.D. from Johns Hopkins, published "Foot-ball and the Physique of Its Devotees from the Point of View of Physical Training" in the *American Journal of Medical Sciences*. Noting the extreme differences between critics who contended that pecuniary rewards and professionalism were ruining the game and enthusiasts who considered football to be "by far the greatest [game] ever invented," Beyer called for more sober, factual studies instead of the continued war of words.[86]

British and American medical journals (*Lancet*, the *British Medical Journal*, the *Journal of the American Medical Association*) had recently reported the numerous injuries and deaths that had been occurring in "football" on both sides of the Atlantic. Beyer believed that because these journals were published for physicians (whom he called "the natural guardians of public health"), the information they contained was likely to be more factual and accurate than much of what had appeared in print. He collected and analyzed measurements of the height, weight, lung capacity, and strength of Annapolis cadets engaged in football, rowing, and gymnastics from 1892 to 1894. The results suggested that both systematic gymnasium drill and rowing produced better results than football; of the two, rowing furnished the best overall training. Football, he concluded, operated with a kind of "natural selection"—the nature of the sport favored men with certain body types. Using data from the Naval Academy, Yale, and Amherst, he found that football players were slightly taller than general students at the fiftieth percentile—and considerably superior in weight, lung capacity, and strength. Questions about any mental benefits of athletics, Beyer held, needed to be investigated by psychologists; however, he was certain that any measurable changes in mental ability would require generations to demonstrate: "the results of Nature's work on mankind are not so easily influenced as to be educated away by an afternoon's practice at foot-ball."[87]

Shortly before Beyer's study appeared, the *Harvard Graduates Magazine* had published the substance of Charles William Eliot's 1892–93 annual report to the board of overseers. By 1894, Harvard's president had become convinced that intercollegiate athletics were aberrations, a blight on college life. While he endorsed activities such as tennis, rowing, "hare and hounds," bicycling, and gymnasium work, Eliot was insistent that the insatiable desires of both students and the general public for "the excitement of frequent contests" and victories had led to appalling evils: overtraining; sprains; loss of teeth; enlargement of joints; "congestions of the brain"; "nervous strain"; a devotion to pecuniary gain; and professionalism. Instead of teaching patience, perseverance, and self-control, the frenetic contests were more likely to blunt the sensibilities of both players and spectators and "dwarf mental and moral preeminence by unduly magnifying physical prowess." Throughout the remainder of his career, the "dean" of America's college presidents would remain an implacable foe of what he believed to be corrupted forms of college sport.[88]

These sentiments were not shared by men like Bigham, Camp, and Bingham, or even Young, Adams, and Walker. And they certainly were not shared by most of America's growing number of sporting enthusiasts. They were only partly shared by physical educators such as Clark Hetherington, who struggled to develop some type of program in which the "educational" ends—that is, ends that emphasized health, fitness, and the inculcation of ethical values—were the central, if not the only, goal of athletics. Eliot's views certainly did not conform to those of the vast majority of students and alumni, who came to have a greater and greater influence on college athletics even as increasing rules and regulations were passed in an effort to bring these contests more fully under the control of college faculties and administrators. Neither were these the sentiments of President Theodore Roosevelt, who declared that he was as interested as the next man in seeing his alma mater victorious. As a Harvard alumnus, the nation's highest elected official, and a devotee of "the strenuous life," Roosevelt finally became exasperated by Eliot's intransigent stand. So did many of Eliot's contemporaries, who found more to praise in collegiate athletics than they did to condemn.[89]

The future was with enthusiasts like Roosevelt, Camp, and those who saw in athletics one of the last bastions for developing strong and courageous men, not with critics like Eliot and the University of California's president Benjamin Ide Wheeler, who found it mortifying that in their sporting ethics Americans seemed decidedly inferior to the English.[90] Increasingly, it was realized that exercise and athletics might make a man stronger and perhaps healthier, although there was concern that health was often sacrificed in the quest for contest victory. As for what the effects of exercise, especially in the form of athletics, might be on a man's ethics and character, the situation was more complex. Among contemporaries, athletics could be beneficial or detrimental depending upon a number of factors, the most important of which were the perspectives and predilections of the speaker. The litany of "sports build character" has been repeated ad infinitum in spite of repeated calls for reform. *American College Athletics* (1929), the report of an investigation commissioned by the Carnegie Foundation for the Advancement of Teaching, declared: "The observer is confronted, on the one hand, with the most lofty ideals and, on the other, by rumors and even well-authenticated statements of questionable practices, deceptions, and hypocrisy." All of the "defects" that could be found in college athletics in 1929, Savage maintained, had their origins in "the twenty years between 1886 and 1906."[91]

Before the overwhelming attractiveness of the intercollegiate—and interscholastic—contest all other forms of sports on campus had paled. The general situation was aptly summed up by Bowdoin's F. N. Whittier in 1904: "Physical training in our schools has been somewhat of a disappointment. For years we have had in mind an ideal system which has been described often, but rarely put in practice. We have looked forward to scientific gymnastics combined with regulated and supervised athletics. Here and there schools have attained this ideal, but have often fallen victims of the Scylla of monotonous drill or the Charybdis of unrestrained, over-strenuous competitive athletics."[92] Although physical educators and others struggled repeatedly to devise programs in which athletics conducted for purposes of health and the development of ethical traits of character predominated, their efforts were persistently overshadowed—and often deflected—by the presence of the all-powerful businesslike model of intercollegiate athletics.

The dominant model was reflected in two articles that Ralph D. Paine contributed to *Century Magazine* in 1905 on the spirit of English and American school sport. A former varsity oarsman and football center at Yale, Paine wrote extensively on the subject of athletics, becoming associate editor of *Outing* in 1906. "Social intercourse between rival camps of Yale and Harvard," he declared, "was as cordial as that between Cossack and Japanese outposts"—a telling analogy as the article was written in the midst of the Russo-Japanese War. "Yale's rowing alumni were no longer welcome at New Haven," he lamented, "because in the businesslike preparation of the eight there must be no distraction." An alumnus of Phillips Andover Academy, Paine observed, decried the change in school sports from a "healthful recreation into a *tour de force* no longer open to the whole school." The colleges and schools offered little of value for the majority of students because, in the gymnasium, the emphasis was on "enforced exercise by scale and chart," and athletics had degenerated to competition for the few.[93]

The National Collegiate Athletic Association (formed in 1906 as the Intercollegiate Athletic Association of the United States) was—and has been—primarily concerned with issuing rules and policies to supervise and regulate transgressions, in spite of repeated proclamations about maintaining "an ethical plane in keeping with the dignity and high purpose of education."[94] Health, strength, and moral rectitude may derive from participation in exercise and athletics, but, during the twentieth century, the *ideal* and the *real* have often been uneasy companions.

Notes

1   E. Anthony Rotundo has described a shift from a standard "rooted in the life of the community and qualities of a man's soul to a standard of manhood based on individual achievement and the male body" ("Body and Soul: Changing Ideals of American Middle Class Manhood, 1770–1920," *Journal of Social History* 16 [1983]: 23). For the nineteenth and early twentieth centuries, the term "gymnastics" must be broadened to include a much more diverse range of calisthenic and exercise forms than it includes in the 1980s.

2   John Bigham, "This Foot-Ball Question," *DePauw Palladium* 1 (1897; reprint, Greencastle, Ind.: Press of Democrat, n.d.), 1.

3   Ibid., 4; Fielding H. Yost, *Football for Player and Spectator* (Ann Arbor, Mich.: University Publishing Co., 1905), 21–22.

4   Bigham, "Foot-Ball Question," 5.

5   Ibid.

6   Walter Camp, "Youth the Time for Physical Development," *New Englander and Yale Review* 9 (1885): 139.

7   In 1929, John Allen Krout dedicated volume 15 of *Annals of American Sport*, part of the Pageant of America series published by Yale University Press, to "Walter Camp, whose faith and vision find fulfillment in these Annals of American Sport."

8   Walter Camp and Lorin Deland, *Football* (Boston: Houghton, Mifflin and Co., 1896), 41–42, 48.

9   Walter Camp, *Walter Camp's Book of College Sports* (1889; reprint, New York: Century Company, 1893), 1–11.

10   Walter Camp, *Football Facts and Figures: A Symposium of Expert Opinions on the Game's Place in American Athletics* (New York: Harper and Brothers, 1894).

11   Charles Kendall Adams, "Moral Aspects of College Life," *Forum* 8 (1889): 673, 674.

12   C. A. Young, "College Athletic Sports," *Forum* 2 (1886): 144; Benjamin Garno, "Health and Rowing," in *Outdoors: A Book of Healthful Pastimes* (Boston: Pope Manufacturing Co., 1893): 64. This small (eighty-page) booklet, which had been prepared by the manufacturers of the Columbia bicycle as a promotional device, discussed tennis, football, baseball, rowing, yachting, canoeing, and cycling.

13   Adams, "Moral Aspects"; Young, "College Athletic Sports"; Garno, "Health and Rowing."

14 *Outdoors*, preface; Norman W. Bingham, ed., *The Book of Athletics and Out-of-Door Sports* (Boston: Lothrop Publishing, 1897), 9–20; J. W. Page, "Sports, Pastimes and Physical Training," in *Sports, Pastimes and Physical Culture*, ed. Andrew Sloan Draper, vol. 6 of *Draper's Self Culture* (New York: Twentieth Century Self Culture Association, 1907), 21.

15 Page, "Sports, Pastimes and Physical Training," 22.

16 See, for example, Howard J. Savage, *American College Athletics* (New York: Carnegie Foundation for the Advancement of Teaching, 1929), and George H. Hanford, *A Report to the American Council on Education on an Inquiry into the Need and Feasibility of a National Study of Intercollegiate Athletics* (Washington, D.C.: American Council of Education, 1974).

17 "Constitution," in *Proceedings of the American Association for the Advancement of Physical Education, Second Annual Meeting at Brooklyn, New York, November 26, 1886* (Brooklyn: Rome Brothers, 1886).

18 See Roberta Park, "Science, Service, and the Professionalization of Physical Education: 1885–1905," *Research Quarterly for Exercise and Sport* (April 1985): 7–20.

19 Isabel C. Barrows, ed., *Physical Training: A Full Report of the Papers and Discussions of the Conference Held in Boston in November, 1889* (Boston: George H. Ellis, 1890); Ellen W. Gerber, *Innovators and Institutions in Physical Education* (Philadelphia: Lea and Febiger, 1971), 308–13; Betty Spears, "The Influential Miss Homans," *Quest* 19 (1979): 46–59.

20 [William T. Harris], "Physical Training," in Barrows, *Physical Training*, 3.

21 Edward M. Hartwell, "The Nature of Physical Training, and the Best Means of Securing Its Ends," in Barrows, *Physical Training*, 20; Camp, *Walter Camp's Book of College Sports*, 2.

22 Barrows, *Physical Training*, 115; "The Boston Conference on Physical Culture," *Boston Medical and Surgical Journal* 121 (1889): 566.

23 Hartwell, "Nature of Physical Training," 5, 16.

24 See Roberta Park, "Physiologists, Physi-cians, and Physical Educators: Nineteenth Century Biology and Exercise, *Hygienic* and *Educative*," *Journal of Sport History* 14 (1987): 28–60; Park, "Too Important to Trust to the Children: The Search for Freedom and *Order* in Children's Play, 1900–1917," in *The Paradoxes of Play*, ed. John Loy (Champagne, Ill.: Leisure Press, 1982), 96–102.

25 *Annual Report of the President of Cornell University for the Academic Year 1887–88* (Ithaca: Published by the university, 1888), 16–19, 111–16. Not everyone agreed that athletics had a positive influence on grades. Paul C. Phillips, director of physical culture at Amherst, reported in 1908 that the scholastic standing of varsity track, baseball, and football teams at Amherst College between 1886 and 1903 had been slightly *below* that of the average student. See "Competitive Athletics and Scholarship," *Science* 27 (1903): 547–53.

26 Roberta Park, "Joseph Neef and William Maclure: Early Pioneers in American Physical Education," *Physical Educator* 31 (1974): 23–26. See also Will S. Monroe, *History of the Pestalozzian Movement in the United States* (Syracuse, N.Y.: C. W. Bardeen, 1907).

27 C. D. Gardette, "Pestalozzi in America," *Galaxy* 2 (1867): 437.

28 Joseph Neef, *Sketch of a Plan and Method of Education . . .* (Philadelphia: Printed for the author, 1808).

29 See Roberta Park, "Harmony and Cooperation: Attitudes Toward Physical Education and Recreation in Utopian Social Thought and American Communitarian Experiments, 1825–1865," *Research Quarterly* 45 (1974): 276–92; The *New Harmony Gazette* (13 December 1826) stated its intention of bringing to the attention of its readers that much-neglected but valuable branch of education—gymnastics—at an early date. See also Albert Fried, *Socialism in America: From the Shakers to the Third International* (Garden City, N.Y.: Anchor Books, 1970).

30 See Roberta Park, "The Attitudes of Leading New England Transcendentalists Toward Healthful Exercise, Active Recreations and Proper Care of the Body, 1830–1860," *Journal of Sport History* 4 (1977): 34–50.

31 [William Russell], "Prospectus," *Ameri-*

can *Journal of Education* 1 (1826): 2–3; "Progress of Physical Education," ibid., 19–23.

32 "Physical Education," *American Journal of Education* 2 (1827): 525–34; see also 289–92, 429–34, 466–71, 487–90. For discussions of various European educational reform efforts, see Roberta Park, "Education as a Concern of the State: Physical Education in National Plans for Education in France, 1763–1795," *Research Quarterly* 44 (1973): 331–45; Park, "Concern for the Physical Education of the Female Sex from 1675 to 1800 in France, England, and Spain," *Research Quarterly* 45 (1974): 104–19; Park, "The 'Enlightenment' in Spain: Expressed Concern for Physical Education in Spanish Educational Thought, 1765–1810," *Canadian Journal of History of Sport and Physical Education* 9 (1978): 1–19. Jacques Ullman, *De la gymnastique aux sports modernes: Histoire des doctrines de l'education physique* (Paris: J. Vrin, 1971), is still one of the more useful sources. See also Horst Ueberhorst, *Geschichte der Leibesübungen* (Berlin: Verlag Bartells und Vernitz, 1972), and Arnd Kruger, *Leibesübungen in Europa I: Die Europaische Gemeinschaft* (London: Arena, 1985).

33 "Physical Education," *American Journal of Education* 2 (1827): 525–34.

34 "On the Health of Literary Men," *North American Review and Miscellaneous Journal* 8 (1818): 177, 179; "A Treatise on Gymnastics: Taken chiefly from the German of F. L. Jahn," *American Quarterly Review* 3 (1828): 144. Beck acknowledged that he had made several modifications to Jahn's original treatise. See Charles Beck, *A Treatise on Gymnastics Taken Chiefly from the German of F. L. Jahn* (Northampton, Mass.: Simeon Butler, 1828).

35 John Jeffries, "Physical Culture, the Result of Moral Obligation," *American Quarterly Review* 1 (1833): 253; see also Roberta Park, "Biological Thought, Athletics, and the Formation of 'A Man of Character,' 1830–1900," in *Manliness and Morality: Images of the Male in the Old and New Worlds, 1800–1950*, ed. J. A. Mangan and James Walvin, (Manchester: University of Manchester Press, 1987).

36 Jack W. Berryman, "John Stuart Skinner and the *American Farmer*, 1819–1829: An Early Proponent of Rural Sports," *Associates National Agriculture Library Today* 1 (1976): 11–32; announcement at the end of the table of contents, *Journal of Health* 1 (1830).

37 Charles Caldwell, *Thoughts on Physical Education: Being a Discourse Delivered to a Convention of Teachers in Lexington, Ky. on the 6th and 7th of November 1833* (Boston: Marsh, Capen and Lyon, 1834), 28–29; John Bell, *Health and Beauty: An Explanation of the Laws of Growth and Exercise; Through Which a Pleasing Contour, Symmetry of Form and Graceful Carriage of the Body are Acquired and the Common Deformities of the Spine and Chest Prevented* (Philadelphia: E. L. Carey and A. L. Hart, 1838), 249.

38 *American Annals of Education and Instruction and Journal of Literary Institutions* (hereafter *Annals of Education*) 1 (1831): 129–33; ibid. 4 (1834): 140–42; William A. Alcott, *The House I Live In; or, The Human Body* (Boston: Light and Stearns, 1837); Alcott, "Anatomy and Physiology: Extracted from *The House I Live In*," *Annals of Education* 4 (1834): 140–42.

39 William A. Alcott, *The Library of Health and Teacher on the Human Constitution* (Boston: George W. Light, 1838), 1, 170–71; Alcott, *The Laws of Health; or, Sequel to "The House I Live In"* (Boston: John P. Jewett, 1857), 23–27. See also James C. Whorton, *Crusaders for Fitness: The History of American Health Reformers* (Princeton: Princeton University Press, 1982); Harvey Green, *Fit for America: Health, Fitness, Sport, and American Society* (New York: Pantheon Books, 1986).

40 "Healthy Children," *Water Cure Journal* 4 (1847): 306; "On Physical Education," ibid. 3 (1847): 11–14; "The Graham System," *Health Journal and Advocate of Physiological Reform* 1 (1840): 23; "Dr. Alcott on Physical Education," ibid. 1 (1840): 36; "Physical Education," ibid. 2 (1841): 28.

41 Andrew Combe, *The Principles of Physiology Applied to the Preservation of Health and to the Improvement of Physical and Mental Education* (New York: Harper and Brothers, 1836), 109–20, 208–9, 216; "Review of Combe's Physiology," *Annals of Education* 4 (1834):

485–91; "Equilibrium of the Physical and the Mental Organs," *Boston Medical and Surgical Journal* 13 (1835): 272.

42 For example, "Exercise," *Boston Medical Intelligencer* 1 (1823): 13; "Gymnastic Exercises for Females," ibid., 698–99; "Different Kinds of Exercise," ibid. 2 (1824): 129, 168; "Gymnastic Exercises," ibid. 4 (1826): 15.

43 "The Boston Gymnasium," *Boston Medical Intelligencer* 5 (1827): 133–34; see also Fred E. Leonard, *Pioneers of Modern Physical Training* (New York: Association Press, 1915), 63–81.

44 Bruce L. Bennett, "The Making of the Round Hill School," *Quest* 4 (1965): 53–63. Lieber became professor of history and political economy at South Carolina College and then of history and political science at Columbia University.

45 See R. Freeman Butts and Lawrence A. Cremin, *A History of Education in American Culture* (New York: Holt, Rinehart and Winston, 1953), 236–89.

46 "Physical Education," *Common School Journal* 1 (1838): 10–11; "Some Defects in Education," *Massachusetts Teacher* 3 (1850): 67, 68; "Physical, Mental, and Social Education," ibid., 87; "Health," ibid., 247. Also, "Physical Education," ibid. 8 (1855): 265–67.

47 "Neglect of Physical Training," *Massachusetts Teacher* 8 (1855): 343–55; Catharine Beecher, *Suggestions Respecting Improvements in Education, Presented to the Trustees of Hartford Female Seminary and Published at Their Request* (Hartford: Packer and Butler, 1829); Beecher, *Letters to the People on Health and Happiness* (New York: Harper and Brothers, 1855); Beecher, *Physiology and Calisthenics for Schools and Families* (New York: Harper and Brothers, 1856), 9–11. Bound with this volume was Beecher's *Calisthenic Exercises for Schools, Families, and Health Establishments, Selected and Arranged from Various Sources* (New York: Harper and Brothers, 1856), in the introduction to which she wrote, "No man can possess much courage whose chest is narrow, and whose lungs are not fully developed. Gymnastics produce cheerfulness and regulate fancy and imagination. They also diminish a predisposition to moral faults that undermine health and bodily purity" (vi).

48 Beecher, *Physiology and Calisthenics*, 12; passim.

49 Russell T. Trall, *The Illustrated Family Gymnasium; Containing the Most Improved Methods of Applying Gymnastic, Calisthenic, Kinesipathic, and Vocal Exercises to the Development of the Bodily Organs, the Invigoration of Their Functions, the Preservation of Health, and the Cure of Diseases and Deformities* (New York: Fowler and Wells, 1857). The Fowler brothers, Orson and Lorenzo, were leading proponents of the pseudoscience of phrenology. In 1844 they entered into partnership with S. R. Wells to become the publishing firm of Fowler and Wells, from which they withdrew in 1863. Although Trall included brief sections on skating, swimming, rowing, and riding, the emphasis was clearly on calisthenics and gymnastics. See also Donald Walker, *British Manly Exercises; In Which Rowing and Sailing Are Now First Discussed* (London, 1834). According to Peter McIntosh, Walker had taken many of his ideas from P. H. Clias, *An Elementary Course of Gymnastic Exercises; Intended to Develop and Improve the Physical Powers of Man* (London: Sherwood, Jones and Co., 1825); see McIntosh, *Physical Education in England Since 1800* (London: G. Bell and Sons, 1952), 78–83.

50 John C. Gunn, *Gunn's New Family Physician: or, Home Book of Health; Forming a Complete Household Guide. Giving Many Valuable Suggestions for Avoiding Disease and Prolonging Life, With Plain Directions in Cases of Emergency, and Pointing Out in Familiar Language the Causes, Symptoms, Treatment and Cure of Diseases Incident to Men, Women and Children with the Simplest and Best Remedies; Presenting a Manual for Nursing the Sick, and Describing Minutely the Properties and Uses of Hundreds of Well-Known Medicinal Plants* (New York: Moore, Wilstach and Baldwin, 1867). The author contended that this was the one hundredth edition! It included three supplementary treatises: "Anatomy, Physiology and Hygiene"; "Domestic and Sanitary Economy"; and "Physical Culture and Develop-

ment," prepared by Charles S. Royce, who identified himself as "Professor of Physical Culture and Hygiene" from Norwalk, Ohio. The "light gymnastics" of Dio Lewis and "some countries of Europe" (probably Sweden) were advocated (1146); W. W. Hall, *The Guide-Board to Health, Peace and Competence; or, The Road to Happy Old Age* (Springfield, Mass.: D. E. Fisk and Co., 1869); Samuel W. Mason, *Manual of Gymnastic Exercises for Schools and Families* (Boston: Crosby and Nichols, 1863); James H. Smart, *A Manual of Free Gymnastic and Dumb-Bell Exercises for the School-Room and Parlor* (Cincinnati: Wilson, Hinkel and Co., 1864); J. Madison Watson, *Watson's Manual of Calisthenics: A Systematic Drill-Book without Apparatus, for Schools, Families, and Gymnasiums; With Music to Accompany the Exercises* (New York: Schermerhorn, Bancroft and Co., 1864); Watson, *Hand-Book of Calisthenics and Gymnastics: A Complete Drill-Book without Apparatus, for Schools, Families, and Gymnasiums; With Music to Accompany the Exercises* (New York: Schermerhorn, Bancroft and Co., 1864).

51 See Fred E. Leonard, *A Guide to the History of Physical Education* (Philadelphia: Lea and Febiger, 1923), 290–308; Robert K. Barney, "Knights of Cause and Exercise: German Forty-Eighters and Turnvereine in the United States During the Ante-Bellum Period," *Canadian Journal of History of Sport* 13 (1982): 62–79; Roberta Park, "German Associational and Sporting Life in the Greater San Francisco Bay Area, 1850–1900," *Journal of the West* 26 (1987): 47–64.

52 Dioclesian Lewis, *The New Gymnastics for Men, Women and Children* (Boston: Ticknor and Fields, 1862); Lewis, *Our Digestion; or, My Jolly Friend's Secret* (Philadelphia: George Maclean, 1872); Gerber, *Innovators and Institutions*, 259–66; *A Synopsis of the Course of Instruction in the Department of Gymnastics of the Northwestern Normal Institute for Physical Education; Being a New System of Light Gymnastics, Compiled from Various Sources with Adaptations and Original Additions* (Chicago: H. A. Newcombe and Co., 1864).

53 *Boston Medical and Surgical Journal* 32 (1860): 106–7; Leonard, *Pioneers*, 89–94.

54 Gerber, *Innovators and Institutions*, 276–82; J. Edmund Welch, "Edward Hitchcock, M.D.: Founder of Physical Education in the College Curriculum" (Ph.D. diss., East Carolina College, 1966); E. Hitchcock and H. H. Seelye, *An Anthropometric Manual, Giving the Average and Mean Physical Measurements and Tests of Male College Students and Methods of Securing Them*, 2d ed. (Amherst, Mass.: J. E. Williams, 1889); B. J. Norton, "The Biometric Defense of Darwinism," *Journal of the History of Biology* 6 (1973): 290–93; Ruth Schwartz Cowan, "Nature and Nurture: The Interplay of Biology and Politics in the Work of Francis Galton," in *Studies in the History of Biology*, ed. William Coleman and Camille Lemoges, vol. 1 (Baltimore: Johns Hopkins University Press, 1977), 133–208.

55 Gerald Geison, "Divided We Stand: Physiologists and Clinicians in the American Context," in *The Therapeutic Revolution: Essays in the Social History of American Medicine*, ed. Morris J. Vogel and Charles E. Rosenberg (Philadelphia: University of Pennsylvania Press, 1979), 67–90; Bruce W. Fye, *The Development of American Physiology: Scientific Medicine in the Nineteenth Century* (Baltimore: Johns Hopkins University Press, 1987); Ronald L. Numbers, ed., *The Education of American Physicians: Historical Essays* (Berkeley: University of California Press, 1980); Thomas Neville Bonner, *American Doctors and German Universities: A Chapter in International Relations, 1870–1914* (Lincoln: University of Nebraska Press, 1963).

56 Park, "Physiologists, Physicians, and Physical Educators"; George W. Fitz, "Problems of Physical Education," *Harvard Graduates Magazine* 2 (1899): 26–31; A. R. Leuf, "Physical Education in Children," *Journal of the American Medical Association* 14 (1890): 493–96; "Physical Education," *Boston Medical and Surgical Journal* 122 (1890): 382–83; William T. Sedgwick and Theodore Hough, "What Training in Physiology and Hygiene May We Reasonably Expect in the Public Schools?" *Science* 18 (1903): 353–60.

57 Melvin L. Adelman, *A Sporting Time: New York City and the Rise of Modern Athletics, 1820–1870* (Urbana: University of Illinois

Press, 1986); William Wood, *Manual of Physical Exercises: Comprising Gymnastics, Rowing, Skating, Fencing, Cricket, Calisthenics, Sailing, Swimming, Sparring, Base Ball, Together with Rules for Training and Sanitary Suggestions* (New York: Harper and Brothers, 1867), 5–7 and passim.

58 Ibid., 185; "The Boat Race," *The Nation* 9 (1869): 188; Guy M. Lewis, "America's First Intercollegiate Sport: The Regattas from 1852 to 1875," *Research Quarterly* 38 (1967): 637–48; Robert K. Barney, "Of Rails and Red Stockings: Episodes in the Expansion of the 'National Pastime' in the American West," *Journal of the West* 17 (1978): 61–70. The visit of the baseball team was so popular in San Francisco that a third "international" cricket match that had been scheduled with a representative team from Vancouver seems not to have been played as a flurry of enthusiasm for baseball followed the Redstockings' local appearance. See Roberta Park, "British Sports and Pastimes in San Francisco, 1850–1900," *British Journal of Sports History* 1 (1984): 300–317.

59 *Athletic Sports for Boys: A Repository of Graceful Recreations for Youth. Containing Complete Instructions in Gymnastics, Limb Exercises, Jumping, and Pole Leaping. Also Full Directions for the Use of Dumb Bells, Indian Clubs, Parallel Bars, the Horizontal Bar, the Trapeze, and the Suspended Ropes; and in the Manly Accomplishments of Skating, Swimming, Rowing, Sailing, Riding, Driving, Angling, Fencing, and the Broad-Sword Exercise* (New York: Dick and Fitzgerald, 1866); *The Boy's Own Book; A Complete Encyclopedia of All Diversions, Athletic, Scientific, and Recreative of Boyhood and Youth,* 12th ed. (London: Vizetelly, Branston and Co. 1837); Charles Peverelly, *The Book of American Pastimes: Containing the History of the Principal Base Ball, Cricket, Rowing, and Yachting Clubs of the United States* (New York: Published by the author, 1866); Bob Considine and Fred G. Jarvis, *The First Hundred Years: A Portrait of the N.Y.A.C.* (London: Macmillan, 1969), 12–13.

60 See John A. Lucas and Ronald A. Smith, *Saga of American Sport* (Philadelphia: Lea and Febiger, 1978); Donald J. Mrozek, *Sport and*

American Mentality: 1880–1910 (Knoxville: University of Tennessee Press, 1983); Benjamin G. Rader, *American Sports: From the Age of Folk Games to the Age of Spectators* (Englewood Cliffs, N.J.: Prentice-Hall, 1983); George H. Benedict, *Hand-Book of Manly Sports* (Chicago: A. G. Spalding and Bros., 1883); James E. Sullivan, *Spalding's Official Rules* (New York: American Sports Publishing Co., 1896). Peter S. Levine, *A. G. Spalding and the Rise of Baseball: The Promise of American Sport* (New York: Oxford University Press, 1985), discusses Spalding's entrepreneurial zeal and the use of "guides" as "a national advertising medium" (75–77). Harry Cornish, *All-Around Athletics* (New York: Association Sports Publishing Co., 1895); Michael C. Murphy, *College Athletics* (New York: American Sports Publishing Co., 1894).

61 See Daniel T. Rodgers, *The Work Ethic in Industrial America, 1850–1920* (Chicago: University of Chicago Press, 1974); Frederick Rudolph, *The American College and University: A History* (New York: Alfred A. Knopf, 1962); Oscar Handlin and Mary F. Handlin, *The American College and American Culture: Socialization as a Function of Higher Education* (New York: McGraw-Hill, 1970).

62 See Roberta Park, "Boys Into Men— State Into Nation: Rites of Passage in Student Life and College Athletics, 1890–1915," in *The Masks of Play*, ed. Brian Sutton-Smith and Diana Kelly-Byrne (West Point, N.Y.: Leisure Press, 1984); Park, "Muscle, Mind and *Agon*: Intercollegiate Debating and Athletics at Harvard and Yale, 1892–1909," *Journal of Sport History* 14 (1987): 263–85.

63 The quarterly journal *Representations* (esp. volume 14, Spring 1986) has devoted considerable attention to "images" of the body, treating the topic from multiple disciplinary perspectives: history, psychology, literary criticism, and so on. See also Roberta Park, "Hermeneutics, Semiotics, and the Nineteenth Century Quest for a Corporeal Self," *Quest* 38 (1986): 33–49; Margaret C. Duncan, "A Hermeneutic of Spectator Sport: The 1976 and 1984 Olympic Games," *Quest* 38 (1986): 50–77; George W. Green, "College Athletics," *New Englander* 35 (1876): 548–60; J. William

White, "A Physician's View of Exercise and Athletics," *Lippincott's Monthly Magazine* 39 (1887): 1008–33.

64 "National Characteristics," *Hours at Home* 1 (1865): 544–48; "The Englishman as a Natural Curiosity," *Lippincott's Magazine* 2 (1868): 447; G. S. Young, "Are Americans Less Healthy Than Europeans?" *Galaxy* 14 (1872): 630–39; T. M. Coan, "Americans— and Some of Their Characteristics," *Putnam's Magazine* 5 (1870): 351–56; John C. Hutchinson, "A Chapter in Uncle Sam's Diversions," *Transatlantic* 6 (1872): 218–28.

65 "Westward Ho!" *North American Review* 169 (1855): 289–324; A. A. Livermore, "Gymnastics," ibid., 52, 65–69.

66 Oliver Wendell Holmes, *The Autocrat of the Breakfast Table* (Boston: Phillips, Sampson and Co., 1859), 197; Thomas Wentworth Higginson, "Barbarism and Civilization," *Atlantic Monthly* 7 (March 1861): 51–61; Higginson, "Gymnastics," ibid., 283–302; Hamilton W. Mabie, "The Most Popular Novels in America," *Forum* 16 (1894). See also Christian Messenger, *Sports and the Spirit of Play in American Fiction: Hawthorne to Faulkner* (New York: Columbia University Press, 1981).

67 Walter Wells, "Strength and How to Use It," *Lippincott's Magazine* 2 (1868): 416–35; H. C. Williston, "Physical Exercise Considered as a Preventative of Disease and as a Curative Agent," *Knickerbocker Magazine* 62 (1863): 1–9. One of the more useful articles on American "nervousness" in the nineteenth century remains Charles E. Rosenberg, "The Place of George M. Beard in Nineteenth-Century Psychiatry," *Bulletin of the History of Medicine* 36 (1966): 245–59; see also Judith Walzer Leavitt and Ronald L. Numbers, eds., *Sickness and Health in America: Readings in the History of Medicine and Public Health* (Madison: University of Wisconsin Press, 1978), and Green, *Fit for America*. The author of an article entitled "Amusements" in *New Englander* for July 1867 noted that attitudes were changing regarding recreations and amusements, provided they were directed to constructive ends: "No one can pretend that billiards, croquet, chess, ten-pins, cards, baseball, and picnics are expressly discountenanced

in the Bible; it does not follow that they are wrong because they are not commanded" (411).

68 Edward M. Hartwell, *Report of the Director of Physical Training—School Document No. 22, 1891* (Boston: Rockwell and Churchill, 1891).

69 Roberta Park, "Edward M. Hartwell and Physical Training at the Johns Hopkins University, 1879–1890," *Journal of Sport History* 14 (1987): 108–19; Edward M. Hartwell, *Report of the Director of Physical Training—School Document No. 4, 1894* (Boston: Rockwell and Churchill, 1894), 63–67, 141–51.

70 James H. McCurdy, *A Bibliography of Physical Training* (Springfield, Mass.: Directors' Society of the Young Men's Christian Associations of North America, 1905); see also Dwight T. Bridges, *Bibliography of Physical Training: English Titles, 1905 to May 1911* (Springfield, Mass.: Physical Directors' Society of the Young Men's Christian Associations of North America, 1912).

71 Alfred M. A. Beale, *Calisthenics and Light Gymnastics for Home and School* (New York: Excelsior Publishing House, 1888); *Manual of School Gymnastics Consisting of Free Gymnastics, Dumb-Bell Exercises, and Aesthetic Exhibition Figures: A Revised and Enlarged Edition of a Manual of Free Gymnastics and Dumb-Bell Exercises by James H. Smart* (New York: American Book Co., 1893); Genevieve Stebbins, *Society Gymnastics and Voice Culture Adapted from the Delsarte System* (New York: Edgar S. Warner, 1890); Alice E. Ives et al., *Our Society: A Complete Treatise of the Usages that Govern the Most Refined Homes and Social Circles, Our Moral, Social, Physical and Business Culture* (Detroit: Darling Brothers and Co., 1891); *The Physical Work of a Young Man's Christian Association*, pamphlet reprinted from chapter 25 of the *Young Man's Christian Association Handbook* (New York: International Committee of the Association, 1891), 3–8.

72 George H. Taylor, *Health by Exercise, Showing What Exercises to Take and How to Remove Special Physical Weakness, Embracing the History and Philosophy of Medical Treatment by This System, Including the Process of Massage, also a Summary of the General Principles of*

Hygiene (New York: Fowler and Wells, 1883); *The Gymnastic Free Exercises of P. H. Ling, Arranged by H. Rothstein*, trans. Mathias Roth (Boston: Ticknor, Reed and Fields, 1853). (Roth was also the author of *The Prevention and Cure of Chronic Diseases by Movements* and had opened an institute in London that treated its clients according to the system devised by Sweden's Per Henrik Ling. On Rothstein and the German opposition to the Swedish system, see Park, "Hartwell . . . at Johns Hopkins.") Baron Nils Posse, *The Special Kinesiology of Educational Gymnastics* (Boston: Lothrop, Lee and Shepard, 1894), v.

73   See Mabel Lee and Bruce L. Bennett, "75 Years of the American Association for Health, Physical Education and Recreation: A Time of Gymnastics and Measurement, 1885–1900," *Journal of Health, Physical Education, Recreation* 31 (1960): 26–33; Hartvig Nissen, *A.B.C. of the Swedish System of Educational Gymnastics: A Practical Hand-Book for School Teachers and the Home* (New York: Educational Publishing Co., 1891). This extremely popular little handbook (107 pages) was reprinted many times. Leonard, *Guide to the History of Physical Education*, 322–36.

74   Leonard, *Guide to the History of Physical Education*, 290–308; Barney, "Knights of Cause and Exercise"; William A. Stecher, ed., *Gymnastics: A Text-Book of the German-American System of Gymnastics, Specially Adapted to the Use of Teachers and Pupils in Public and Private Schools and Gymnasiums* (Boston: Lothrop, Lee and Shepard, 1895). Stecher was secretary of the Committee on Physical Training of the North American Gymnastic Union.

75   Bruce L. Bennett, "Dudley A. Sargent—A Man for All Seasons," *Quest* 19 (1979): 33–45; Bennett, "The Life of Dudley Allen Sargent, M.D., and His Contributions to Physical Education" (Ph.D. diss., University of Michigan, 1947).

76   It is not clear whether Sargent derived much personal income from these sales. However, he, Luther Halsey Gulick, and J. Gardiner Smith, both also doctors, had rather different views about whether it was appropriate for a medical man to use his name in connec-

tion with a patent (see response to Sargent's "Is the Teaching of Physical Education a Trade or a Profession?" in *Proceedings of the American Association for the Advancement of Physical Education, Boston 1891* [Ithaca, N.Y.: Andrus and Church, 1891], esp. 22–24); Dudley Allen Sargent, "The Physical Proportions of the Typical Man," *Scribner's Magazine* 2 (1887): 3–17; Sargent, "The Physical Characteristics of the Athlete," ibid., 541–61; Sargent, "The Physical Development of Women," ibid. 5 (1889): 172–85; editor's introduction to Dudley Allen Sargent, "Physical Training at Harvard," in *Draper's Self Culture*, 348.

77   William Blaikie, *How to Get Strong and How to Stay So* (New York: Harper and Brothers, 1879); Blaikie, *How to Get Strong and How to Stay So*, rev. ed. (New York: Harper and Brothers, 1902).

78   Blaikie, *How to Get Strong*, rev. ed., esp. 91–103. For example, see Edwin Checkley, *A Natural Method of Physical Training: Making Muscle and Reducing Flesh Without Diet or Apparatus* (Brooklyn: Wm. C. Bryant and Co., 1890). *Educational Review* for July 1891 noted, "The growing popularity of physical culture has given us of late many interesting manuals, but none of greater value to the average lay reader than that of Mr. Checkley, which is already in its seventh edition" (192). Checkley called most systems "physical straining" rather than "physical training."

79   Edward M. Hartwell, *On the Physiology of Exercise* (Boston: Cupples, Upham, and Co., 1887), reprinted from *Boston Medical and Surgical Journal*, 31 March and 7 April 1887. Hartwell, "Nature of Physical Training"; Hartwell, "On Physical Training," *Report of the Commissioner of Education for 1897–98*, vol. 1 (Washington, D.C.: U.S. Government Printing Office, 1891).

80   Edward M. Hartwell, "Physical Training, Its Function and Place in Education," *American Physical Education Review* 2 (1897): 133–51.

81   Ibid.; see, for example, N. S. Shaler, "The Athletic Problem in Education," *Atlantic Monthly* 63 (1889): 79–88; Luther Halsey Gulick, "Some Psychical Aspects of Physical

Exercise," *Popular Science Monthly* 52 (1898): 793–808; Park, "Physiologists, Physicians and Physical Educators."

82 Blaikie, *How to Get Strong*, rev. ed., 112–15, 120–24.

83 Ralph D. Paine, "The Spirit of School and College Sport: American and English Rowing," *Century Magazine* 70 (1905): 483–503.

84 "Some Tendencies in Modern Sport," *Quarterly Review* 199 (1904): 151–52.

85 Francis A. Walker, "College Athletics," *Harvard Graduates Magazine* 2 (1893): 1–18. Walker's remarks were reprinted elsewhere, for example in *Physical Education* 3 (1894): 14–16, a journal of the YMCA.

86 Henry G. Beyer, "Foot-ball and the Physique of Its Devotees from the Point of View of Physical Training," *American Journal of Medical Sciences* 108 (1894): 306–22; Beyer, "The Influence of Exercise on Growth," *American Physical Education Review* 1 (1896): 76–87.

87 Beyer, "Foot-ball and the Physique," 321.

88 "President Eliot's Report of 1892–93," *Harvard Graduates Magazine* 2 (1893): 374–83. See also Ronald A. Smith, "Harvard and Columbia and a Reconsideration of the 1905 Football Crisis," *Journal of Sport History* 8 (1981): 5–19.

89 Theodore Roosevelt, *The Strenuous Life: Essays and Addresses* (New York: Century Company, 1900). See also George M. Frederickson, *The Inner Civil War: Northern Intellectuals and the Crisis of the Union* (New York: Harper Brothers, 1965); Theodore Roosevelt, *The Rough Riders: A History of the First United States Volunteer Cavalry* (Philadelphia: Gebbie and Co., 1903), especially chapter 1; J. William White, "Football and Its Critics," *Outlook* 81 (1905): 662–69.

90 Charles William Eliot to Benjamin Ide Wheeler, 8 February 1906 and 19 September 1906, Bancroft Library, University of California; see also Roberta Park, "From Football to Rugby—and Back, 1906–1919: The University of California–Stanford University Response to the 'Football Crisis of 1905,'" *Journal of Sport History* 11 (1984): 5–40.

91 Savage, *American College Athletics*, 32, 29.

92 F. N. Whittier, "Physical Training for the Mass of Students," *American Physical Education Review* 9 (1904): 23–37.

93 Ralph D. Paine, "The Spirit of School and College Sport: English and American Rowing," and "The Spirit of School and College Sport: English and American Football," *Century Magazine* 70 (1905): 99–116.

94 Palmer E. Pierce, "The Intercollegiate Athletic Association of the United States," *Proceedings of the Third Annual Convention Held at New York City, New York, January 2, 1909*, 27.

Contributors

Harvey Green is professor of history and coordinator of public history programs at Northeastern University. He is former chief historian and vice president for interpretation at the Strong Museum in Rochester, New York. Green holds a doctorate in history from Rutgers University and is the author of *The Light of the Home: An Intimate View of the Lives of Women in Victorian America* (1983) and *Fit for America: Health, Fitness, Sport, and American Society* (1986), both published by Pantheon Books.

Kathryn Grover is director and editor in the office of publications and technical services at the Strong Museum in Rochester, New York. She holds masters degrees in journalism from the University of Michigan and in American history from Boston University. She has edited several books in American social and cultural history, including *Dining in America,* a collection of essays published in 1987 by the University of Massachusetts Press in conjunction with the Strong Museum.

Michael R. Harris is a museum specialist in the Division of Medical Sciences at the National Museum of American History, where he has worked since 1973. A pharmacist in his initial training, Harris has done graduate work in the history of pharmacy and the history of science and technology at Johns Hopkins University, George Washington University, and the University of Wisconsin.

T. J. Jackson Lears is professor of history at Rutgers University. Lears received his doctorate in history from Yale University, has been professor of history at the University of Missouri at Columbia, and was at the Smithsonian Institution's National

Museum of American History before joining the Rutgers faculty. He is author of *No Place of Grace: Antimodernism and the Transformation of American Culture*, published by Pantheon Books in 1981. He is currently at work on a book on American advertising and culture between 1880 and 1960, forthcoming from Pantheon Books.

Donald J. Mrozek is professor of history at Kansas State University, where he has taught since 1972. He is the author of *Sport and American Mentality, 1880–1910* (Knoxville: University of Tennessee Press, 1983) and received his doctorate from Rutgers University.

Roberta J. Park is professor of physical education and chair of the department of physical education at the University of California at Berkeley. She received her doctorate in education and history from Berkeley and has coedited the volume *Play, Games and Sports in Cultural Contexts* (Champaign, Ill.: Human Kinetics, 1983).

James C. Whorton is professor of biomedical history at the University of Washington School of Medicine and author of *Crusaders for Fitness: The History of American Health Reformers* (Princeton: Princeton University Press, 1982). His doctorate is from the University of Wisconsin.